A MORE PERFECT UNION

A More Perfect Union

Documents in U.S. History

Third Edition

Volume II: Since 1865

Paul F. Boller, Jr.

Professor Emeritus, Texas Christian University

Ronald Story

University of Massachusetts, Amherst

Houghton Mifflin Company   **Boston**

Dallas   Geneva, Illinois   Palo Alto   Princeton, New Jersey

To Martin and Eliza

Sponsoring Editor: John Weingartner
Project Editor: Celena Sun
Senior Production Coordinator: Renée Le Verrier
Senior Manufacturing Coordinator: Marie Barnes
Marketing Manager: Diane Gifford

Cover: Plaster model of the Statue of Liberty by Frédéric Auguste Bartholdi,
approved by the French-American Committee in 1875. Cover art courtesy of
National Park Service: Statue of Liberty National Monument.

Text credit: Pages 241–244. Reprinted from *The Feminine Mystique* by Betty
Friedan, by permission of W.W. Norton & Company, Inc. Copyright © 1963 by
Betty Friedan. Copyright renewed 1991.

ISBN: 0-395-59172-4

Library of Congress: 91-72006

CDEFGHIJ-AH-95432

CONTENTS

◆

♦ CHAPTER THREE

The Minorities

♦ ───── CHAPTER FOUR ─────

Empire and Uplift

◆ ── CHAPTER FIVE ──────────

Crisis and Hope

◆ ── CHAPTER SIX ──────────

Protracted Conflict

◆ CHAPTER SEVEN

Uncertain Trumpets

◆ ───── CHAPTER EIGHT

Modern Times

PREFACE

◆

Our two-volume reader, *A More Perfect Union: Documents in U.S. History*, presents students with the original words of speeches and testimony, political and legal writings, and literature that have reflected, precipitated, and implemented pivotal events of the past four centuries. The readings in Volume I cover the era from the founding of the Virginia and Massachusetts Bay colonies to Reconstruction. Volume II begins with the post-Civil War period, repeating some of the first volume's final readings, and concludes with contemporary selections. We are pleased with the reception that *A More Perfect Union* has received, and we have worked toward refining the contents of this new edition.

About a third of the material is new to this edition. New selections in Volume I include, for example, "Address to John Smith" by Powhatan and "The Examination of Anne Hutchinson" from the seventeenth century and Lydia Maria Child's "That Class of Americans Called Africans" and Elizabeth Palmer Peabody's "Plan of Brook Farm" from the nineteenth century. Many new selections have been added to Volume II. Among them are "Chief Joseph's Story" and Robert Hunt's "Bessemer Steel" from the late nineteenth century as well as Harry Blackmun's opinion in *Roe* v. *Wade* and George Bush on the war with Iraq.

The readings in these volumes represent a blend of social and political history, along with some cultural and economic trends, suitable for introductory courses in American history. We made our selections with three thoughts in mind. First, we looked for famous documents with a lustrous place in the American tradition—the Gettysburg Address, for example, or Franklin D. Roosevelt's First Inaugural Address. These we chose for their great mythic quality, as expressions of fundamental sentiments with which students should be familiar. Second, we looked for writings that caused something to happen or had an impact when they appeared. Examples include the Virginia slave statutes, Thomas Paine's *The Crisis*, the Emancipation Proclamation, and Earl Warren's opinion in *Brown* v. *Board of Education of Topeka*—all of them influential pieces, some of them famous as well. Third, we looked for documents that seemed to reflect important attitudes or developments. Into this group fall Thomas Hart Benton's racial views as well as the writings of Upton Sinclair on industrial Chicago and of Martin Luther King, Jr. on Vietnam. In this category, where the need for careful selection from a wide field was most apparent, we looked especially for thoughtful pieces with a measure of fame and influence. Horace Mann's statement on schools reflected common attitudes; it also caused something to happen and is a well-known reform statement. We have also tried to mix a few unusual items into the stew, as with the "Report of the Joint Committee on Reconstruction" and a *Playboy* interview with Germaine Greer.

We have edited severely in places, mostly when the document is long or contains extraneous material or obscure references. We have also, in some cases, modernized spelling and punctuation.

Each document has a lengthy headnote that summarizes the relevant trends of the era, provides a specific setting for the document, and sketches the life of the author. There are also "Questions to Consider" to guide students through the prose and suggest ways of thinking about the selections. In addition, we have eliminated the Counterpoints. Reviewers wanted to see more selections and believed the Counterpoints to be less useful.

We would like to thank the following people who reviewed the manuscript for one or both volumes:

John K. Alexander, University of Cincinnati; George Flynn, Texas Tech University; Marty Haas, Adelphi University; Michael Krenn, University of Miami; Lisa Lane, Miracosta College; C. Elizabeth Raymond, University of Nevada-Reno; James Oliver Robertson, University of Connecticut; Henry J. Sage, Northern Virginia Community College; Robert Smith, University of Toledo; and John Scott Wilson, University of South Carolina.

We also wish to express our appreciation to the editorial staff of Houghton Mifflin Company for their hard and conscientious work in producing these volumes. We owe a particular debt of gratitude to Celena Sun, who was a model of efficiency, intelligence, and tact throughout the project; to John Weingartner and Jeff Greene, who advised without commanding; and to Jean Woy, under whose auspices earlier editions of this collection first saw the light of day and whose continued presence at Houghton Mifflin was both energizing and reassuring.

P.F.B.
R.S.

A More Perfect Union

Capitol in ruins. The ruins of the South Carolina capitol building in Columbia after General Sherman's passage through the city in early 1865. (Chicago Historical Society)

CHAPTER ONE

◆

Reconstructing the Union

1
◆

BINDING WOUNDS

In June 1864, when the Republicans nominated Abraham Lincoln for a second term, the end of the war seemed as far away as ever. Northerners were shocked at the heavy casualties reported from battlefields in Virginia, and criticism of the administration had become so harsh that in mid-August Lincoln was convinced he would not be reelected. The Radical Republicans, who spoke for the antislavery faction of the party, condemned him as "politically, militarily, and financially a failure" and for a time backed John C. Frémont for the presidency. The Northern Democrats nominated General George B. McClellan, a former federal commander, and adopted a platform calling for the immediate cessation of hostilities and the restoration of the Union by a negotiated peace. Lincoln was so sure McClellan would defeat him that he wrote a secret memorandum explaining how he would cooperate with the new president after the election in order to save the Union.

But a series of federal victories—the closing of Mobile Bay, the capture of Atlanta, and the routing of Southern forces in the Shenandoah Valley—led public opinion to swing back rapidly to Lincoln. Republican newspapers began ridiculing the "war-is-a-failure" platform of the Democrats, and Frémont decided to drop out of the campaign. Lincoln's prediction that he would not be reelected proved wrong. On election day he won a plurality of nearly half a million votes and carried every state in the Union except Kentucky, Delaware, and New Jersey.

In his second inaugural address on March 4, 1865, Lincoln singled out slavery as the cause of the Civil War and stated that its eradication was inevitable. He expressed hope for a speedy end to the conflict, called for "malice toward none" and "charity for all," and looked forward to the day when Americans would achieve a "just and lasting peace" among themselves and with all nations. On April 9, Lee surrendered to Grant at Appomattox; two days later Lincoln made his last public address, outlining his reconstruction policy. He had never considered the South to be outside of the Union and hoped for a speedy reconciliation. On April 14, at his last cabinet meeting, he urged the cabinet members to put aside all thoughts of hatred and revenge. That evening he was shot.

Questions to Consider. Lincoln's second inaugural address is commonly regarded as one of the greatest addresses ever made by an American president. Why do you think this is so? What did he regard as the basic issue of the Civil War? What irony did he see in the attitude of the contestants? What use of the Bible did he make? Do you think this was likely to appeal to Americans in 1865?

◆

Second Inaugural Address (1865)

ABRAHAM LINCOLN

FELLOW-COUNTRYMEN:—At this second appearing to take the oath of the presidential office there is less occasion for an extended address than there was at the first. Then a statement somewhat in detail of a course to be pursued seemed fitting and proper. Now, at the expiration of four years, during which public declarations have been constantly called forth on every point and phase of the great contest which still absorbs the attention and engrosses the energies of the nation, little that is new could be presented. The progress of our arms, upon which all else chiefly depends, is as well known to the public as to myself, and it is, I trust, reasonably satisfactory and encouraging to all. With high hope for the future, no prediction in regard to it is ventured.

On the occasion corresponding to this four years ago all thoughts were anxiously directed to an impending civil war. All dreaded it, all sought to avert it. While the inaugural address was being delivered from this place, devoted altogether to *saving* the Union without war, insurgent agents were in the city seeking to *destroy* it without war—seeking to dissolve the Union and divide effects by negotiation. Both parties deprecated war, but one of them would *make* war rather than let the nation survive, and the other would *accept* war rather than let it perish, and the war came.

One eighth of the whole population was colored slaves, not distributed generally over the Union, but localized in the Southern part of it. These slaves constituted a peculiar and powerful interest. All knew that this interest was somehow the cause of the war. To strengthen, perpetuate, and extend this interest was the object for which the insurgents would

From James D. Richardson, ed., *A Compilation of the Messages and Papers of the Presidents* (Government Printing Office, Washington, D.C., 1897–1907), VIII: 3477–3478.

End of the war. Anticipating the final triumph of Union arms, New York City staged a huge triumphal procession on March 6, 1865, two days after Lincoln's second inauguration. (Courtesy Dover Pictorial Archive Series, *New York in the 19th Century* by John Grafton, © 1980 Dover Publications, Inc.)

rend the Union even by war, while the Government claimed no right to do more than to restrict the territorial enlargement of it. Neither party expected for the war the magnitude nor the duration which it has already attained. Neither anticipated that the *cause* of the conflict might cease with or even before the conflict itself should cease. Each looked for an easier triumph, and a result less fundamental and astounding. Both read the same Bible and pray to the same God, and each invokes His aid against the other. It may seem strange that any men should dare to ask a just God's assistance in wringing their bread from the sweat of other men's faces, but let us judge not, that we be not judged. The prayers of both could not be answered. That of neither has been answered fully. The Almighty has His own purposes. "Woe unto the world because of offenses; for it must needs be that offenses come, but woe to that man by whom the offense cometh." If we shall suppose that American slavery is one of those offenses which, in the providence of God, must needs come, but which, having continued through His appointed time, He now wills to remove, and that He gives to both North and South this terrible war as the woe due to those by whom the offense came, shall we discern therein any departure from those divine attributes which the believers in a living

God always ascribe to Him? Fondly do we hope, fervently do we pray, that this mighty scourge of war may speedily pass away. Yet, if God wills that it continue until all the wealth piled by the bondsman's two hundred and fifty years of unrequited toil shall be sunk, and until every drop of blood drawn with the lash shall be paid by another drawn with the sword, as was said three thousand years ago, so still it must be said, "The judgments of the Lord are true and righteous altogether."

With malice toward none, with charity for all, with firmness in the right as God gives us to see the right, let us strive on to finish the work we are in, to bind up the nation's wounds, to care for him who shall have borne the battle and for his widow and his orphan, to do all which may achieve and cherish a just and lasting peace among ourselves and with all nations.

2

◆

A HELPING HAND

The Thirteenth Amendment, which became part of the Constitution in 1865, freed about four million slaves in the South. But with freedom came uncertainty, insecurity, and perplexity. Unlike the peasants of France and Russia, who stayed on the land on which they had been working when they were freed from serfdom, the former American slaves were cast adrift at the end of the Civil War with no means of livelihood. They found themselves without property, legal rights, education, training, and any experience as independent farmers or laborers. Thousands began roaming the countryside looking for work and ways to survive. The first year of freedom brought hunger, disease, suffering, and death.

The freedmen did receive some assistance from the federal government after the war. In March 1865, Congress established the Bureau of Refugees, Freedmen, and Abandoned Lands (commonly called the Freedmen's Bureau) to provide them with food, clothing, shelter, and medical aid. Under the direction of General Oliver O. Howard (the "Christian General"), the Freedmen's Bureau also established schools and colleges for young blacks, founded savings banks, set up courts to protect their civil rights, and tried to get them jobs and fair contracts of employment. During its seven years of existence (1865–1872), the bureau spent more than $15 million for food and other aid and over $6 million on schools and educational work, and gave medical attention to nearly half a million patients. Bureau agents also registered black voters and encouraged political participation. The hostility of Southern whites and the growing indifference of whites in the North, however, negated much of the bureau's work.

The report excerpted below was written by Colonel Eliphalet Whittlesey, assistant bureau commissioner for North Carolina, in October 1865. Whittlesey later became a general and moved to Washington, where he served as a trustee of the national Freedman's Savings Bank. In North Carolina where blacks made up only a third of the population and therefore only a third of the potential voters, the Republican party and the national government soon began to lose political control. By 1871 the white Democratic party once again controlled the state, ending Reconstruction there.

Questions to Consider. Southern whites argued repeatedly that the fundamental objective of the Freedmen's Bureau was not to help the needy but to punish its foes by transforming Southern racial and economic relations. Does Whittlesey's report support this contention? Who received federal assistance in 1865? On what grounds was assistance given? Who made the decisions? Did Whittlesey sound like the commander of an occupying army? Of the bureau's four goals, which did he seem to feel were most urgent? Was he optimistic? Which of its goals was the bureau most likely to achieve in the short run?

◆

Report on the Freedmen's Bureau (1865)

On the 22d of June I arrived at Raleigh with instructions from you to take the control of all subjects relating to "refugees, freedmen, and the abandoned lands" within this State. I found these subjects in much confusion. Hundreds of white refugees and thousands of blacks were collected about this and other towns, occupying every hovel and shanty, living upon government rations, without employment and without comfort, many dying for want of proper food and medical supplies. A much larger number, both white and black, were crowding into the towns, and literally swarming about every depot of supplies to receive their rations. My first effort was to reduce this class of suffering and idle humanity to order, and to discover how large a proportion of these applicants were really deserving of help. The whites, excepting "loyal refugees," were referred to the military authorities. To investigate the condition of refugees and freedmen and minister to the wants of the destitute, I saw at once would require the services of a large number of efficient officers. As fast as suitable persons could be selected, application was made to the department and district commanders for their detail, in accordance with General Order No. 102, War Department, May 31, 1865. In many cases these applications were unsuccessful because the officers asked for could not be spared. The difficulties and delays experienced in obtaining the help needed for a proper organization of my work will be seen from the fact that upon thirty-four written requests, in due form, only eleven officers have been detailed by the department and district commanders. . . .

With this brief history of my efforts to organize the bureau, I proceed to state

From *Report of the Joint Committee on Reconstruction, 1st Session, 39th Congress* (Government Printing Office, Washington, D.C., 1866), II: 186–192.

An early class at Hampton Institute. Uniformed African-American students in class at Virginia's Hampton Institute, founded in 1868 with white philanthropic help to "train selected Negro youth who should go out and teach and lead their people." (Gift of Leonard Kirstein, The Museum of Modern Art, NY)

The Design and Work Proposed

In my circulars Nos. 1 and 2 (copies of which are herewith enclosed) the objects to be attained are fully stated. All officers of the bureau are instructed—

1. To aid the destitutes, yet in such a way as not to encourage dependence.
2. To protect freedmen from injustice.
3. To assist freedmen in obtaining employment and fair wages for their labor.
4. To encourage education, intellectual and moral.

Under these four divisions the operations of the bureau can best be presented.

Relief Afforded

It was evident at the outset that large numbers were drawing rations who might support themselves. The street in front of the post commissary's office was blocked up with vehicles of all the descriptions peculiar to North Carolina, and with people who had come from the country around, in some instances from a distance of sixty miles, for government rations. These were destitute whites, and were supplied by order of the department commander. Our own headquarters, and every office of the bureau, was besieged from morning till night by freedmen, some coming many miles on foot, others in wagons and carts. The rations issued would scarcely last till they reached home, and in many instances they were sold before leaving the town, in exchange for luxuries. To correct these evils, orders were issued that no able-bodied man or woman should receive supplies, except such as were known to be industrious, and to be entirely destitute. By constant inquiry and effort the throng of beggars was gradually removed. The homeless and helpless were gathered in camps, where shelter and food could be furnished, and the sick collected in hospitals, where they could receive proper care. . . .

Protection

Regarding this bureau as the appointed instrument for redeeming the solemn pledge of the nation, through its Chief Magistrate, to secure the rights of freedmen, I have made every effort to protect them from wrong. Suddenly set free, they were at first exhilarated by the air of liberty, and committed some excesses. To be sure of their freedom, many thought they must leave the old scenes of oppression and seek new homes. Others regarded the property accumulated by their labor as in part their own, and demanded a share of it. On the other hand, the former masters, suddenly stripped of their wealth, at first looked upon the freedmen with a mixture of hate and fear. In these circumstances some collisions were inevitable. The negroes were complained of as idle, insolent, and dishonest; while they complained that they were treated with more cruelty than when they were slaves. Some were tied up and whipped without trial; some were driven from their homes without pay for their labor, without clothing or means of support; others were forbidden to leave on pain of death, and a few were shot or otherwise murdered. All officers of the bureau were directed, in accordance with your circular No. 5, to investigate these difficulties between the two classes, to settle them by counsel and arbitration as far as possible, to punish light offences by fines or otherwise, and to report more serious cases of crime to the military authorities for trial. The exact number of cases heard and decided cannot be given; they have been so numerous that no complete record could be kept; one officer reported that he had heard and disposed of as many as 180 complaints in a single day. The method pursued may be best presented by citing a few cases and the action thereon. From the report of Captain James, for August, I quote the following:

"Reports had reached me of the way in which David Parker, of Gates county, treated his colored people, and I determined to ascertain for myself their truth. Accordingly, last Monday, August 20, accompanied by a guard of six men from this post, (Elizabeth City,) I proceeded to his residence, about forty miles distant. He is very wealthy. I ascertained, after due investigation, and after convincing his colored people that I was really their friend, that the worst reports in regard to him were true. He had twenty-three negroes on his farm, large and small. Of these, fourteen were field-hands; they all bore unmistakable evidence of the way they had been worked; very much undersized, rarely exceeding, man or women, 4 feet 6 inches—men and women of thirty and forty years of age looking like boys and girls. It has been his habit for years to work them from sunrise to sunset, and often long after, only stopping one hour for dinner—food always cooked for them to save time. He had, and has had for many years, an old colored man, one-eyed and worn out in the service, for an over-seer or 'over-looker,' as he called himself. In addition, he has two sons at home, one of whom has made it a point to be with them all summer long—not so much to superintend as to drive. The old colored overseer always went behind the gang with a cane or whip, and woe betide the unlucky wretch who did not continually do his part; he had been brought up to work, and had not the least pity for any one who could not work as well as he.

"Mr. Parker told me that he had hired his people for the season: that directly after the surrender of General Lee he called them up and told them they were free; that he was better used to them than to others, and would prefer hiring them; that he would give them board and two suits of clothing to stay with him till the 1st day of January, 1866, and one Sunday suit at the end of that time; that they consented willingly—in fact, preferred to remain with him, & c. But from his people I learned that though he did call them up, as stated, yet when one of them demurred at the offer his son James flew at him and cuffed and kicked him; that after that they were all 'perfectly willing to stay'; they were watched night and day; that Bob, one of the men, had been kept chained nights; that they were actually afraid to try to get away. There was no complaint of the food nor much of the clothing, but they were in constant terror of the whip. Only three days before my arrival, Bob had been stripped in the field and given fifty lashes for hitting Adam, the colored over-looker, while James Parker stood by with a gun, and told him to run if he wanted to, he had a gun there. About four weeks before, four of them who went to church and returned before sunset were treated to twenty-five lashes each. Some were beaten or whipped almost every day. Having ascertained these and other similar facts, I directed him to call them up and pay them for the first of May last up to the present time. I investigated each case, taking into consideration age, family, physical condition, & c., estimating their work from $8 down, and saw him pay them off then and there, allowing for clothing and medical bill. I then arrested him and his two sons, and brought them here, except Dr. Joseph Parker, whose sister is very sick, with all the colored people I thought necessary as witnesses, intending to send them to Newbern for trial. But on account of the want of immediate transportation I concluded to release them on their giving a bond in the sum of $2,000 to Colonel E. Whittlesey, assistant commissioner for the State of North Carolina, and to his successors in office, conditioned as follows:

"That whereas David Parker and James Parker have heretofore maltreated their colored people, and have enforced the compulsory system instead of the free labor system: Now, therefore, if they, each of them, shall hereafter well and kindly treat, and cause to be treated, the hired laborers under their or his charge, and shall adopt the free labor system in lieu of the compulsory system, then this bond to be void and of no effect; otherwise to remain in full force and effect, with good security."

Lieutenant Colonel Clapp, superintendent central district, reports three cases of cruel beating, which have been investigated, and the offenders turned over to the military authorities for trial; besides very many instances of defrauding freedmen of their wages. . . .

The following cases are taken from the report of Captain Barritt, assistant commissioner, at Charlotte:

"Morrisson Miller charged with whipping a girl Hannah (colored.) Found guilty. Action: ordered to pay said Hannah fifty bushels of corn towards supporting herself and children, two of said children being the offspring of Miller.

"Wm. Wallace charged with whipping Martha (colored.) Plead guilty. Action: fined said Wallace $15, with assurance that if the above offense was repeated, the fine would be doubled.

"Council Best attempts to defraud six families of their summer labor, by offering to sell at auction the crop on his leased plantation. Action: sent military force and stopped the sale until contract with laborers was complied with."

A hundred pages of similar reports might be copied, showing, on the one side, that many freedmen need the presence of some authority to enforce upon them their new duties; and on the other, that so far from being true that "there is no county in which a freedman can be imposed upon," there is no county in which he is not oftener wronged; and these wrongs increase just in proportion to their distance from United States authorities. There has been great improvement, during the quarter, in this respect. The efforts of the bureau to protect the freedmen have done much to restrain violence and injustice. Such efforts must be continued until civil government is fully restored, just laws enacted, or great suffering and serious disturbance will be the result.

Industry

Contrary to the fears and predictions of many, the great mass of colored people have remained quietly at work upon the plantations of their former masters during the entire summer. The crowds seen about the towns in the early part of the season had followed in the wake of the Union army, to escape from slavery. After hostilities ceased these refugees returned to their homes, so that but few vagrants can now be found. In truth, a much larger amount of vagrancy exists among the whites than among the blacks. It is the almost uniform report of officers of the bureau that freedmen are industrious.

The report is confirmed by the fact that out of a colored population of nearly 350,000 in the State, only about 5,000 are now receiving support from the government. Probably some others are receiving aid from kindhearted men who have enjoyed the benefit of their services from childhood. To the general quiet and industry of this people there can be no doubt that the efforts of the bureau have contributed greatly. I have visited some of the larger towns, as Wilmington, Newbern, Goldsborough, and both by public addresses and private instructions counselled the freedmen to secure employment and maintain themselves. Captain James has made an extensive tour through the eastern district for the same purpose, and has exerted a most happy influence. Lieutenant Colonel Clapp has spent much of his time in visiting the county seats of the central district, and everywhere been listened to by all classes with deep interest. Other officers have done much good in this way. They have visited plantations, explained the difference between slave and free labor, the nature and the solemn obligation of contracts. The chief difficulty met with has been a want of confidence between the two parties. The employer, accustomed only to the system of compulsory labor, is slow to believe that he can secure fruitful services by the stimulus of wages. The laborer is unwilling to trust the promises of those for whom he had toiled all his days without pay; hence but few contracts for long periods have been effected. The bargains for the present year are generally vague, and their settlement as the crops are gathered in requires much labor. In a great majority of cases the landowners seem disposed to do justly, and even generously; and when this year's work is done, and the proceeds divided, it is hoped that a large number of freedmen will enter into contracts for the coming year. They will, however, labor much more cheerfully for money, with prompt and frequent payments, than for a share of the crop, for which they must wait twelve months. A large farmer in Pitt county hires hands by the job, and states that he never saw negroes work so well. Another in Lenoir county pays monthly, and is satisfied so far with the experiment of free labor. Another obstacle to long contracts was found in the impression which had become prevalent to some degree, *i.e.*, that lands were to be given to freedmen by the government. To correct this false impression I published a circular, No. 3, and directed all officers of the bureau to make it as widely known as possible. From the statistical reports enclosed, it will be seen that during the quarter 257 written contracts for labor have been prepared and witnessed; that the average rate of wages, when paid in money, is from $8 to $10 per month; that 128 farms are under the control of the bureau and cultivated for the benefit of freedmen; that 8,540 acres are under cultivation, and 6,102 are employed. Many of the farms were rented by agents of the treasury as abandoned lands, previous to the establishing of this bureau, and were transferred to us with the leases upon them. Nearly all have been restored to their owners, under the President's proclamation of amnesty, and our tenure of the few that remain is so uncertain that I have not deemed it prudent to set apart any for use of refugees and freedmen, in accordance with the act of Congress approved March 3, 1865. But many freedmen are taking this matter into their own hands, and renting lands from the owners for one or more years. . . .

Education

The quarter has been one of vacation rather than active work in this department. Still some progress has been made, and much done to prepare for the coming autumn and winter. Rev. F. A. Fiske, a Massachusetts teacher, has been appointed superintendent of education, and has devoted himself with energy to his duties. From his report it will be seen that the whole number of schools, during the whole or any part of the quarter, is 63, the number of teachers 85, and the number of scholars 5,624. A few of the schools are self-supporting, and taught by colored teachers, but the majority are sustained by northern societies and northern teachers. The officers of the bureau have, as far as practicable, assigned buildings for their use, and assisted in making them suitable; but the time is nearly past when such facilities can be given. The societies will be obliged hereafter to pay rent for school-rooms and for teachers' homes. The teachers are engaged in a noble and self-denying work. They report a surprising thirst for knowledge among the colored people—children giving earnest attention and learning rapidly, and adults, after the day's work is done, devoting the evening to study. In this connexion it may be mentioned, as a result of moral instruction, that 512 marriages have been reported and registered, and 42 orphans provided with good homes.

3

◆

KLANSMEN OF THE CAROLINAS

Reconstruction developed in a series of moves and countermoves. In a white Southern backlash to Union victory and emancipation came the "black codes" for coercing black laborers and President Andrew Johnson's pardon of Confederate landowners. Then in a Northern backlash to these codes and pardons came the Civil Rights bills, the sweeping Reconstruction Acts of 1867, and the Fourteenth and Fifteenth Amendments, all designed to guarantee black political rights. White Southerners reacted to these impositions in turn with secret night-time terrorist or "night rider" organizations designed to shatter Republican political power. Congress tried to protect Republican voters and the freedmen with the Force Acts of 1870 allowing the use of the army to prevent physical assaults, but Northern willingness to commit troops and resources to the struggle was waning. By the mid-1870s only three states remained in Republican hands, and within three years racist Democrats controlled these, too. The night riders had turned the tide.

Although numerous secret societies for whites appeared in the Reconstruction South—including the Order of the White Camelia (Louisiana), the Pale Faces (Tennessee), the White Brotherhood (North Carolina), and the Invisible Circle (South Carolina)—the largest and most influential society, and the one that spawned these imitators, was the Ku Klux Klan, the so-called Invisible Empire. The Klan began in Tennessee in 1866 as a young men's social club with secret costumes and rituals similar to those of the Masons, the Odd-Fellows, and other popular societies. In 1867, however, following passage of the Reconstruction Acts, anti-Republican racists began to see the usefulness of such a spookily secret order, and the Klan was reorganized to provide for "dens," "provinces" (counties), and "realms" (states), all under the authority of a "Grand Wizard," who in 1867 was believed to have been Nathan B. Forrest, a former slave trader and Confederate general.

The Klan structure was probably never fully established because of the disorganized conditions of the postwar South. Other societies with different names emerged, and the Reconstruction-era "Ku-Klux" may have disbanded as a formal entity in the early 1870s. But it clearly survived in spirit and in loosely formed groups, continuing to terrorize

Republicans and their allies among the newly enfranchised freedmen into the 1870s and sowing fear among the black families who composed, after all, the labor force on which the white planters still depended. The excerpt reprinted below includes congressional testimony by David Schenck, a member of the North Carolina Klan seeking to portray it in the best possible light, followed by testimony from Elias Hill, a South Carolina black man victimized by a local "den" of the Klan. Schenck and Hill were testifying before a joint Senate-House committee concerned with antiblack terrorism.

Questions to Consider. The oath taken by David Schenck emphasizes the Klan's religious, constitutional, and benevolent qualities, whereas Elias Hill's story reveals its terrorist features. Are there elements in the Klan oath that seem to hint at or justify the use of violence? Why does the oath contain the phrases "original purity," "pecuniary embarrassments," and "traitor's doom"? What "secrets of this order" could deserve death? What position did Hill hold in the black community? Did the Klansmen seem to be assaulting him because of his condition or because of his position in the black community? Why did they ask Hill to pray for them? Would it be fair or accurate to call the Ku Klux Klan a terrorist organization that succeeded?

◆

Report of the Joint Committee on Reconstruction (1872)

A select committee of the Senate, upon the 10th of March, 1871, made a report of the result of their investigation into the security of person and property in the state of North Carolina. . . . A sub-committee of their number proceeded to the State of South Carolina, and examined witnesses in that State until July 29. . . .

David Schenck, esq., a member of the bar of Lincoln County, North Carolina . . . was initiated in October, 1868, as a member of the Invisible Empire . . . In his own words: "We were in favor of constitutional liberty as handed down to us by our forefathers. I think the idea incorporated was that we were opposed to the [fourteenth and fifteenth] amendments to the Constitution. I desire to explain in regard to that that it was not to be—at least, I did not intend by that that it should be—forcible resistance, but a political principle."

The oath itself is as follows:

From *Report of the Joint Select Committee to Inquire into the Condition of Affairs in the Late Insurrectionary States* (Government Printing Office, Washington, D.C., 1872), 25–27, 44–47.

I, (name,) before the great immaculate Judge of heaven and earth, and upon the Holy Evangelist of Almighty God, do, of my own free will and accord, subscribe to the following sacred, binding obligation:

I. I am on the side of justice and humanity and constitutional liberty, as bequeathed to us by our forefathers in its original purity.

II. I reject and oppose the principles of the radical [Republican] party.

III. I pledge aid to a brother of the Ku-Klux Klan in sickness, distress, or pecuniary embarrassments. Females, friends, widows, and their households shall be the special objects of my care and protection.

IV. Should I ever divulge, or cause to be divulged, any of the secrets of this order, or any of the foregoing obligations, I must meet with the fearful punishment of death and traitor's doom, which is death, death, death, at the hands of the brethren. . . .

Elias Hill of York County, South Carolina, is a remarkable character. He is crippled in both legs and arms, which are shriveled by rheumatism; he cannot walk, cannot help himself . . . ; was in early life a slave, whose freedom was purchased by his father. . . . He learned his letters and to read by calling the school children into the cabin as they passed, and also learned to write. He became a Baptist preacher, and after the war engaged in teaching colored children, and conducted the business correspondence of many of his colored neighbors. . . . We put the story of his wrongs in his own language:

"On the night of the 5th of May, after I had heard a great deal of what they had done in that neighborhood, they came . . . to my brother's door, which is in the same yard, and broke open the door and attacked his wife, and I heard her screaming and mourning. I could not understand what they said, for they were talking in an outlandish and unnatural tone, which I had heard they generally used at a negro's house. They said, 'Where's Elias?' She said, 'He doesn't stay here; yon is his house.' I had heard them strike her five or six licks. Someone then hit my door. . . .

"They carried me into the yard between the houses, my brother's and mine, and put me on the ground. . . . 'Who did that burning? Who burned our houses?' I told them it was not me. I could not burn houses. Then they hit me with their fists, and said I did it, I ordered it. They went on asking me didn't I tell the black men to ravish all the white women. No, I answered them. They struck me again. . . . 'Haven't you been preaching and praying about the Ku-Klux? Haven't you been preaching political sermons? Doesn't a [Republican Party newspaper] come to your house? Haven't you written letters?' Generally one asked me all the questions, but the rest were squatting over me—some six men I counted as I lay there. . . . I told them if they would take me back into the house, and lay me in the bed, which was close adjoining my books and papers, I would try and get it. They said I would never go back to that bed, for they were going to kill me. . . . They caught my leg and pulled me over the yard, and then left me there, knowing I could not walk nor crawl. . . .

"After they had stayed in the house for a considerable time, they came back to where I lay and asked if I wasn't afraid at all. They pointed pistols at me all around my head once or twice, as if they were going to shoot me. . . . One caught me by the leg and hurt me, for my leg for forty years has been drawn each year, more and more, and I made moan when it hurt so. One said, 'G–d d—n it, hush!' He had a horsewhip, [and] I reckon he struck me eight cuts right on the hip bone; it was almost the only place he could hit my body, my legs are so short. They all had disguises. . . . One of them then took a strap, and buckled it around my neck and said, 'Let's take him to the river and drown him.' . . .

"Then they said, 'Look here! Will you put a card in the paper to renounce all republicanism? Will you quit preaching?' I told them I did not know. I said that to save my life. . . . They said if I did not they would come back the next week and kill me. [After more licks with the strap] one of them went into the house where my brother and sister-in-law lived, and brought her to pick me up. As she stooped down to pick me up one of them struck her, and as she was carrying me into the house another struck her with a strap. . . . They said, 'Don't you pray against Ku-Klux, but pray that God may forgive Ku-Klux. Pray that God may bless and save us.' I was so chilled with cold lying out of doors so long and in such pain I could not speak to pray, but I tried to, and they said that would do very well, and all went out of the house. . . ."

Satisfied that he could no longer live in that community, Hill wrote to make inquiry about the means of going to Liberia. Hearing this, many of his neighbors desired to go also. . . . Others are still hoping for relief, through the means of this sub-committee.

4

◆

A KIND OF REUNION

Despite Congress's seizure of control over Reconstruction policy and Ulysses S. Grant's defeat of Andrew Johnson for the presidency in 1868, Radical Reconstruction—the garrisoning of the South, the disfranchisement of former rebels, and the control of Southern state governments by Republican votes—did not last long in most places. During President Grant's first term of office, the white-dominated Democratic Party gained control of North Carolina, Tennessee, and Virginia, the three ex-Confederate states with the lowest percentage of black population. During Grant's second term, Democrats seized control of Alabama, Arkansas, Georgia, Mississippi, and Texas. That left Republican governments (and federal troops) in Florida, Louisiana, and South Carolina, three states with large black populations.

Those states mattered greatly in national politics. During the election of 1876 both parties resorted to fraud. Two sets of electoral returns came in from the three states, and it was necessary for Congress to set up an electoral commission to decide whether Rutherford B. Hayes, the Republican candidate, or Samuel J. Tilden, the Democratic standard bearer, had won. By a strict party vote of 8 to 7, the commission awarded all 20 disputed electoral votes to the Republicans. Hayes became president, with 185 votes to Tilden's 184. In the end, Southern Democrats reached a compromise with Northern Republicans. The Democrats agreed to accept the commission's decision and the Republicans promised to withdraw the remaining federal troops from the South. In April 1877, the last federal soldiers left the South. Solid Democratic control—and stepped-up measures to disfranchise black voters—quickly followed.

Although political maneuvering was important in finally killing Republican Reconstruction, the underlying reason it died was simply that Northerners were losing the will to suppress an increasingly violent white South. The nation's approaching centennial celebration in 1876 triggered an especially strong outpouring of sentiment in favor of improving sectional feelings by withdrawing the troops, even if withdrawal meant the resurgence of the Democratic Party. That, in turn, would permit an overdue rebonding of the century-old republic. The following unsigned editorial ran in the August 1875 issue of *Scribner's*

Monthly, an influential, generally Republican, New York magazine. It expressed, with unusual eloquence, this emotional yearning for peace.

Questions to Consider. What was the occasion of the *Scribner's* editorial? Was this a natural time to consider troop withdrawals? What, in the view of the editor, was the major accomplishment of the Civil War? What specific political theory had been tested and defeated? When addressing the "men of the South," was the editor speaking to all Southern men? What did the phrase "brotherly sympathy" mean? Was it naive or was it realistic for the writer to think that the upcoming centennial could "heal all the old wounds" and "reconcile all the old differences"? Would Abraham Lincoln have agreed with the spirit of this editorial?

◆

What the Centennial Ought to Accomplish (1875)

SCRIBNER'S MONTHLY

We are to have grand doings next year. There is to be an Exposition. There are to be speeches, and songs, and processions, and elaborate ceremonies and general rejoicings. Cannon are to be fired, flags are to be floated, and the eagle is expected to scream while he dips the tip of either pinion in the Atlantic and the Pacific, and sprinkles the land with a new baptism of freedom. The national oratory will exhaust the figures of speech in patriotic glorification, while the effete civilizations of the Old World, and the despots of the East, tottering upon their tumbling thrones, will rub their eyes and sleepily inquire, "What's the row?" The Centennial is expected to celebrate in a fitting way—somewhat dimly apprehended, it is true—the birth of a nation.

Well, the object is a good one. When the old colonies declared themselves free, they took a grand step in the march of progress; but now, before we begin our celebration of this event, would it not be well for us to inquire whether we have a nation? In a large number of the States of this country there exists not only a belief that the United States do not constitute a nation, but a theory of State rights which forbids that they ever shall become one. We hear about the perturbed condition of the Southern mind. We hear it said that multitudes there are just as disloyal as they were during the civil war. This, we believe, we are justified in denying. Before the war they had a theory of State rights. They fought to establish that theory, and they now speak of the result as "the lost cause."

Miss Liberty's torch. A display at the great 1876 Centennial Exposition, Philadelphia. (Samuel Castner Collection/Free Library of Philadelphia)

They are not actively in rebellion, and they do not propose to be. They do not hope for the re-establishment of slavery. They fought bravely and well to establish their theory, but the majority was against them; and if the result of the war emphasized any fact, it was that *en masse* the people of the United States constitute a nation—indivisible in constituents, in interest, in destiny. The result of the war was without significance, if it did not mean that the United States constitute a nation which cannot be divided; which will not permit itself to be divided; which is integral, indissoluble, indestructible. We do not care what theories of State rights are entertained outside of this. State rights, in all the States, should be jealously guarded, and, by all legitimate means, defended. New York should be as jealous of her State prerogatives as South Carolina or Louisiana; but this theory which makes of the Union a rope of sand, and of the States a collection of petty nationalities that can at liberty drop the bands which hold them together, is forever exploded. It has been tested at the point of the bayonet. It went down in blood, and went down for all time. Its adherents may mourn over the fact, as we can never cease to mourn over the events which accompanied it, over the sad, incalculable cost to them and to those who opposed them. The great point with them is to recognize the fact that, for richer or poorer, in sickness and health, until death do us part, these United States constitute a nation; that we are to live, grow, prosper, and suffer together, united by bands that cannot be sundered.

Unless this fact is fully recognized throughout the Union, our Centennial will be but a hollow mockery. If we are to celebrate anything worth celebrating, it is the birth of a nation. If we are to celebrate anything worth celebrating, it should be by the whole heart and united voice of the nation. If we can make the Centennial an occasion for emphasizing the great lesson of the war, and universally assenting to the results of the war, it will, indeed, be worth all the money expended upon and the time devoted to it. If around the old Altars of Liberty we cannot rejoin our hands in brotherly affection and national loyalty, let us spike the cannon that will only proclaim our weakness, put our flags at half-mast, smother our eagles, eat our ashes, and wait for our American aloe to give us a better blossoming.

A few weeks ago, Mr. Jefferson Davis, the ex-President of the Confederacy, was reported to have exhorted an audience to which he was speaking to be as loyal to the old flag of the Union now as they were during the Mexican War. If the South could know what music there was in these words to Northern ears—how grateful we were to their old chief for them—it would appreciate the strength of our longing for a complete restoration of the national feeling that existed when Northern and Southern blood mingled in common sacrifice on Mexican soil. This national feeling, this national pride, this brotherly sympathy *must be restored;* and accursed be any Northern or Southern man, whether in power or out of power, whether politician, theorizer, carpet-bagger, president-maker or plunderer, who puts obstacles in the way of such a restoration. Men of the South, we want you. Men of the South, we long for the restoration of your peace and your prosperity. We would see your cities thriving, your homes happy, your plantations teeming with plenteous harvests, your schools overflowing, your wisest statesmen leading you, and all causes and all memories of discord wiped out forever. You do not believe this? Then you do not know the heart of the North. Have you cause of complaint against the politicians? Alas! so have we. Help us, as loving and loyal American citizens, to make our politicians better. Only remember and believe that there is nothing that the North wants so much to-day, as your recognition of the fact that the old relations between you and us are forever restored—that your hope, your pride, your policy, and your destiny are one with ours. Our children will grow up to despise our childishness, if we cannot do away with our personal hates so far, that in the cause of an established nationality we may join hands under the old flag.

To bring about this reunion of the two sections of the country in the old fellowship, should be the leading object of the approaching Centennial. A celebration of the national birth, begun, carried on, and finished by a section, would be a mockery and a shame. The nations of the world might well point at it the finger of scorn. The money expended upon it were better sunk in the sea, or devoted to repairing the waste places of the war. Men of the South, it is for you to say whether your magnanimity is equal to your valor—whether you are as reasonable as you are brave, and whether, like your old chief, you accept that definite and irreversible result of the war which makes you and yours forever members of the great American nation with us. Let us see to it, North and South, that the Centennial heals all the old wounds, reconciles all the old differences, and furnishes the occasion for such a reunion of the great American nationality, as shall make our celebration an expression of fraternal good-will among all sections and all States, and a corner-stone over which shall be reared a new temple to national freedom, concord, peace, and prosperity.

5

◆

AFTERMATH

Frederick Douglass regarded the Declaration of Independence as a "watchword of freedom." But he was tempted to turn it to the wall, he said, because its human rights principles were so shamelessly violated. A former slave himself, Douglass knew what he was talking about. Douglass thought that enslaving blacks fettered whites as well and that the United States would never be truly free until it ended chattel slavery. During the Civil War, he had several conversations with Lincoln, urging him to make emancipation his major aim. He also put unremitting pressure on the Union army to accept black volunteers, and after resistance to admitting blacks into the army gave way, he toured the country encouraging blacks to enlist and imploring the government to treat black and white soldiers equally in matters of pay and promotion.

Douglass had great hopes for his fellow blacks after the Civil War. He demanded they be given full rights—political, legal, educational, and economic—as citizens. He also wanted to see the wall of separation between the races crumble and see "the colored people of this country, enjoying the same freedom [as whites], voting at the same ballot-box, using the same cartridge-box, going to the same schools, attending the same churches, travelling in the same street cars, in the same railroad cars, on the same steam-boats, proud of the same country, fighting the same war, and enjoying the same peace and all its advantages." He regarded the Republican party as the "party of progress, justice and freedom" and at election time took to the stump and rallied black votes for the party. He was rewarded for these services by appointment as marshal of the District of Columbia in 1877, as recorder of deeds for the District in 1881, and as minister to Haiti in 1889. But he was also asked by Republican leaders to keep a low profile, was omitted from White House guest lists, and was excluded from presidential receptions even though one duty of the District marshal was to introduce the guests at White House state occasions.

Douglass was puzzled and then upset by the increasing indifference of Republican leaders to conditions among blacks after the Civil War. In 1883 he attended a convention of blacks in Louisville, Kentucky, which met to discuss their plight and reaffirm their demand for full civil rights. In his keynote address, which is reprinted here, Douglass vividly portrayed the discrimination and persecution his people encountered, but he continued to believe that "prejudice, with all its malign accomplishments, may yet be removed by peaceful means."

Born into slavery in Maryland in 1817, Frederick Augustus Washington Bailey learned to read and write despite efforts to keep him illiterate. In 1838 he managed to escape to freedom and adopted the name Frederick Douglass. Shortly afterward he became associated with William Lloyd Garrison and developed into such an articulate spokesman for the antislavery cause that people doubted he had ever been a slave. In 1845 he published his *Narrative of the Life of Frederick Douglass, an American Slave,* naming names, places, dates, and precise events to convince people he had been born in bondage. Douglass continued to be an articulate spokesman for the black cause throughout his life. Shortly before his death in 1895 a college student asked him what a young black could do to help the cause. "Agitate! Agitate! Agitate!" Douglass is supposed to have told him.

Questions to Consider. In the following address Douglass was speaking to a convention of blacks in Louisville, but his appeal was primarily to American whites. How did he try to convince them that blacks deserved the same rights and opportunities as all Americans? How powerful did he think the color line was? What outrages against his people did he report? What was his attitude toward the Republican party, which he had so faithfully served? Were the grievances he cited largely economic or were they social and political in nature?

◆

Address to the Louisville Convention (1883)

FREDERICK DOUGLASS

Born on American soil in common with yourselves, deriving our bodies and our minds from its dust, centuries having passed away since our ancestors were torn from the shores of Africa, we, like yourselves, hold ourselves to be in every sense Americans, and that we may, therefore, venture to speak to you in a tone not lower than that which becomes

From Philip Foner, ed., *The Life and Writings of Frederick Douglass* (4 v., International Publishers, New York, 1955), IV: 373–392. Reprinted by permission.

Frederick Douglass. Douglass's greatest work came before and during the Civil War. One of the most eloquent and magnetic of all the abolitionist leaders, he contributed enormously to the antislavery cause. During the Civil War he pressed hard for the enlistment of blacks to fight in the Union armies on an equal footing with whites. After the war he continued his efforts for civil rights, including black suffrage. For his services to the Republican party he received appointments as secretary to the Santo Domingo commission, marshal and recorder of deeds for the District of Columbia, and U.S. minister to Haiti. (National Portrait Gallery, Smithsonian Institution, Washington, D.C.)

earnest men and American citizens. Having watered your soil with our tears, enriched it with our blood, performed its roughest labor in time of peace, defended it against enemies in time of war, and at all times been loyal and true to its best interests, we deem it no arrogance or presumption to manifest now a common concern with you for its welfare, prosperity, honor and glory. . . .

It is our lot to live among a people whose laws, traditions, and prejudices have been against us for centuries, and from these they are not yet free. To assume that they are free from these evils simply because they have changed their laws is to assume what is utterly unreasonable and contrary to facts. Large bodies move slowly. Individuals may be converted on the instant and change their whole course of life. Nations never. Time and events are required for the conversion of nations. Not even the character of a great political organization can be changed by a new platform. It will be the same old snake though in a new skin. Though we have had war, reconstruction and abolition as a nation, we still linger in the shadow and blight of an extinct institution. Though the colored man is no longer subject to be bought and sold, he is still surrounded by an adverse sentiment which fetters all his movements. In his downward course he meets with no resistance, but his course upward is resented and resisted at every step of his progress. If he comes in ignorance, rags, and wretchedness, he conforms to the popular belief of his character, and in that character he is welcome. But if he shall come as a gentleman, a scholar, and a statesman, he is hailed as a contradiction to the national faith concerning his race, and his coming is resented as impudence. In the one case he may provoke contempt and derision, but in the other he is an affront to pride, and provokes malice.

He is rejected by trade unions, of every trade, and refused work while he lives, and burial when he dies, and yet he is asked to forget his color, and forget that which everybody else remembers. If he offers himself to a builder as a mechanic, to a client as a lawyer, to a patient as a physician, to a college as a professor, to a firm as a clerk, to a Government Department as an agent, or an officer, he is sternly met on the color line, and his claim to consideration in some way is disputed on the ground of color.

Not even our churches, whose members profess to follow the despised Nazarene, whose home, when on earth, was among the lowly and de-spised, have yet conquered this feeling of color madness, and what is true of our churches is also true of our courts of law. Neither is free from this all-pervading atmosphere of color hate. The one describes the Deity as impartial, no respecter of persons, and the other the Goddess of Justice as blindfolded, with sword by her side and scales in her hand held evenly between high and low, rich and low, white and black, but both are the images of American imagination, rather than American practices.

Taking advantage of the general disposition in this country to impute crime to color, white men *color* their faces to commit crime and wash off the hated color to escape punishment. In many places where the commission of crime is alleged against one of our color, the ordinary processes of law are set aside as too slow for the impetuous justice of the infuriated populace. They take the law into their own bloody hands and proceed to whip, stab, shoot, hang, or burn the alleged culprit, without the intervention of courts, counsel, judges, juries, or witnesses. In such cases it is not the business of the accusers to prove guilt, but it is for the accused to prove his innocence, a thing hard for him to do in these infernal Lynch courts. A man accused, surprised, frightened, and captured by a motley crowd, dragged with a rope about his neck in midnight-darkness to the nearest tree, and told in the coarsest terms of profanity to prepare for death, would be more than human if he did not, in his terror-stricken appearance, more confirm suspicion of guilt than the contrary. Worse still, in the presence of such hell-black outrages, the pulpit is usually dumb, and the press in the neighborhood is silent or openly takes side with the mob. There are occasional cases in which white men are lynched, but one sparrow does not make a summer. Every one knows that what is called Lynch law is peculiarly the law for colored people and for nobody else. If there were no other grievance than this horrible and barbarous Lynch law custom, we should be justified in assembling, as we have now done, to expose and denounce it. But this is not all. Even now, after twenty years of so-called emancipation, we are subject to lawless raids of midnight riders, who, with blackened faces, invade our homes and perpetrate the foulest of crimes upon us and our families. This condition of things is too flagrant and notorious to require specifications or proof.

Thus in all the relations of life and death we are met by the color line. While we recognize the color line as a hurtful force, a mountain barrier to our progress, wounding our bleeding feet with its flinty rocks at every step, we do not despair. We are a hopeful people. This convention is a proof of our faith in you, in reason, in truth and justice—our belief that prejudice, with all its malign accomplishments, may yet be removed by peaceful means; that, assisted by time and events and the growing enlightenment of both races, the color line will ultimately become harmless. When this shall come it will then only be used, as it should be, to distinguish one variety of the human family from another. It will cease to have any civil, political, or moral significance, and colored conventions will then be dispensed with as anachronisms, wholly out of place, but not till then. Do not marvel that we are discouraged. The faith within us has a rational basis, and is confirmed by facts. When we consider how deep-seated this feeling against us is; the long centuries it has been forming; the forces of avarice which have been marshaled to sustain it; how the language and literature of the country have been pervaded with it; how the church, the press, the play-house, and other influences of the country have been arrayed in its support, the progress toward its extinction must be considered vast and wonderful. . . .

We do not believe, as we are often told, that the Negro is the ugly child of the national family, and the more he is kept out of sight the better it will be for him. You know that liberty given is never so precious as liberty sought for and fought for. The man outraged is the man to make the outcry. Depend upon it, men will not care much for a people who do not care for themselves. Our meeting here was opposed by some of our members, because it would disturb the peace of the Republican party. The suggestion came from coward lips and misapprehended the character of that party. If the Republican party cannot stand a demand for justice and fair play, it ought to go down. We were men before that party was born, and our manhood is more sacred than any party can be. Parties were made for men, not men for parties.

The colored people of the South are the laboring people of the South. The labor of a country is the source of its wealth; without the colored laborer to-day the South would be a howling wilderness, given up to bats, owls, wolves, and bears. He was the source of its wealth before the war, and has been the source of its prosperity since the war. He almost alone is visible in her fields, with implements of toil in his hands, and laboriously using them to-day.

Let us look candidly at the matter. While we see and hear that the South is more prosperous than it ever was before and rapidly recovering from the waste of war, while we read that it raises more cotton, sugar, rice, tobacco, corn, and other valuable products than it ever produced before, how happens it, we sternly ask, that the houses of its laborers are miserable huts, that their clothes are rags, and their food the coarsest and scantiest? How happens it that the land-owner is becoming richer and the laborer poorer?

The implication is irresistible—that where the landlord is prosperous the laborer ought to share his prosperity, and whenever and wherever we find this is not the case there is manifestly wrong somewhere. . . .

Flagrant as have been the outrages committed upon colored citizens in respect to their civil rights, more flagrant, shocking, and scandalous still have been the outrages committed upon our political rights by means of bull-dozing and Kukluxing, Mississippi plans, fraudulent courts, tissue ballots, and the like devices. Three States in which the colored people out-number the white population are without colored representation and their political voice suppressed. The colored citizens in those States are virtually disfranchised, the Constitution held in utter contempt and its provisions nullified. This has been done in the face of the Republican party and successive Republican administrations. . . .

This is no question of party. It is a question of law and government. It is a question whether men shall be protected by law, or be left to the mercy of cyclones of anarchy and bloodshed. It is whether the Government or the mob shall rule this land; whether the promises solemnly made to us in the constitution be manfully kept or meanly and flagrantly broken. Upon this vital point we ask the whole people of the United States to take notice that whatever of political power we have shall be exerted for no man of any party who will not, in advance of election, promise to use every power given him by the Government, State or National, to make the black man's path to the ballot-box as straight, smooth and safe as that of any other American citizen. . . .

We hold it to be self-evident that no class or color should be the exclusive rulers of this country. If there is such a ruling class, there must of course be a subject class, and when this condition is once established this Government of the people, by the people, and for the people, will have perished from the earth.

Extension of the Brooklyn Bridge. Workmen demolishing buildings to make way for the extension of the monumental Brooklyn Bridge, whose tower dwarfs the old waterfront structures, across the East River from Brooklyn to New York City. (Courtesy Dover Pictorial Archive Series, *New York in the 19th Century* by John Grafton, © 1980 Dover Publications, Inc.)

CHAPTER TWO

◆

The Age of Industry

6

◆

THE GOSPEL OF PRODUCTION

During the last part of the nineteenth century the United States experienced remarkable industrial development. In 1860 it was largely a nation of farms, villages, small businesses, and small-scale manufacturing establishments; by 1900 it had become a nation of cities, machines, factories, offices, shops, and powerful business combinations. Between 1860 and 1900, railroad trackage increased, annual production of coal rose steadily, iron and steel production soared, oil refining flourished, and development of electric power proceeded apace. "There has never been in the history of civilization," observed economist Edward Atkinson in 1891, "a period, or a place, or a section of the earth in which science and invention have worked such progress or have created such opportunity for material welfare as in these United States in the period which has elapsed since the end of the Civil War." By the end of the century, America's industrial production exceeded that of Great Britain and Germany combined, and the United States was exporting huge quantities of farm and factory goods to all parts of the world. The country had become one of the richest and most powerful nations in history.

More than any other single element, steel permitted and laid the foundation for industrialization. The process of steel production powered industrial development, and the key to rising steel production was the adaptation of the so-called Bessemer process to American conditions. As the following article by Robert Hunt shows, the emergence of mass steel manufacture by this method involved a dynamic interplay between foreign and domestic production ideas, patent law, firm capitalization and competition, creative marketing, and, perhaps most important, constant technical adaptation on the factory floor.

At the other end of the production scale was Andrew Carnegie, the "King of Steel." Carnegie liked to boast of the accomplishments of efficient business organization in the American steel industry, as he did in the excerpt below from *Triumphant Democracy* (1886), a best seller. "Two pounds of ironstone mined upon Lake Superior and transported nine hundred miles to Pittsburgh; one pound and a half of coal, mined and manufactured into coke, and transported to Pittsburgh; one-half pound of lime, mined and transported to Pittsburgh; a small amount of manganese ore mined in Virginia and brought to Pittsburgh—and these four pounds of materials manufactured into one pound of steel, for which the consumer pays one cent." Carnegie preached what he called a "gospel of wealth." His gospel emphasized individual initiative, private property, competition, and the accumulation of wealth in the hands of those with superior ability and energy. But, acknowledging that wealth was the product of society as well as of individual effort, he also maintained that rich people had an obligation to spend their surplus wealth for the good of the community. The "man who dies rich," he asserted, "dies disgraced."

Born in 1838 to a Bucks County, Pennsylvania, physician, Robert W. Hunt ran a drugstore, worked in a local iron-rolling mill, and studied chemistry in Philadelphia before joining the Union Army. After the war Hunt helped introduce the Bessemer method to the Cambria Iron Company of Johnstown, Pennsylvania. He was later the general superintendent of the Albany and Rensselaer Iron and Steel Company of Troy, New York. He wrote and lectured frequently on matters concerning steel and belonged to numerous scientific societies. He died in Chicago in 1923.

Andrew Carnegie, the son of a handloom weaver, was born in Scotland in 1835. With his family, he moved to Allegheny, Pennsylvania, at the age of twelve and got a job in a textile mill at $1.20 a week. During this period he studied telegraphy, a skill that landed him a position as the personal secretary and telegrapher of a leading railroad executive. Carnegie was himself a railroad executive for a time, then amassed a fortune selling bonds, dealing in oil, and building bridges. In 1873 he concentrated his efforts on steel and gradually built his Carnegie Steel Company into a massive industrial giant. In 1901 he sold the firm to J. P. Morgan, who made it the core of the world's first billion-dollar company, the United States Steel Corporation. Over the next two decades Carnegie gave away some $350 million for libraries and other public works. He died in Lenox, Massachusetts, in 1919.

Questions to Consider. In reading Robert Hunt's article, note that, according to Hunt, many steps resulted in the sharp increases in steel productivity. How important were the original inventors (Henry Bessemer in England and William Kelly in the United States) to this result? How important was finding large-scale financial backing? In Hunt's eyes, what single innovation produced the biggest jump in productivity? Who was responsible for that innovation? Why did the owners of existing blast furnaces seem to resist the new product? How important was the presence of skilled labor to the development of the new system? Was Hunt entitled to attribute the revolution in steelmaking to "American push"?

The excerpt from *Triumphant Democracy* is typical of the many articles and books Andrew Carnegie wrote celebrating the American system. He thought America's republican institutions were far more favorable to economic progress than were the monarchical institutions of the Old World. Why did Carnegie think life "has become vastly better worth living" than it was a century before? What particular aspects of American life did he single out for special mention? In what ways did he think life in the United States was better than life in Europe? Was he writing mainly about the life of the average or the well-to-do American? How did he relate America's economic achievements to democracy?

◆

Bessemer Steel (1877)

ROBERT HUNT

The memorable features of American history have been rapidly emerging during the last century, and notably so since 1860; and they are by no means confined to political or to any one branch of scientific development. Of all the industrial arts, none show a greater change or a mightier progress than the Bessemer manufacture. And this year, while we are celebrating the first centennial of our national life, we can also celebrate the first decennial of American Bessemer practice. While not forgetting or under-valuing what has been done in other countries, I have thought that a brief history of the introduction and development of the Pneumatic or Bessemer process[1] in America would be of interest.

In 1863 the Kelly Pneumatic Process Company was formed and an arrangement entered into with William Kelly, who had taken out letters-patent. . . .

Previous to the application of William Kelly for a patent, Henry Bessemer, of England, had taken out patents dated February 12th, 1856, and August 25th, 1856, in this country. Kelly claimed priority in the discovery of the principles of the process, and the Patent-office allowed his claim by granting him his patents.

In the autumn of 1862 Mr. Alexander L. Holley, while in England, was impressed with the importance of Mr. Bessemer's invention, and so fully foresaw its future, that, upon his return to the United States, he induced

From Robert W. Hunt, 'A History of the Bessemer Manufacture in America," *Transactions of the American Institute of Mining Engineers* 5 (1876–1877), 201–216.

1. **The Bessemer process:** A process that makes steel from pig iron by burning out carbon and other impurities by means of a blast of air forced through the molten metal.

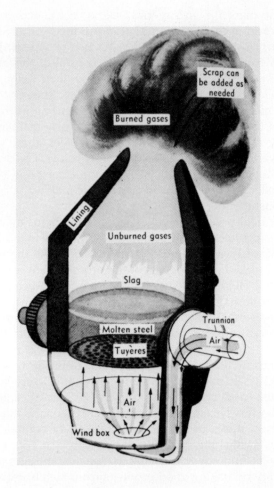

Bessemer converter. A simplified diagram, including the trunnions on which the bucket pivoted and the tuyeres through which forced air was blown into the molten iron, of a Bessemer converter, the single most important ingredient in the vast expansion of 19th-century American steel production. (Courtesy American Iron and Steel Institute)

Messrs. John A. Griswold and John F. Winslow, of Troy, New York, to join him in endeavoring to possess Bessemer's American patents. . . .

But, before entering into chronological details of subsequent works, I must here state that, after building the first experimental plant at Troy, Mr. Holley seems to have at once broken loose from the restraints of his foreign experience, and to have been impressed with the capabilities of the new process. The result is that mainly through his inventions and modifications of the plant we, in America, are today enabled to stand at the head of the world in respect of amount of product.

But to return to the detailed history. As before stated, there were, in 1865, the two rival organizations claiming control of the process in this country,—the Kelly Process Company, through their Kelly and Mushet's patents, and Messrs. Winslow, Griswold & Holley, through their Bessemer and Holley American patents. Both parties felt strong in their respective positions, and in possessing the necessary means to maintain them. But, after spending large sums of money in counsel fees, they . . . combined their respective interests, the Bessemer, or Winslow, Griswold & Holley, party taking 70 per cent., and the Kelly Process Company 30 per cent. of all royalties collected. To this wise compromise may we attribute the subsequent establishment of many works. . . .

But great difficulty was even yet experienced in inducing capitalists and manufacturers to attempt the introduction of the new manufacture. While the metal produced was wonderful in its qualities, still the necessary first outlay was so large, and the details of the process were so uncertain, and the time-honored prejudice against anything new held such powerful sway, that our people hesitated, doubted, and waited. Wonderful tales came to us of what was being done abroad, and some venture-some railway managers even dared to import and place in their tracks trial lots of foreign Bessemer rails.

Messrs. Winslow, Griswold & Holley had, from the very first erection of their works, wisely pursued the plan of extending every facility to blast-furnace owners, in all parts of the country, to have their irons tried for steel; and under this system many brands were tried, and most were found wanting. These failures to obtain good results, of course, built up still greater barriers against the spread of the process. . . . But still it was this very blind using of unknown irons that first opened the eyes of steelmakers to the possibility of making good products from metals pronounced unfit by the then authorities. . . .

After building the original experimental plant at Troy, Mr. A. L. Holley seems to have appreciated that the manufacture was capable of a development far beyond that which had been attained. . . . The result of his thought gave us the present accepted type of American Bessemer plant. He did away with the English deep pit and raised the vessels so as to get working space under them on the ground floor; he substituted top-supported hydraulic cranes for the more expensive counter-weighted English ones, and put three ingot cranes around the pit instead of two, and thereby obtained greater area of power. He changed the location of the vessels as related to the pit and melting-house. He modified the ladle crane, and worked all the cranes and the vessels from a single point; he substituted cupolas for reverberatory furnaces, and last, but by no means least, introduced the intermediate or accumulating ladle which is placed on scales, and thus insures accuracy of operation by rendering possible the weighing of each charge of melted iron, before pouring it into the converter. These points cover the radical features of his innovations. After building such a plant, he began to meet the difficulties of details in manufacture, among the most serious of which was the short duration of the vessel bottoms, and the time required to cool off the vessels to a point at which it was possible for workmen to enter and make new bottoms. After many experiments, the result was the Holley Vessel Bottom, which, either in its form as patented, or in a modification of it as now used in all American works, has rendered possible, as much as any other one thing, the present immense production. . . .

[Following other improvements] Mr. Holley had become a consulting Bessemer engineer. Many discussions and consultations took place between Mr. George Fritz, Mr. Holley, and the writer, as to the possibility of increasing the product of the [Cambria, Pennsylvania,] works. Among other things, tapping cinder from the cupolas was thought of, and decided upon. These works had already placed their turn's work at nine instead of eight heats.[2] The Cambria works applied the cinder tap, and the production went up to the unanticipated amount of thirty heats, or one hundred and fifty tons in twenty-four hours. Grand as we thought this, it is only about one-half of the present yield of each of several works. During all this time many details were modified, and as the new ways proved successful they were adopted in the regular practice. I think one thing which had a strong bearing on the increased production was the labor organization of the Cambria works. In compliance with the policy decided upon, I started the converting works without a single man who had ever seen even the outside of Bessemer works, and, with a very few exceptions, they were not even skilled rolling-mill men, but on the contrary were selected from intelligent laborers. The result was that we had willing pupils with no prejudices, and without any reminiscences of what they had done in the old country or at any other works. Of course when one works went ahead, the others had to follow. . . .

While I am not able to mention all of the very many good things accomplished by the gentlemen at each and all the various works, I am, at the same time, well aware they have all done their share toward achieving the great end; and, fortunately, their mutual relations have been so pleasant, that each one's experiences have been freely imparted to the others. This has done wonders to advance the science. But without one element, all skill and all mechanical talent would have been wasted, and with it nearly all things have been possible. That element has been, and is, "American push."

---

2. **A "heat":** About five tons of molten steel.

◆

Triumphant Democracy (1886)

ANDREW CARNEGIE

A community of toilers with an undeveloped continent before them, and destitute of the refinements and elegancies of life—such was the picture presented by the Republic sixty years ago. Contrasted with that of today, we might almost conclude that we were upon another planet and subject to different primary conditions. The development of an unequaled transportation system brings the products of one section to the doors of another, the tropical fruits of Florida and California to Maine, and the ice of New England to the Gulf States. Altogether life has become vastly better worth living than it was a century ago.

Among the rural communities, the change in the conditions is mainly seen in the presence of labor-saving devices, lessening the work in house and field. Mowing and reaping machines, horse rakes, steam plows and threshers, render man's part easy and increase his productive power. Railroads and highways connect him with the rest of the world, and he is no longer isolated or dependent upon his petty village. Markets for his produce are easy of access, and transportation swift and cheap. If the roads throughout the country are yet poor compared with those of Europe, the need of good roads has been rendered less imperative by the omnipresent railroad. It is the superiority of the iron highway in America which has diverted attention from the country roads. It is a matter of congratulation, however, that this subject is at last attracting attention. Nothing would contribute so much to the happiness of life in the country as such perfect roads as those of Scotland. It is a difficult problem, but its solution will well repay any amount of expenditure necessary. [British historian Thomas] Macaulay's test of the civilization of a people—the condition of their roads—must be interpreted, in this age of steam, to include railroads. Communication between great cities is now cheaper and more comfortable than in any other country. Upon the principal railway lines, the cars—luxurious drawng-rooms by day, and sleeping chambers by night—are ventilated by air, warmed and filtered in winter, and cooled in summer. Passenger steamers upon the lakes and rivers are of gigantic size, and models of elegance.

It is in the cities that the change from colonial conditions is greatest. Most of these—indeed all, excepting those upon the Atlantic coast—have been in great measure the result of design instead of being allowed, like Topsy, to "just grow." In these modern days cities are laid out under definite, far-seeing plans; consequently the modern city presents symmetry

From Andrew Carnegie, *Triumphant Democracy* (Scribners, New York, 1886), 164–183.

Andrew Carnegie. Carnegie was perhaps the country's most famous indus-
trialist of the late 1800s. Certainly he was its richest, with a fortune of a half-
billion dollars. But he was also its most articulate spokesman, producing widely
read books and articles. Furthermore, as an immigrant's son who later en-
dowed hundreds of public libraries, Carnegie exemplified two cherished American ideals: self-help in the accumulation of wealth, and stewardship in the
disposal of it. (Andrew Carnegie, *Triumphant Democracy*, Scribners, NY)

of form unknown in mediaeval ages. The difference is seen by contrasting
the crooked cowpaths of old Boston with the symmetrical, broad streets
of Washington or Denver. These are provided with parks at intervals for
breathing spaces; amply supplied with pure water, in some cases at enormous expense; the most modern ideas are embodied in their sanitary arrangements; they are well lighted, well policed, and the fire departments
are very efficient. In these modern cities an extensive fire is rare. The
lessening danger of this risk is indicated by the steady fall in the rate of
fire insurance.

The variety and quality of the food of the people of America excels that
found elsewhere, and is a constant surprise to Europeans visiting the States.
The Americans are the best-fed people on the globe. Their dress is now of
the richest character—far beyond that of any other people, compared class
for class. The comforts of the average American home compare favorably

with those of other lands, while the residences of the wealthy classes are unequaled. The first-class American residence of today in all its appointments excites the envy of the foreigner. One touch of the electric button calls a messenger; two bring a telegraph boy; three summon a policeman; four give the alarm of fire. Telephones are used to an extent undreamt of in Europe, the stables and other out-buildings being connected with the mansion; and the houses of friends are joined by the talking wire almost as often as houses of business. Speaking tubes connect the drawing-room with the kitchen; and the dinner is brought up "piping hot" by a lift. Hot air and steam pipes are carried all over the house; and by the turning of a tap the temperature of any room is regulated to suit the convenience of the occupant. A passenger lift is common. The electric light is an additional home comfort. Indeed, there is no palace or great mansion in Europe with half the conveniences and scientific appliances which characterize the best American mansions. New York Central Park is no unworthy rival of Hyde Park and the Bois de Boulogne in its display of fine equipages; and in winter the hundreds of graceful sleighs dashing along the drives form a picture. The opera-houses, theatres, and public halls of the country excel in magnificence those of other lands, if we except the latter constructions in Paris and Vienna, with which the New York, Philadelphia, and Chicago opera-houses rank. The commercial exchanges, and the imposing structures of the life insurance companies, newspaper buildings, hotels, and many edifices built by wealthy firms, not only in New York but in the cities of the West, never fail to excite the Europeans' surprise. The postal system is equal in every respect to that of Europe. Mails are taken up by express trains, sorted on board, and dropped at all important points without stopping. Letters are delivered several times a day in every considerable town, and a ten-cent special delivery stamp insures delivery at once by special messenger in the large cities. The uniform rate of postage for all distances, often exceeding three thousand miles, is only two cents . . . per ounce.

In short, the conditions of life in American cities may be said to have approximated those of Europe during the sixty years of which we are speaking. Year by year, as the population advances, the general standard of comfort in the smaller Western cities rises to that of the East. Herbert Spencer [an English philosopher] was astonished beyond measure at what he saw in American cities. "Such books as I had looked into," said he, "had given me no adequate idea of the immense developments of material civilization which I have found everywhere. The extent, wealth, and magnificence of your cities, and especially the splendors of New York, have altogether astonished me. Though I have not visited the wonder of the West, Chicago, yet some of your minor modern places, such as Cleveland, have sufficiently amazed me by the marvelous results of one generation's activity. Occasionally, when I have been in places of some ten thousand inhabitants, where the telephone is in general use, I have felt somewhat ashamed of our own unenterprising towns, many of which, of fifty thousand inhabitants and more, make no use of it."

Such is the Democracy; such its conditions of life. In the presence of such a picture can it be maintained that the rule of the people is subversive of government and religion? Where have monarchical institutions developed a community so delightful in itself, so intelligent, so free from crime or pauperism—a community in which the greatest good of the greatest number is so fully attained, and one so well calculated to foster the growth of self-respecting men—which is the end civilization seeks?

> "For ere man made us citizens
> God made us men."

The republican is necessarily self-respecting, for the laws of his country begin by making him a man indeed, the equal of other men. The man who most respects himself will always be found the man who most respects the rights and feelings of others.

The rural democracy of America could be as soon induced to sanction the confiscation of the property of its richer neighbors, or to vote for any violent or discreditable measure, as it could be led to surrender the President for a king. Equal laws and privileges develop all the best and noblest characteristics, and these always lead in the direction of the Golden Rule. These honest, pure, contented, industrious, patriotic people really do consider what they would have others do to them. They ask themselves what is fair and right. Nor is there elsewhere in the world so conservative a body of men; but then it is the equality of the citizen—just and equal laws— republicanism, they are resolved to conserve. To conserve these they are at all times ready to fight and, if need be, to die; for, to men who have once tasted the elixir of political equality, life under unequal conditions could possess no charm.

To every man is committed in some degree, as a sacred trust, the manhood of man. This he may not himself infringe or permit to be infringed by others. Hereditary dignities, political inequalities, do infringe the right of man, and hence are not to be tolerated. The true democrat must live the peer of his fellows, or die struggling to become so.

The American citizen has no further need to struggle, being in possession of equality under the laws in every particular. He has not travelled far in the path of genuine Democracy who would not scorn to enjoy a privilege which was not the common birthright of all his fellows.

7

◆

LABOR'S VISION

The decades following the Civil War brought an enormous expansion of activity in railroads, coal, steel, and other basic industries. This rapid rise in the development of America's natural resources was accompanied by a sharp rise in the country's per capita wealth and income and, in the long run, a higher standard of living for most people. But it resulted in other things as well: greater wealth and power for "capitalists," as the new leaders of industry were called; a deterioration in conditions for many workers; and a society repeatedly torn by class conflict.

The Noble Order of the Knights of Labor, formed as a secret workingmen's lodge in 1869, represented an early response to these trends. Secrecy seemed essential at first because of the hostility of employers toward labor unions. Not until 1881 did the Knights of Labor abandon secrecy and announce its objectives to the world. Its slogan was "An injury to one is the concern of all." The Knights took pride in their admission of all workers—regardless of race, sex, or level of skill—and in their moderate, public-spirited vision of a cooperative economic order. These factors, together with their support of successful railroad strikes, swelled the Knights of Labor membership rolls to nearly 800,000 by 1886. After that, however, a wave of antiradicalism, combined with internal problems and the loss of several bitter industrial struggles, sent membership plummeting. By 1900 the organization was gone. It was replaced by two other labor organizations: the American Federation of Labor (AFL), founded in 1886, which organized skilled labor and struck over wages and working conditions, and the Industrial Workers of the World (IWW), founded in 1905, which appealed to the unskilled and stood for industrial reorganization. The AFL, which opposed most of the Knights principles, endured; the IWW, which shared many of them, did not.

The American Federation of Labor was a combination of national craft unions with an initial membership of about 140,000. It was the result of craft disagreement with the Knights of Labor partly over tactics and partly over leadership. The unions that comprised the AFL were central players in a nationwide campaign in support of an eight-hour workday. Centered in Chicago but spreading rapidly to other cities, the campaign (whose major statement appears below) culminated in a series of mass strikes and demonstrations on May 1, 1886. The campaign failed in its efforts to impose a uniform eight-hour day throughout American industry. It succeeded, however, in making a shortened workday one of the cardinal ongoing demands of union organizers and negotiators. When major breakthroughs in union representation and influence came during the 1930s and 1940s, eight hours—"nine to five" with an hour for lunch—became in fact the standard workday everywhere.

Because the Knights of Labor was at first a secret organization, the preamble to its constitution, reprinted below, contained asterisks instead of the organization's name. The author of the preamble was Terence V. Powderly, Grand Master Workman of the Knights from 1879 to 1893. Powderly was born in Carbondale, Pennsylvania, in 1849 to Irish immigrant parents. After ten years as a railroad laborer and machinist, he became active in union affairs, joining the Knights in 1874 and rising rapidly in the organization. He was also a political activist during these years. He served as mayor of Scranton, Pennsylvania, supporting many prolabor candidates in the 1880s, though, like most American labor leaders, he refused to support a separate labor party. After the Knights' decline, Powderly studied law and then served in the Federal Bureau of Immigration. He died in Washington, D.C., in 1924.

The president of the AFL in 1886 and a key figure in the Eight-Hour Association, was Samuel Gompers. Gompers was a German-born cigarmaker who emigrated to New York City with his parents at age thirteen. At first a strong socialist, he became a leader of the Cigarmakers' Union in the 1870s, moving it away from social and political reform and toward "pure and simple unionism" based on demands for higher wages, benefits, and security. Gompers was president of the AFL every year but one from 1886 to 1924. During this time, he built an organization that was both powerful and conservative—one that was hostile to radicalism, party alignments, and the admission of the unskilled. He died in San Antonio, Texas, in 1924.

Questions to Consider. What general objectives did the Knights preamble set forth? What do the Knights' practical demands reveal about working conditions in America during the Gilded Age (the period from 1870 to 1890)? To what extent was the preamble idealistic? How radical was it? Does the preamble explain why the Knights barred doctors, lawyers, bankers, gamblers, and liquor dealers from membership, although it allowed farmers, merchants, and small capitalists to join? If you wanted to quote something from the preamble giving the gist of the Knights' philosophy, which passage would you select? The statement of the Eight-Hour Association opened with a demand to reduce the workday from ten hours to eight. How long had the standard workday been ten hours? Was the ten-hour workday a national standard in 1886? How, according to the statement, would the U.S. economy be able to tolerate so drastic a shrinkage in the work-week? For whose eyes does this portion of the statement appear to have been written? How could a shorter workday benefit laborers? Who besides the individual workers would benefit from the new day?

◆

Preamble to the Constitution of the Knights of Labor (1878)

The recent alarming development and aggression of aggregated wealth, which, unless checked, will invariably lead to the pauperization and hope-less degradation of the toiling masses, render it imperative, if we desire to enjoy the blessings of life, that a check should be placed upon its power and upon unjust accumulation, and a system adopted which will secure to the laborer the fruits of his toil; and as this much-desired object can only be accomplished by the thorough unification of labor, and the united efforts of those who obey the divine injunction that "In the sweat of thy brow shalt thou eat bread," we have formed the ***** with a view of securing the organization and direction, by co-operative effort, of the power of the industrial classes; and we submit to the world the object sought to be accomplished by our organization, calling upon all who believe in securing "the greatest good to the greatest number" to aid and assist us:—

I. To bring within the folds of organization every department of productive industry, making knowledge a standpoint for action, and in-dustrial and moral worth, not wealth, the true standard of individual and national greatness.

II. To secure to the toilers a proper share of the wealth that they create; more of the leisure that rightfully belongs to them; more societary advantages; more of the benefits, privileges, and emoluments of the world; in a word, all those rights and privileges necessary to make them capable of enjoying, appreciating, defending, and perpetuating the blessing of good government.

III. To arrive at the true condition of the producing masses in their educational, moral, and financial condition, by demanding from the various governments the establishment of bureaus of Labor Statistics.

IV. The establishment of co-operative institutions, productive and distributive.

From Terence V. Powderly, *Thirty Years of Labor* (Excelsior Publishing House, Columbus, Ohio, 1890), 243–246.

V. The reserving of the public lands—the heritage of the people—for the actual settler;—not another acre for railroads or speculators.

VI. The abrogation of all laws that do not bear equally upon capital and labor, the removal of unjust technicalities, delays, and discriminations in the administration of justice, and the adopting of measures providing for the health and safety of those engaged in mining, manufacturing, or building pursuits.

VII. The enactment of laws to compel chartered corporations to pay their employees weekly, in full, for labor performed during the preceding week, in the lawful money of the country.

VIII. The enactment of laws giving mechanics and laborers a first lien on their work for their full wages.

IX. The abolishment of the contract system on national, state, and municipal work.

X. The substitution of arbitration for strikes, whenever and wherever employers and employees are willing to meet on equitable grounds.

XI. The prohibition of the employment of children in workshops, mines, and factories before attaining their fourteenth year.

XII. To abolish the system of letting out by contract the labor of convicts in our prisons and reformatory institutions.

XIII. To secure for both sexes equal pay for equal work.

XIV. The reduction of the hours of labor to eight per day, so that the laborers may have more time for social enjoyment and intellectual improvement, and be enabled to reap the advantages conferred by the labor-saving machinery which their brains have created.

XV. To prevail upon governments to establish a purely national circulating medium, based upon the faith and resources of the nation, and issued directly to the people, without the intervention of any system of banking corporations, which money shall be a legal tender in payment of all debts, public or private.

◆

Statement of the Eight-Hour Association (1886)

The Eight-Hour Association asks for a reduction of all daily toil from ten hours to eight, for the reason that such reduction of time will give opportunity for two more men to work for every eight now employed. In other words, the work now performed by eight men will require ten men to achieve the same result. This will be twenty more men employed for every eighty, thus giving immediate, and for some years, constant labor to all who are willing and able to work.

From *John Swinton's Paper* (May 2, 1886).

Strikebreakers dragged from a train in Pittsburgh, 1877. The 1877 railroad strike was the first nationwide strike. Two weeks of fierce fighting left hundreds dead and damage in the millions of dollars. Industrial conflicts continued to convulse the industry in the 1880s, with workers sometimes winning concessions and sometimes losing them.

That every one shall have steady employment at good wages, working eight hours daily, it is necessary that all agree and unite in this movement. In order for each workman to prosper it is essential that all other workmen prosper; because all people support each other by exchanging each others' production and services. Therefore everybody who has commodities or services for sale is interested in having everybody else have a sufficient income from his own earnings to make a mutual exchange. United action in this effort means not only strength but prosperity for all.

The advocates of eight hours for a day's labor advise all workers to take for this number of hours an eight-hour price, allowing the law of supply and demand to regulate wages in the future. We fully believe that while merchants, manufacturers and all employers will be benefited, the wages for laborers will soon be higher than ever heretofore, for the following reasons: A reduction of one-fifth of laboring-time for all that work will make a reduction of one-fifth of all kinds of products in the near future, which will make proportionate scarcity. With scarcity will come advance in prices for every commodity, giving merchants and manufacturers a fair profit, and wage-workers an advance in wages. Ere long, all being employed, the production will be as great as now, but, all earning wages, the consumption and demand will be greater than now, so that prices and wages will still continue better than at present.

Eight hours, instead of ten, means a gain of two hours each day—more than one day each week—*seventy-eight days a year!*—a time sufficient to enable every unlettered person to learn to read and write; time in which every foreigner can learn to speak the English language and familiarize himself with his political duty as an American citizen. The extra time thus gained in the year will afford every workingman not only a sufficient recreation, but opportunity to attend the State and county fairs, the National Exposition, and make a visit to the childhood home, with time to spare for a journey to Europe.

This appeal is in the interest of capital as well as labor. The plain facts are that the strikes, lock-outs, business failures, general business depression throughout the world, overflowing prisons and poor-houses, are the result of the producing power of the country being far in excess of the practical ability to consume. We make, raise and produce more than we can readily eat, wear, or dispose of. This results, first, in a falling of prices; then a lowering of wages, succeeded by strikes and resistance of wage-workers, and a final discharge of workmen into idleness. Then, as men are unable to buy, there is a great under-consumption, goods piling up on one side, while great want and destitution exist on the other. To remedy this, productive power, temporarily, must be lessened. To do this by destroying machinery is barbarous. It is wiser far to accomplish this result, and benefit all mankind, by lessening the hours in which machines and men labor in the work of production. . . .

The advantage of eight hours to the laboring classes will be (1st) employment; (2d) steady employment; (3d) better wages; (4th) relief from anxiety that comes from idleness and poverty; (5th) an opportunity to lay aside the means for the purchase of a home; (6th) opportunity to see and get acquainted with the family by day-light; (7th) more time for intellectual improvement; (8th) a chance for outdoor recreation on the secular day, without being compelled to take Sunday for that purpose; (9th) the ability to obtain respectable dress and make a good appearance, whereby encouragement is given to attend church and social gatherings, resulting in intellectual, moral and spiritual improvement. . . .

To fully lay this matter before the people, through literature, discussion, lecture, sermon and study, *we recommend Saturday, April 24, 1886, as a general holiday for the laboring classes, preparatory to inaugurating the Eight-Hour Movement seven days afterwards, on the first day of May.*

In this effort we fervently invoke the aid of the press, the clergy, leg-islators, teachers, employers, and all persons in authority. Give us em-ployment for the idle masses who are struggling for bread; give us a chance to send pauper and criminal back to shop, and field, and factory, where they may get an honest living; give us back again health and bloom for the sunken-eyed, starving sewing-woman; give us homes for working-people, and a chance to earn them; give us an honest opportunity for every human being to possess the reasonable comforts of life—GIVE US EIGHT HOURS!

8

◆

RURAL REVOLT

Rapid agricultural expansion was a crucial part of the nation's amazing economic growth in the late nineteenth century. Yet in this expansive era, average farm income went down and the farmer gradually lost pre-eminent status in American society. Farmers in the Midwest suffered from bad weather, and farmers in the South, from weevils and other pests. Everywhere growers received lower prices because of overproduction but paid higher borrowing and shipping costs because of what they saw as greedy and unresponsive banks and railroads. This network of "capitalist" transportation and finance quickly became a target of rural frustration, and farmers joined organizations such as the Grange and the Farmers' Alliance to promote their own interests.

In 1890, state alliances in the Midwest formed political parties to challenge the Republicans and Democrats; in the South, alliance members, faced with the difficult problem of race relations, sought to take over the Democratic party. Encouraged by local victories, however, the alliances created a national People's, or Populist, party in 1892 and ran James B. Weaver of Iowa for president. The Populists promised to restore the government (which they charged was controlled by the captains of industry and finance) "to the hands of the plain people." In their 1892 platform they called for a series of political reforms that would democratize the American system: the popular election of senators, the initiative, the referendum, and the secret ballot. They also made economic demands: government ownership of the railroad, telegraph,and telephone industries; a graduated income tax; shorter working hours for labor (to win urban allies); and an increase in the amount of money circulating in the country (particularly by means of the free coinage of silver), which, by producing inflation, would raise farm prices and ease the farmers' debt burdens.

The People's party did remarkably well for a new party. Weaver carried four states (for a total of twenty-two electoral votes) in 1892 and received over a million popular votes. The Populists also succeeded in electing a number of congressmen and some state officials. Although most Populist officeholders were in the Midwest and Rocky Mountain states, the achievement of the Southern wing of the party was perhaps the more remarkable because it was biracial. Indeed, despite widespread violence against them, the Populists in the South gained a significant black following on the basis of such appeals as the one by Thomas E. Watson of Georgia reprinted below. By 1896, however, the party found its Southern supporters being harassed and murdered and its banking and currency program everywhere being taken over by the Democrats. Thus the People's party, like the Knights of Labor, soon ceased to exist.

Thomas E. Watson, the Populists' foremost Southern leader, was born near Thomson, Georgia, in 1856. A schoolteacher and later a successful lawyer, Watson entered politics as a Democrat, but was elected to Congress in 1890 as a Farmers' Alliance candidate. He lost his reelection bid as a Populist in 1892, but remained active in the party's affairs and served as its vice-presidential candidate in 1896. Increasingly disillusioned with the prospects for agrarian reform, Watson grew more intolerant with age and eventually supported black disfranchisement and segregation. He died in Washington, D.C., in 1922, two years after his election to the U.S. Senate.

Questions to Consider. In this essay, which appeared in a national journal in 1892, Watson asked both races to leave their old party affiliations. What were these affiliations and how do you explain them? What did Watson think the two races had in common economically? How much validity was there in his contention that the two races "are kept apart" so that they "may be separately fleeced of [their] earnings" or in his insistence that material self-interest would bring them together? What sectional appeal did he make? What position did he take on the question of social equality? How much truth is there in his assumption that class interests cut across racial lines?

◆

Populism in the South (1892)

THOMAS E. WATSON

The key to the new political movement called the People's Party has been that the Democratic farmer was as ready to leave the Democratic ranks as the Republican farmer was to leave the Republican ranks. In exact pro-

From Thomas E. Watson, "The Negro Question in the South," *Arena,* 35(1892), 541–544, 548–550.

portion as the West received the assurance that the South was ready for a new party, it has moved. In exact proportion to the proof we could bring that the West had broken Republican ties, the South has moved. Without a decided break in both sections, neither would move. With that decided break, both moved.

The very same principle governs the race question in the South. The two races can never act together permanently, harmoniously, beneficially, till each race demonstrates to the other a readiness to leave old party affiliations and to form new ones, based upon the profound conviction that, in acting together, both races are seeking new laws which will benefit both. On no other basis under heaven can the "Negro Question" be solved. . . .

The white tenant lives adjoining the colored tenant. Their houses are almost equally destitute of comforts. Their living is confined to bare necessities. They are equally burdened with heavy taxes. They pay the same high rent for gullied and impoverished land.

They pay the same enormous prices for farm supplies. Christmas finds them both without any satisfactory return for a year's toil. Dull and heavy and unhappy, they both start the plows again when "New Year's" passes.

Now the People's Party says to these two men, "You are kept apart that you may be separately fleeced of your earnings. You are made to hate each other because upon that hatred is rested the keystone of the arch of financial despotism which enslaves you both. You are deceived and blinded that you may not see how this race antagonism perpetuates a monetary system which beggars both."

This is so obviously true it is no wonder both these unhappy laborers stop to listen. No wonder they begin to realize that no change of law can benefit the white tenant which does not benefit the black one likewise; that no system which now does injustice to one of them can fail to injure both. Their every material interest is identical. The moment this becomes a conviction, mere selfishness, the mere desire to better their conditions, escape onerous taxes, avoid usurious charges, lighten their rents, or change their precarious tenements into smiling, happy homes, will drive these two men together, just as their mutually inflamed prejudices now drive them apart.

Suppose these two men now to have become fully imbued with the idea that their material welfare depends upon the reforms we demand. Then they act together to secure them. Every white reformer finds it to the vital interest of his home, his family, his fortune, to see to it that the vote of the colored reformer is freely cast and fairly counted.

Then what? Every colored voter will be thereafter a subject of industrial education and political teaching.

Concede that in the final event, a colored man will vote where his material interests dictate that he should vote; concede that in the South the accident of color can make no possible difference in the interests of farmers, croppers, and laborers; concede that under full and fair discussion the people can be depended upon to ascertain where their interests lie— and we reach the conclusion that the Southern race question can be solved by the People's Party on the simple proposition that each race will be led by self-interest to support that which benefits it, when so presented that neither is hindered by the bitter party antagonisms of the past.

Let the colored laborer realize that our platform gives him a better guaranty for political independence; for a fair return for his work; a better chance to buy a home and keep it; a better chance to educate his children and see them profitably employed; a better chance to have public life freed from race collisions; a better chance for every citizen to be considered as a *citizen* regardless of color in the making and enforcing of laws,—let all this be fully realized, and the race question in the South will have settled itself through the evolution of a political movement in which both whites and blacks recognize their surest way out of wretchedness into comfort and independence.

The illustration could be made quite as clearly from other planks in the People's Party platform. On questions of land, transportation and finance, especially, the welfare of the two races so clearly depends upon that which benefits either, that intelligent discussion would necessarily lead to just conclusions.

Why should the colored man always be taught that the white man of his neighborhood hates him, while a Northern man, who taxes every rag on his back, loves him? Why should not my tenant come to regard me as his friend rather than the manufacturer who plunders us both? Why should we perpetuate a policy which drives the black man into the arms of the Northern politician? . . .

To the emasculated individual who cries "Negro supremacy!" there is little to be said. His cowardice shows him to be a degeneration from the race which has never yet feared any other race. Existing under such conditions as they now do in this country, there is no earthly chance for Negro domination, unless we are ready to admit that the colored man is our superior in will power, courage, and intellect.

Not being prepared to make any such admission in favor of any race the sun ever shone on, I have no words which can portray my contempt for the white men, Anglo-Saxons, who can knock their knees together, and through their chattering teeth and pale lips admit that they are afraid the Negroes will "dominate us."

The question of social equality does not enter into the calculation at all. That is a thing each citizen decides for himself. No statue ever yet drew the latch of the humblest home—or ever will. Each citizen regulates his own visiting list—and always will.

The conclusion, then, seems to me to be this: the crushing burdens which now oppress both races in the South will cause each to make an effort to cast them off. They will see a similarity of cause and a similarity of remedy. They will recognize that each should help the other in the work of repealing bad laws and enacting good ones. They will become political allies, and neither can injure the other without weakening both. It will be to the interest of both that each should have justice. And on these broad lines of mutual interest, mutual forbearance, and mutual support the present will be made the steppingstone to future peace and prosperity.

9

◆

SIDE EFFECTS

Industrialization brought, among other things, the factory system: big machines in large buildings where thousands of workers did specialized tasks under strict supervision. The factory system vastly increased America's output of such products as glass, machinery, newspapers, soap, cigarettes, beef, and beer. Factories thus provided innumerable new goods and millions of new jobs for Americans. But factories also reduced workers' control over their place of work, made the conditions of labor more dangerous, and played no small part in destroying the dignity of that labor. The first part of the following excerpt from Upton Sinclair's novel *The Jungle* offers a glimpse into the factory system as it operated in a Chicago meat-packing plant around 1905.

Industrialization produced not only big factories but also big cities, particularly in the Northeast and Midwest. Sinclair therefore took pains to show the role of industry and new production techniques in creating urban transportation and other services. The second part of the excerpt suggests a few of the links between industrial growth and Chicago's leaders—the so-called gray wolves who controlled the city's government and businesses. Here again, Sinclair indicates the high toll in human life exacted by unrestrained development.

The Jungle caused a sensation when it was first published. The pages describing conditions in Chicago's meat-packing plants aroused horror, disgust, and fury, and sales of meat dropped precipitously. "I aimed at the public's heart," said Sinclair ruefully, "and hit it in the stomach." President Theodore Roosevelt ordered a congressional investigation of meat-packing plants in the nation, and Congress subsequently passed the Meat Inspection Act. But Sinclair, a socialist, did not seek to inspire reform legislation. He was concerned mainly with dramatizing the misery of workers under the capitalist mode of production and with winning recruits to socialism.

Upton Sinclair was born in Baltimore, Maryland, in 1878. After attending college in New York City, he began to write essays and fiction, experiencing his first real success with the publication of *The Jungle* in 1906. Dozens of novels on similar subjects—the coal and oil industries, newspapers, the liquor business, the persecution of radicals, the threat of dictatorship—poured from his pen in the following years, though none had the immediate impact of *The Jungle*. Sinclair's style, with its emphasis on the details of everyday life, resembles the realism of other writers of the time. But he also wrote as a "muckraker" (as Theodore Roosevelt called journalists who wrote exposés), trying to alert readers to the deceit and corruption then prevalent in American life. Unlike most muckrakers, however, Sinclair was politically active, running in California in the 1920s as a socialist candidate for the U.S. Congress. In 1934 he won the Democratic nomination for governor with the slogan "End Poverty in California"(EPIC), but he lost the election. During World War II he was a warm supporter of President Franklin D. Roosevelt and wrote novels about the war, one of which won a Pulitzer Prize. Not long before Sinclair's death in 1968 in Bound Brook, New Jersey, President Lyndon Johnson invited him to the White House to be present at the signing of the Wholesome Meat Act.

Questions to Consider.   *The Jungle* has been regarded as propaganda, not literature, and has been placed second only to Harriet Beecher Stowe's *Uncle Tom's Cabin* in its effectiveness as a propagandistic novel. Why do you think the novel caused demands for reform rather than converts to socialism? What seems more shocking in the passages from the novel reprinted below, the life of immigrant workers in Chicago in the early twentieth century or the filthy conditions under which meat was prepared for America's dining tables? What did Sinclair reveal about the organization of the work force in Chicago's meat-packing plants? Sinclair centered his story on a Lithuanian worker named Jurgis Rudkus and his wife, Ona. In what ways did he make Jurgis's plight seem typical of urban workers of his time? Why did Jurgis deny that he had ever worked in Chicago before? What did Sinclair reveal about the attitude of employers toward labor unions at that time?

◆

The Jungle (1906)

UPTON SINCLAIR

There was another interesting set of statistics that a person might have gathered in Packingtown—those of the various afflictions of the workers. When Jurgis had first inspected the packing plants with Szedvilas, he had marveled while he listened to the tale of all the things that were made out of the carcasses of animals and of all the lesser industries that were maintained there; now he found that each one of these lesser industries was a

From Upton Sinclair, *The Jungle* (Doubleday, Page and Co., New York, 1906), 116–117, 265–269. Published in the British Commonwealth by Penguin Books, Ltd. Reprinted by permission of the Estate of Upton Sinclair.

A meat packing house. Trimmers wielding razor-sharp knives in a Chicago packing house in 1892, more than a decade before the publication of *The Jungle*. (From *Views in the Chicago Stock Yards and Packing Industry*, published by A. Wittemann, NY, 1892; photo from Chicago Historical Society)

separate little inferno, in its way as horrible as the killing-beds, the source and fountain of them all. The workers in each of them had their own peculiar diseases. And the wandering visitor might be skeptical about all the swindles, but he could not be skeptical about these, for the worker bore the evidence of them about on his own person—generally he had only to hold out his hand.

There were the men in the pickle rooms, for instance, where old Antanas had gotten his death; scarce a one of these had not some spot of horror on his person. Let a man so much as scrape his finger pushing a truck in the pickle rooms, and he might have a sore that would put him out of the world; all the joints in his fingers might be eaten by the acid, one by one. Of the butchers and floormen, the beef boners and trimmers, and all those who used knives, you could scarcely find a person who had the use of his thumb; time and time again the base of it had been slashed, till it was a mere lump of flesh against which the man pressed the knife to hold it. The hands of these men would be criss-crossed with cuts, until you could no longer pretend to count them or to trace them. They would have no nails—they had worn them off pulling hides; their knuckles were swollen so that their fingers spread out like a fan. There were men who worked in the cooking rooms, in the midst of steam and sickening odors, by artificial light; in these rooms the germs of tuberculosis might live for two years, but the supply was renewed every hour. There were the beef luggers, who carried two-hundred-pound quarters into the refrigerator cars, a fearful kind of work, that began at four o'clock in the morning, and that wore out the most powerful man in a few years. There were those who worked in the chilling rooms, and whose special disease was rheumatism; the time limit that a man could work in the chilling rooms was said to be five years. There were the wool pluckers, whose hands went to pieces even sooner than the hands of the pickle men; for the pelts of the sheep had to be painted with acid to loosen the wool, and then the pluckers had to pull out this wool with their bare hands, till the acid had eaten their fingers off. There were those who made the tins for the canned meat, and their hands, too, were a maze of cuts, and each cut represented a chance for blood poisoning. Some worked at the stamping machines, and it was very seldom that one could work long there at the pace that was set, and not give out and forget himself, and have a part of his hand chopped off. There were the "hoisters," as they were called, whose task it was to press the lever which lifted the dead cattle off the floor. They ran along upon a rafter, peering down through the damp and the steam, and as old Durham's architects had not built the killing room for the convenience of the hoisters, at every few feet they would have to stoop under a beam, say four feet above the one they ran on, which got them into the habit of stooping, so that in a few years they would be walking like chimpanzees. Worst of any, however, were the fertilizer men, and those who served in the cooking rooms. These people could not be shown to the visitor—for the odor of a fertilizer man would scare any ordinary visitor at a hundred yards, and as for the other men, who worked in tank rooms full of steam and in some of which there were open vats near the level of the floor, their peculiar trouble was that they fell into the vats; and when they were fished out, there was never enough of them left to be worth exhibiting—sometimes they would be overlooked for days, till all but the bones of them had gone out to the world as Durham's Pure Leaf Lard!

* * * * *

Early in the fall Jurgis set out for Chicago again. All the joy went out of tramping as soon as a man could not keep warm in the hay; and, like many thousands of others, he deluded himself with the hope that by coming early he could avoid the rush. He brought fifteen dollars with him, hidden away in one of his shoes, a sum which had been saved from the saloon-keepers, not so much by his conscience, as by the fear which filled him at the thought of being out of work in the city in the wintertime.

He traveled upon the railroad with several other men, hiding in freight cars at night, and liable to be thrown off at any time, regardless of the speed of the train. When he reached the city he left the rest, for he had money and they did not, and he meant to save himself in this fight. He would bring to it all the skill that practice had brought him, and he would stand, whoever fell. On fair nights he would sleep in the park or on a truck or an empty barrel or box, and when it was rainy or cold he would stow himself upon a shelf in a ten-cent lodging-house, or pay three cents for the privileges of a "squatter" in a tenement hallway. He would eat at free lunches, five cents a meal, and never a cent more—so he might keep alive for two months and more, and in that time he would surely find a job. He would have to bid farewell to his summer cleanliness, of course, for he would come out of the first night's lodging with his clothes alive with vermin. There was no place in the city where he could wash even his face, unless he went down to the lake front—and there it would soon be all ice.

First he went to the steel mill and the harvester works, and found that his places there had been filled long ago. He was careful to keep away from the stockyards—he was a single man now, he told himself, and he meant to stay one, to have his wages for his own when he got a job. He began the long, weary round of factories and warehouses, tramping all day, from one end of the city to the other, finding everywhere from ten to a hundred men ahead of him. He watched the newspapers, too—but no longer was he to be taken in by the smooth-spoken agents. He had been told of all those tricks while "on the road."

In the end it was through a newspaper that he got a job, after nearly a month of seeking. It was a call for a hundred laborers, and though he thought it was a "fake," he went because the place was near by. He found a line of men a block long, but as a wagon chanced to come out of an alley and break the line, he saw his chance and sprang to seize a place. Men threatened him and tried to throw him out, but he cursed and made a disturbance to attract a policeman, upon which they subsided, knowing that if the latter interfered it would be to "fire" them all.

An hour or two later he entered a room and confronted a big Irishman behind a desk.

"Ever worked in Chicago before?" the man inquired; and whether it was a good angel that put it into Jurgis's mind, or an intuition of his sharpened wits, he was moved to answer, "no, sir."

"Where do you come from?"

"Kansas City, sir."

"Any references?"

"No sir. I'm just an unskilled man, I've got good arms."

"I want men for hard work—it's all underground, digging tunnels for telephones. Maybe it won't suit you."

"I'm willing, sir—anything for me. What's the pay?"

"Fifteen cents an hour."

"I'm willing, sir."

"All right; go back there and give your name."

So within half an hour he was at work, far underneath the streets of the city. The tunnel was a peculiar one for telephone wires; it was about eight feet high, and with a level floor nearly as wide. It had innumerable branches—a perfect spider-web beneath the city; Jurgis walked over half a mile with his gang to the place where they were to work. Stranger yet, the tunnel was lighted by electricity, and upon it was laid a double-tracked, narrow gauge railroad!

But Jurgis was not there to ask questions, and he did not give the matter a thought. It was nearly a year afterward that he finally learned the meaning of this whole affair. The City Council had passed a quiet and innocent little bill allowing a company to construct telephone conduits under the city streets; and upon the strength of this, a great corporation had proceeded to tunnel all Chicago with a system of railway freight subways. In the city there was a combination of employers, representing hundreds of millions of capital, and formed for the purpose of crushing the labor unions. The chief union which troubled it was the teamsters'; and when these freight tunnels were completed, connecting all the big factories and stores with the railroad depots, they would have the teamsters' union by the throat. Now and then there were rumors and murmurs in the Board of Aldermen, and once there was a committee to investigate—but each time another small fortune was paid over, and the rumors died away; until at last the city woke up with a start to find the work completed. There was a tremendous scandal, of course; it was found that the city records had been falsified and other crimes committed, and some of Chicago's big capitalists got into jail—figuratively speaking. The aldermen declared that they had had no idea of it all, in spite of the fact that the main entrance to the work had been in the rear of the saloon of one of them. . . .

In a work thus carried out, not much thought was given to the welfare of the laborers. On an average, the tunneling cost a life a day and several manglings; it was seldom, however, that more than a dozen or two men heard of any one accident. The work was all done by the new boring-machinery, with as little blasting as possible; but there would be falling rocks and crushed supports and premature explosions—and in addition all the dangers of railroading. So it was that one night, as Jurgis was on his way out with his gang, an engine and a loaded car dashed round one of the innumerable right-angle branches and struck him upon the shoulder, hurling him against the concrete wall and knocking him senseless.

When he opened his eyes again it was to the clanging of the bell of an ambulance. He was lying in it, covered by a blanket, and it was heading its way slowly through the holiday-shopping crowds. They took him to the county hospital, where a young surgeon set his arm, then he was washed and laid upon a bed in a ward with a score or two more of maimed and mangled men.

10

◆

THE MANAGERIAL SPIRIT

Mass production involved two steps: the substitution of machines for the human hand in manufacturing; and the substitution of steam, electric, or other nonanimal power for human energy to drive the machines. The place where these two things occurred was the factory. Factories first appeared in the New England textile industry of the early nineteenth century. By 1900 they were the chief feature of the urban landscape, dominating every industry from meatpacking, steel, and clothing to paper, cigarettes, and automobiles. Factories had reached huge proportions, with thousands of workers—"hands"—in many places.

In spite of the best efforts of industrialists to simplify and mechanize the processes of production, human labor remained a central element in manufacturing. This was especially true where workers possessed skills that could not easily be mechanized or where unions were strong enough to resist management authority. It was true as well in the case of the unskilled laborer unwilling or unable to perform rote tasks efficiently. The human element was also a central concern in large nonmanufacturing businesses, such as department stores, mail-order houses, insurance firms, and telegraph companies, which employed clerical and white-collar workers away from the shop floor.

A great interest therefore arose in management technique and theory, an interest that led to the establishment of schools of business administration, the appearance of management journals, and the emergence of management consultants. By far the most important management theory of the period took the form of the "scientific management" principles of Frederick W. Taylor. Taylor was an industrial engineer who believed it was possible to establish more realistic times for doing most industrial tasks, thus reducing labor-management friction and boosting productivity. Taylor's system involved time-and-motion studies, analysis of work flows, divided foremanship, and other techniques. But, as he argued in the following testimony before Congress as well as in numerous books and articles, scientific management (or "Taylorism") was more than the sum of these parts.

Born in 1856 in Germantown, Pennsylvania, Frederick Taylor apprenticed to a pattern maker and went to work in various Philadelphia factories, eventually becoming chief engineer in a steel mill. In the mill, he began to take notes on worker tasks and output. Concluding that bosses usually expected too much from workers, he devised better machinery and also systematized the time allotted for every task in the making of steel. Productivity at the mill rose sharply, and Taylor's ideas quickly spread throughout industrial America, including Bethlehem Steel Company and other corporate giants. Notorious in some labor circles for saying that a "first-class man is the same as a first-class horse" and for making other remarks considered demeaning, Taylor resigned his management post to devote himself to popularizing his ideas on industrial engineering and administration. The titles of his books suggest the tenor and focus of his thinking: *Note on Belting* (1893), *The Adjustment of Wages to Efficiency* (1896), *Shop Management* (1903), *On the Art of Cutting Metals* (1906), and *The Principles of Scientific Management* (1911). Taylor died in Philadelphia in 1915.

Questions to Consider. Taylor delivered the following remarks in 1911 to a House of Representatives Special Committee on Shop Management. Why might Congress have established such a committee at that time? Even though "Taylorism" was widely identified with efficiency devices such as time and motion study and premium and bonus systems, he took great pains to say that scientific management was more than this. What larger principle was he trying to assert? Why do you think managers generally liked Taylor's ideas more than workers did, even though he argued that his methods would benefit everyone?

◆

The Essentials of Scientific Management (1911)

FREDERICK TAYLOR

Scientific management is not any efficiency device, not a device of any kind for securing efficiency; nor is it any bunch or group of efficiency devices. It is not a new system of figuring costs; it is not a new scheme of paying men; it is not a piecework system; it is not a bonus system; it is not a premium system; it is no scheme for paying men; it is not holding a stop watch on a man and writing things down about him; it is not time study; it is not motion study nor an analysis of the movement of men; it

U.S. Congress, House Special Committee to Investigate the Taylor and Other Systems of Shop Management (1911), *Hearings*, vol. 3 (Washington: Government Printing Office, 1912), pp. 1386-1389.

is not the printing and ruling and unloading of a ton or two of blanks on a set of men and saying, "Here's your system; go use it." It is not divided foremanship or functional foremanship; it is not any of the devices which the average man calls to mind when scientific management is spoken of. The average man thinks of one or more of these things when he hears the words "scientific management" mentioned, but scientific management is not any of these devices. I am not sneering at cost-keeping systems, at time study, at functional foremanship, nor at any new and improved scheme of paying men, nor at any efficiency devices, if they are really devices that make for efficiency. I believe in them, but what I am emphasizing is that these devices in whole or in part are not scientific management; they are useful adjuncts to scientific management, so are they also useful adjuncts of other systems of management.

Now, in its essence, scientific management involves a complete mental revolution on the part of the working man engaged in any particular establishment or industry—a complete mental revolution on the part of these men as to their duties toward their work, toward their fellow man, and toward their employers. And it involves the equally complete mental revolution on the part of those on the management's side—the foreman, the superintendent, the owner of the business, the board of directors—a complete mental revolution on their part as to their duties toward their fellow workers in the management, toward their workmen, and toward all of their daily problems. And without this complete mental revolution on both sides scientific management does not exist.

That is the essence of scientific management, this great mental revolution. . . .

I think it is safe to say that in the past a great part of the thought and interest both of the men, on the sides of the management, and of those on the side of the workmen in manufacturing establishments has been centered upon what may be called the proper division of the surplus resulting from their joint efforts, between the management on the one hand, and the workmen on the other hand. The management have been looking for as large a profit as possible for themselves, and the workmen have been looking for as large wages as possible for themselves, and that is what I mean by the division of the surplus. Now, this question of the division of the surplus is a very plain and simple one (for I am announcing no great fact in political economy or anything of that sort). Each article produced in the establishment has its definite selling price. Into the manufacture of this article have gone certain expenses, namely the cost of materials, the expenses connected with selling it, and certain indirect expenses, such as the rent of the building, taxes, insurance, light and power, maintenance of machinery, interest on the plant, etc. Now, if we deduct these several expenses from the selling price, what is left over may be called the surplus. And out of this surplus comes the profit to the manufacturer on the one hand, and the wages of the workmen on the other hand. And it is largely upon the division of this surplus that the attention of the workmen and of the management has been centered in the past. . . .

The great revolution that takes place in the mental attitude of the two parties under scientific management is that both sides take their eyes off the division of the surplus as the all-important matter, and together turn their attention toward increasing the size of the surplus until this surplus becomes so large that it is unnecessary to quarrel over how it shall be divided. They come to see that when they stop pulling against one another, and instead both turn and push shoulder to shoulder in the same direction, the size of the surplus created by their joint efforts is truly astounding. They both realize that when they substitute friendly cooperation and mutual helpfulness for antagonism and strife they are together able to make this surplus so enormously greater than it was in the past that there is ample room for a large increase in wages for the workmen and an equally great increase in profits for the manufacturer. This, gentlemen, is the beginning of the great mental revolution which constitutes the first step toward scientific management. . . .

There is, however, one more change in viewpoint which is absolutely essential to the existence of scientific management. Both sides must recognize as essential the substitution of exact scientific investigation and knowledge for the old individual judgment or opinion, either of the workman or the boss, in all matters relating to the work done in the establishment. And this applies both as to the methods to be employed in doing the work and the time in which each job should be done.

Scientific management cannot be said to exist, then, in any establishment until after this change has taken place in the mental attitude of both the management and the men, both as to their duty to cooperate in producing the largest possible surplus and as to the necessity for substituting exact scientific knowledge for opinions or the old rule of thumb or individual knowledge.

These are the two absolutely essential elements of scientific management.

Welcome to a new world. A formidable Miss Liberty at the New York docks to greet a family of Jewish "greenhorns"—an Americanism for someone fresh off the boat from the old country. (YIVO Institute for Jewish Research)

CHAPTER THREE

◆

The Minorities

11

◆

INDIAN AUTUMN

Conflict between whites and Native Americans began with the first colonial landings and continued undiminished into the late nineteenth century. At that time, the United States finally completed its conquest of the continent and extended its authority over all the lands formerly held by the indigenous peoples. After the Civil War, whites began moving in large numbers along the new rail lines west of the Mississippi River. As part of this movement, the U.S. Army fought continuous wars against the larger and more combative Native American nations— notably the Comanche, Apache, Kiowa, Cheyenne, and Sioux. The army also harassed most of the smaller nations. Native Americans won occasional victories, for example, the Sioux victory over former Civil War General George A. Custer at the Little Bighorn in 1876. Most of the time, however, the tribespeople fell victim to U.S. Army's superior organization, supplies, and firepower. Whites' slaughter of the vast buffalo herds on which the Native Americans had based their lives— thirteen million buffalo had been killed by 1883—virtually ensured that the tribes would be crushed. The last major military clash between the government and the Native Americans came with the slaughter of scores of Sioux families in 1890 at Wounded Knee, South Dakota.

The Plains peoples were confined almost entirely to reservations. These large tracts of land had been set aside by the U.S. government as places where, with the protection and economic aid of the Indian Office, the Plains peoples might continue their nomadic communal ways. But this policy was a failure. Tribal ranks, already severely depleted by the Plains wars, were further thinned by the growing scarcity of buffalo. Moreover, large tribes were often widely divided on scattered reservations, where resident U.S. government agents usually proved unwilling or unable to prevent looting by white settlers and theft of funds earmarked for tribal assistance.

"Chief Joseph's Story," excerpted below, is a commentary on events during the 1870s. It describes both the encounters—peaceful and otherwise—of the Nez Percés[1] of the Oregon and Idaho country with

---

1. "Nez Percé," like "Joseph," was a European-American name imposed by American explorers in place of the tribal name.

U.S. settlers and authorities and the betrayals that accompanied those encounters. Born about 1840, "Young Joseph" was the son of a chief of a major Nez Percé band, who had also been named Joseph by white missionaries. The father had refused to cede tribal lands to the U.S. government following the discovery of gold in the Oregon country, and he passively resisted white efforts to settle the area. When his father died in 1873, "Young Joseph"—named Hinmatonyalatkit, or Thunder Traveling Over The Mountains, in his native tongue—continued the policy of noncooperation. In early 1877 General O. O. Howard ordered the Nez Percés off the land, promising them a reservation elsewhere in the Oregon region. "Young Joseph," seeking to protect his people, agreed to leave, but other Nez Percés did not. A skirmish quickly escalated into a series of pitched battles that decimated the tribe. After armed resistance and a masterly retreat of 1,500 miles, "Young Joseph" surrendered in October 1877. He and his band were sent to Indian Territory, then in 1885 to Washington state. Chief "Young Joseph," by now a figure of legendary proportions to Native Americans and whites alike, died in 1904.

Questions to Consider. What were the key features in the history of relations between Native Americans and whites, as "Young Joseph" told it? In "Young Joseph's" eyes, was the U.S. Army merely an arm of westward expansion or was it an autonomous agent? Given the Nez Percé beliefs (as the chief summarized them), do you think the Americans' westward advance could have occurred without wrecking the tribal nations? In his policy proposals at the end of the passage, was "Young Joseph" advocating a policy of assimilation, separate but equal status, ethnic autonomy, or simple justice? Was his vision practical at that time? Can you see any alternative that might have suited both sides?

◆

Chief Joseph's Story (1879)

YOUNG JOSEPH

My friends, I have been asked to show you my heart. I am glad to have a chance to do so. I want the white people to understand my people. Some of you think an Indian is like a wild animal. This is a great mistake. I will tell you about our people, and then you can judge whether an Indian is a man or not. I believe much trouble and blood would be saved if we opened

From "Chief Joseph's Own Story," *North American Review* (April 1879), 415–433.

Young Joseph. A late 19th-century Nez Percé chief. (Smithsonian Institution, Washington, D.C.)

our hearts more. I will tell you in my way how the Indian sees things. The white man has more words to tell you how they look to him, but it does not require many words to speak the truth. What I have to say will come from my heart, and I will speak with a straight tongue. Ah-cum-kin-i-ma-me-hut (the Great Spirit) is looking at me, and will hear me.

My name is In-mut-too-yah-lat-lat (Thunder-traveling-over-the-mountains). I am chief of the Wal-lam-wat-kin band of Chute-pa-lu, or Nez Percés (nose-pierced Indians). I was born in eastern Oregon, thirty-eight winters ago. My father was chief before me. When a young man he was called Joseph by Mr. Spalding, a missionary. He died a few years ago. There was no stain on his hands of the blood of a white man. He left a good name on the earth. He advised me well for my people.

Our fathers gave us many laws, which they had learned from their fathers. These laws were good. They told us to treat all men as they treated us; that we should never be the first to break a bargain; that it was a disgrace to tell a lie; that we should speak only the truth; that it was a shame for one man to take from another his wife, or his property, without paying for it. We were taught to believe that the Great Spirit sees and hears everything, and that He never forgets; that hereafter He will give every man a spirit-home according to his deserts; if he has been a good man, he will have a good home; if he has been a bad man, he will have a bad home. This I believe, and all my people believe the same.

The first white men of your people who came to our country were named Lewis and Clarke. They also brought many things that our people had never seen. They talked straight, and our people gave them a great feast, as a proof that their hearts were friendly. These men were very kind. They made presents to our chiefs and our people made presents to them. We had a great many horses of which we gave them what they needed, and they gave us guns and tobacco in return. All the Nez Percés made friends with Lewis and Clarke, and agreed to let them pass through their country, and never to make war on white men. This promise the Nez Percés have never broken. . . .

Next there came a white officer who invited all the Nez Percés to a treaty council. After the council was opened he made known his heart. He said there were a great many white people in the country, and many more would come; that he wanted the land marked out so that the Indians and white men could be separated. If they were to live in peace it was necessary, he said, that the Indians should have a country set apart for them, and in that country they must stay. My father, who represented his band, refused to have anything to do with the council, because he wished to be a free man. He claimed that no man owned any part of the earth, and a man could not sell what was not his own. . . .

For a short time we lived quietly. But this could not last. White men had found gold in the mountains around the land of the winding water. They stole a great many horses from us, and we could not get them back because we were Indians. . . . We could have avenged our wrongs many times, but we did not. Whenever the Government has asked us to help them against other Indians we have never refused. When the white men were few and we were strong we could have killed them off, but the Nez Percés wished to live at peace. . . .

Year after year we have been threatened, but no war was made upon my people until General Howard came to our country two years ago and told us that he was the white war-chief of all that country. He said: "I have a great many soldiers at my back. I am going to bring them up here, and then I will talk to you again. I will not let white men laugh at me the next time I come. The country belongs to the Government, and I intend to make you go upon the reservation."

I remonstrated with him against bringing more soldiers to the Nez Percé country. He had one house full of troops all the time at Fort Lapwei. . . .

When the party arrived there General Howard sent out runners and called all the Indians to a grand council. In the council General Howard informed us in a haughty spirit that he would give my people thirty days to go back home, collect all their stock, and move on to the reservation, saying, "If you are not here in that time, I shall consider that you want to fight, and will send my soldiers to drive you on." . . .

When I returned to Wallowa I found my people very much excited upon discovering that the soldiers were already in the Wallowa Valley. We held a council, and decided to move immediately to avoid bloodshed. . . .

We gathered all the stock we could find, and made an attempt to move. We left many of our horses and cattle in Wallowa, and we lost several hundred in crossing the river. All my people succeeded in getting across in safety. Many of the Nez Percés came together in Rocky Cañon to hold a grand council. . . .

Again I counseled peace, and I thought the danger was past. We had not complied with General Howard's order because we could not, but we intended to do so as soon as possible. I was leaving the council to kill beef for my family when news came that a young man whose father had been killed had gone out with several hot-blooded young braves and killed four white men. He rode up to the council and shouted: "Why do you sit here like women? The war has begun already." [Following many battles] I went to General [Colonel Nelson] Miles and gave up my gun, and said, "From where the sun now stands I will fight no more." . . .

Words do not pay for my dead people. They do not pay for my country, now overrun by white men. They do not protect my father's grave. They do not pay for my horses and cattle. Good words will not give me back my children. Good words will not make good the promise of your War Chief, General Miles, [of reservation land in Idaho]. Good words will not give my people good health and stop them from dying. Good words will not get my people a home where they can live in peace and take care of themselves. I am tired of talk that comes to nothing. . . .

I know that my race must change. We cannot hold our own with the white men as we are. We only ask an even chance to live as other men live. We ask to be recognized as men. We ask that the same law shall work alike on all men. If the Indian breaks the law, punish him by the law. If the white man breaks the law, punish him also.

Let me be a free man—free to travel, free to stop, free to work, free to trade where I choose, free to choose my own teachers, free to follow the religion of my fathers, free to think and talk and act for myself—and I will obey every law, or submit to the penalty.

Whenever the white man treats the Indian as they treat each other, then we shall have no more wars. We shall be all alike—brothers of one father and one mother, with one sky above us and one country around us, and one government for all. Then the Great Spirit Chief who rules above will smile upon this land, and send rain to wash out the bloody spots made by brothers' hands upon the face of the earth. For this time the Indian race are waiting and praying. I hope that no more groans of wounded men and women will ever go to the ear of the Great Spirit Chief above, and that all people may be one people..

In-mut-too-yah-lat-lat has spoken for his people.

Young Joseph

12

◆

NEWCOMERS

The sprawling city was as fundamental a fact of life as the great West or the bitter South in the late nineteenth century, and most Americans found it simultaneously exciting and unsettling. Cities were exciting because they symbolized prosperity and progress, cardinal virtues of the country for decades if not centuries. These urban centers were full of good and novel things to buy and do in a land lusting to do both. But cities were also unsettling—seething (so it seemed) with greedy landlords, corrupt politicians, and radical workers. Most unsettling of all, they were populated by foreigners, not "real" Americans—immigrants from a dozen lands, speaking as many languages and exhibiting as many objectionable habits. These new migrants spilled out from the waterfronts of New York, Baltimore, or Chicago into vast impoverished tenement districts that strained not only public morality but also public order and public health. They may have been lovers of liberty "yearning to be free," as it said on the Statue of Liberty, but they were also "huddled masses."

For most Americans, New York City—the country's largest city and chief port of European debarkation—was the epitome of the immigrant city. No U.S. city could claim more foreign-born inhabitants or more crowded housing conditions. Relatively little open space remained for new residential or business construction. But New York was more than an immigrant center; it was also the publishing and literary capital of the United States. By 1890, hundreds of reporters and writers lived in the city, working for dozens of newspapers and magazines, not counting the foreign-language press. When the United States developed an appetite for urban coverage, New York had a thriving industry to supply it.

Jacob Riis, a Danish immigrant, was a pioneer in the field of urban exposé journalism. Riis, who arrived in New York in 1870, wandered in semipoverty for several years before becoming a city police reporter, first for the *New York Tribune,* then for the *Evening Sun.* His beat was the lower East Side, a teeming immigrant district. For twenty-two years, until 1899, his office was directly across from police headquarters. Here, he wrote, "I was to find my lifework." But Riis was more than a reporter; he became a reformer, determined not only to describe slum life but to improve it. His goal was partly to establish better building codes, but chiefly to ensure that all immigrants learned English and were assimilated thoroughly into American life. This path, after all, was the one that Jacob Riis himself had followed. *How the Other Half Lives,* which first appeared as a series of newspaper essays (one of which is excerpted below), was a weapon in Riis's crusade.

Jacob Riis, born in Ribe, Denmark, in 1849, was educated by his father and became an apprentice carpenter before emigrating to the United States in 1870. By 1890 he had become one of the best-known, most colorful newspapermen in New York. *How the Other Half Lives,* which Riis illustrated with startling photographs of slum conditions, made him a byword in the nation as well. Among its readers was another budding reformer and member of the New York City police board—Theodore Roosevelt, who befriended Riis, accompanied him on forays into the slums, and supported his reform efforts. Riis carried on his crusade in later books, including several on immigrant children, and saw significant improvements in slum schools and recreational facilities. He died in Barre, Massachusetts, in 1914.

Questions to Consider. Modern readers will instantly notice Riis's constant use of stereotypes in discussing various immigrant groups. Why might an intelligent, sympathetic reporter of the 1890s resort to such stereotypes? How could such an author be seen (as Riis was) as a champion of liberal social reform? Riis was a reporter, not a social scientist. Are his descriptions and explanations of group social mobility persuasive? When he explains why immigrant groups tend to form separate enclaves, is he persuasive? Would a writer about homelessness in the 1990s approach the task as Riis did?

◆

How the Other Half Lives (1890)

JACOB RIIS

When once I asked the agent of a notorious Fourth Ward alley how many people might be living in it I was told: One hundred and forty families, one hundred Irish, thirty-eight Italian, and two that spoke the German tongue. Barring the agent herself there was not a native-born individual in the court. The answer was characteristic of the cosmopolitan character of lower New York, very nearly so of the whole of it, wherever it runs to alleys and courts. One may find for the asking an Italian, a German, a

From Jacob Riis, *How the Other Half Lives* (Scribner's, New York, 1907), 14–21.

Homeless shelters. A Jacob Riis photograph of the denizens of Jersey Street, New York City, who paid, according to Riis, as little as a dollar a month to sleep in these so-called "piggeries" of old boards and discarded tin. (Jacob Riis Collection/The Museum of the City of New York)

French, African, Spanish, Bohemian, Russian, Scandinavian, Jewish, and Chinese colony. Even the Arab, who peddles "holy earth" from the Battery as a direct importation from Jerusalem, has his exclusive preserves at the lower end of Washington Street. The one thing you shall vainly ask for in the chief city of America is a distinctively American community. . . .

They are not here. In their place has come this queer conglomerate mass of heterogeneous elements, ever striving and working like whiskey and water in one glass, and with the like result: final union and a prevailing taint of whiskey. The once unwelcome Irishman has been followed in his turn by the Italian, the Russian Jew, and the Chinaman, and has himself taken a hand at opposition, quite as bitter and quite as ineffectual, against these later hordes. Wherever these have gone they have crowded him out, possessing the block, the street, the ward with their denser swarms. But the Irishman's revenge is complete. Victorious in defeat over his recent as over his more ancient foe, the one who opposed his coming no less than the one who drove him out, he dictates to both their politics, and, secure in possession of the offices, returns the native his greeting with interest, while collecting the rents of the Italian whose house he has bought with the profits of his saloon. . . .

In justice to the Irish landlord it must be said that like an apt pupil he was merely showing forth the result of the schooling he had received, reenacting, in his own way, the scheme of the tenements. It is only his frankness that shocks. The Irishman does not naturally take kindly to tenement life, though with characteristic versatility he adapts himself to its conditions at once. It does violence, nevertheless, to the best that is in him, and for that very reason of all who come within its sphere soonest corrupts him. The result is a sediment, the product of more than a generation in the city's slums, that, as distinguished from the larger body of his class, justly ranks at the foot of tenement dwellers, the so-called "low Irish." . . .

An impulse toward better things there certainly is. The German rag-picker of thirty years ago, quite as low in the scale as his Italian successor, is the thrifty tradesman or prosperous farmer of today.

The Italian scavenger of our time is fast graduating into exclusive control of the corner fruit-stands, while his black-eyed boy monopolizes the boot-blacking industry in which a few years ago he was an intruder. The Irish hod-carrier in the second generation has become a bricklayer, if not the Alderman of his ward, while the Chinese coolie is in almost exclusive possession of the laundry business. The reason is obvious. The poorest immigrant comes here with the purpose and ambition to better himself and, given half a chance, might be reasonably expected to make the most of it. To the false plea that he prefers the squalid homes in which his kind are housed there could be no better answer. . . .

As emigration from east to west follows the latitude, so does the foreign influx in New York distribute itself along certain well-defined lines that waver and break only under the stronger pressure of a more gregarious race or the encroachments of inexorable business. A feeling of dependence upon mutual effort, natural to strangers in a strange land, unacquainted with its language and customs, sufficiently accounts for this.

The Irishman is the true cosmopolitan immigrant. All-pervading, he shares his lodging with perfect impartiality with the Italian, the Greek, and the "Dutchman," yielding only to sheer force of numbers, and objects equally to them all. A map of the city, colored to designate nationalities, would show more stripes than on the skin of a zebra, and more colors than any rainbow. The city on such a map would fall into two great halves, green for the Irish prevailing in the West Side tenement districts, and blue for the Germans on the East side. But intermingled with these ground colors would be an odd variety of tints that would give the whole the appearance of an extraordinary crazy-quilt. From down in the Sixth Ward, upon the site of the old Collect Pond that in the days of the fathers drained the hills which are no more, the red of the Italian would be seen forcing its way northward along the line of Mulberry Street to the quarter of the French purple on Bleecker Street and South Fifth Avenue, to lose itself and reappear, after a lapse of miles, in the "Little Italy" of Harlem, east of Second Avenue. Dashes of red, sharply defined, would be seen strung through the Annexed District, northward to the city line. On the West Side the red would be seen overrunning the old Africa of Thompson Street, pushing the black of the negro rapidly uptown, against querulous but unavailing protests, occupying his home, his church, his trade, and all with merciless impartiality.

Hardly less aggressive than the Italian, the Russian and Polish Jew, having overrun the district between Rivington and Division Streets, east of the Bowery, to the point of suffocation, is filling the tenements of the old Seventh Ward to the river front, and disputing with the Italian every foot of available space in the back alleys of Mulberry Street. The two races, differing hopelessly in much, have this in common: they carry their slums with them wherever they go, if allowed to do it. Little Italy already rivals its parent, the "Bend," in foulness. Other nationalities that begin at the bottom make a fresh start when crowded up the ladder. Happily both are manageable, the one by rabbinical, the other by the civil law. Between the dull gray of the Jew, his favorite color, and the Italian red, would be seen squeezed in on the map a sharp streak of yellow, marking the narrow boundaries of Chinatown. Dovetailed in with the German population, the poor but thrifty Bohemian might be picked out by the sombre hue of his life as of his philosophy, struggling against heavy odds in the big human bee-hives of the East Side. Colonies of his people extend northward, with long lapses of space, from below the Cooper Institute more than three miles. The Bohemian is the only foreigner with any considerable representation in the city who counts no wealthy man of his race, none who has not to work hard for a living, or has got beyond the reach of the tenement.

Down near the Battery the West Side emerald would be soiled by a dirty stain, spreading rapidly like a splash of ink on a sheet of blotting paper, headquarters of the Arab tribe, that in a single year has swelled from the original dozen to twelve hundred, intent, every mother's son, on trade and barter. Dots and dashes of color here and there would show where the Finnish sailors worship their djumala (God), the Greek pedlars the ancient name of their race, and the Swiss the goddess of thrift. And so on to the end of the long register, all toiling together in the galling fetters of the tenement. Were the question raised who makes the most of life thus mortgaged, who resists most stubbornly its levelling tendency—knows how to drag even the barracks upward a part of the way at least toward the ideal plane of the home—the palm must be unhesitatingly awarded the Teuton. The Italian and the poor Jew rise only by compulsion. The Chinaman does not rise at all; here, as at home, he simply remains stationary. The Irishman's genius runs to public affairs rather than domestic life; wherever he is mustered in force the saloon is the gorgeous centre of political activity. The German struggles vainly to learn his trick; his Teutonic wit is too heavy, and the political ladder he raises from his saloon usually too short or too clumsy to reach the desired goal. The best part of his life is lived at home, and he makes himself a home independent of the surroundings, giving the lie to the saying, unhappily become a maxim of social truth, that pauperism and drunkenness naturally grow in the tenements. He makes the most of his tenement, and it should be added that whenever and as soon as he can save up money enough, he gets out and never crosses the threshold of one again.

13

◆

YELLOW PERIL

In 1882, Congress passed the Chinese Exclusion Act, prohibiting Chinese workers from entering this country for a period of ten years. As the date of expiration approached, however, pressure from powerful sources mounted for renewing the law. Leading the fight was the Immigration Committee of the House of Representatives, under the chairmanship of Representative Herman Stump of Maryland, who produced a stream of witnesses describing how the Chinese used drugs, committed crimes, and lusted after American women. Stump distilled the most important parts of this testimony in the report, reprinted below, that accompanied the committee's recommendation that the exclusion act be renewed.

The committee and its witnesses were persuasive. Not only did Congress extend the law for another ten years, but in 1893 President Grover Cleveland named Representative Stump superintendent of immigration. The exclusion act and Stump's appointment in turn set the stage for a treaty between the United States and China, signed in 1894, barring the immigration of Chinese laborers for ten years from the date of the exchange of ratifications. Those who had left the United States were permitted to return, provided they had wives, children, parents, or property worth $1,000 in this country. The treaty gave China the right to exclude American workers (of which there were none in China), but not American merchants and officials (who were numerous and important there). Chinese were thus all but barred from American soil, even as the Statue of Liberty (a gift of France) was unveiled in 1886 to welcome immigrants from Europe.

By 1900, Japanese workers, too, were entering the United States in sizable numbers; outcries against the "yellow peril" were again raised in the West. The so-called Gentleman's Agreement of 1907 between Washington and Tokyo instantly reduced the flow of unskilled Japanese laborers into the United States.

Questions to Consider. The congressional report of 1892 argued that the Chinese presence in the United States was a threat to American "institutions." What institutions did the Immigration Committee seem most concerned about? Why does the report mention the "vegetable" diets of the Chinese? One aim of the committee was evidently to reduce the "smuggling" of Chinese aliens into the country. Why might such smuggling have taken place,, and why did immigration officers seem unable to prevent it? The committee based much of its argument on the idea that the Chinese either could not or would not assimilate. Assuming that this lack of assimilation was a genuine problem, what alternatives might the committee have explored besides exclusion?

In studying the United States–China Treaty of 1894, consider the following points. First, although the document has racist overtones, it did not expel the Chinese already living in the United States or deny them citizenship rights; nor did it prevent all Chinese from entering this country. Compare this variety of racism with that depicted by Frederick Douglass toward blacks, who were exploited and disfranchised. What factors prevented a similar sequestration, disfranchisement, or exclusion of the Chinese? Second, what forces seem to have produced this treaty?

◆

Congressional Report on Immigration (1892)

There is urgent necessity for prompt legislation on the subject of Chinese immigration. The exclusion act approved May 6, 1882, and its supplement expires by limitation of time on May 6, 1892, and after that time there will be no law to prevent the Chinese hordes from invading our country in number so vast, as soon to outnumber the present population of our flourishing States on the Pacific slope. . . .

The popular demand for legislation excluding the Chinese from this country is urgent and imperative and almost universal. Their presence here is inimical to our institutions and is deemed injurious and a source of danger. They are a distinct race, saving from their earnings a few hundred dollars and returning to China. This they succeed in doing in from five to ten years by living in the most miserable manner, when in cities and towns in crowded tenement houses, surrounded by dirt, filth, corruption, pollution, and prostitution; and gambling houses and opium joints abound. When used as cooks, farm-hands, servants, and gardeners, they are more cleanly in habits and manners. They, as a rule, have no families here; all are men, save a few women, usually prostitutes. They have no attachment to our country, its laws or its institutions, nor are they interested in its prosperity. They never assimilate with our people, our manners, tastes, religion, or ideas. With us they have nothing in common.

Living on the cheapest diet (mostly vegetable), wearing the poorest clothing, with no family to support, they enter the field of labor in competition with the American workman. In San Francisco, and in fact throughout the whole Pacific slope, we learn from the testimony heretofore alluded

Chinese-American merchant. A late 19th-century Chinese-American dry goods store, San Francisco. (The Bancroft Library)

to, that the Chinamen have invaded almost every branch of industry; manufacturers of cigars, cigar boxes, brooms, tailors, laundrymen, cooks, servants, farmhands, fishermen, miners and all departments of manual labor, for wages and prices at which white men and women could not support themselves and those dependent upon them. Recently this was a new country, and the Chinese may have been a necessity at one time, but now our own people are fast filling up and developing this rich and highly favored land, and American citizens will not and can not afford to stand idly by and see this undesirable race carry away the fruits of the labor which justly belongs to them. A war of races would soon be inaugurated; several times it has broken out, and bloodshed has followed. The town of Tacoma, in 1887, banished some 3,000 Chinamen on twenty-four hours' notice, and no Chinaman has ever been permitted to return.

Our people are willing, however, that those now here may remain, protected by the laws which they do not appreciate or obey, provided strong provision be made that no more shall be allowed to come, and that the smuggling of Chinese across the frontiers be scrupulously guarded against, so that gradually, by voluntary departures, death by sickness, accident, or old age, this race may be eliminated from this country, and the white race fill their places without inconvenience to our own people or to the Chinese, and thus a desirable change be happily and peacefully accomplished. It was thought that the exclusion act of 1882 would bring about this result; but it now appears that although at San Francisco the departures largely exceed the arrivals, yet the business of smuggling Chinese persons across the lines from the British Possessions and Mexico has so greatly increased that the number of arrivals now exceed the departures. This must be effectually stopped.

◆

The United States–China Treaty of 1894

Whereas, On the 17th day of November, A.D. 1880, and of Kwanghali the sixth year, tenth moon, fifteenth day, a treaty was concluded between the United States and China for the purpose of regulating, limiting, or suspending the coming of Chinese laborers to, and their residence in, the United States; and

Whereas, The two Governments desire to cooperate in prohibiting such emigration and to strengthen in other ways the bonds of friendship between the two countries; and,

Whereas, The two Governments are desirous of adopting reciprocal measures for the better protection of the citizens or subjects of each within the jurisdiction of the other. . . .

Article I The high-contracting parties agree that for a period of ten years beginning with the date of the exchange of the ratifications of this convention, the coming, except under the conditions hereinafter specified, of Chinese laborers to the United States shall be absolutely prohibited.

Article II The preceding article shall not apply to the return to the United States of any registered Chinese laborer who has a lawful wife, child, or parent in the United States, or property therein of the value of $1,000, or debts of like amount due him and pending settlement. Nevertheless, every such Chinese laborer shall, before leaving the United States, deposit, as a condition of his return, with the Collector of Customs of the district from which he departs, a full description in writing of his family, or property, or debts, as aforesaid, and shall be furnished by said Collector with such certificate of his right to return under this treaty as the laws of the United States may now or hereafter prescribe and not inconsistent with the provisions of this treaty, and should the written description aforesaid be proved

From *The New York Times*, November 19, 1894.

to be false, the right of return thereunder, or of continued residence after return, shall in each case be forfeited. And such right of return to the United States shall be exercised within one year from the date of leaving the United States, but such right of return to the United States may be extended for an additional period, not to exceed one year in cases where, by reason of sickness or other cause of disability beyond his control, such Chinese laborer shall be rendered unable sooner to return, which facts shall be fully reported to the Chinese Consul at the port of departure, and by him certified, to the satisfaction of the Collector of the port at which such Chinese subjects shall land in the United States. And no such Chinese laborer shall be permitted to enter the United States by land or sea without producing to the proper officer of the customs the return certificate herein required.

Article III The provisions of this convention shall not affect the right at present enjoyed of Chinese subjects, being officials, teachers, students, merchants, or travelers for curiosity or pleasure, but not laborers, of coming to the United States and residing therein. To entitle such Chinese subjects as are above described to admission into the United States, they may produce a certificate from their Government or the Government where they last resided, vizéd [endorsed] by the diplomatic or Consular representative of the United States in the country or port whence they depart. It is also agreed that Chinese laborers shall continue to enjoy the privilege of transit across the territory of the United States in the course of their journey to or from other countries, subject to such regulations by the Government of the United States as may be necessary to prevent said privilege of transit from being abused.

Article IV In pursuance of Article III, of the immigration treaty between the United States and China, signed at Pekin [Beijing] of the 17th day of November, 1880, (the 15th day of the tenth moon of Kwanghali, sixth year,) it is hereby understood and agreed that Chinese laborers or Chinese of any other class, either permanently or temporarily residing in the United States, shall have for the protection of their persons and property all rights that are given by the laws of the United States to citizens of the most favored nation, excepting the right to become naturalized citizens. And the Government of the United States reaffirms its obligations, as stated in said Article III, to exert all its power to secure protection to the person and property of all Chinese subjects in the United States.

Article V The Government of the United States, having, by an act of Congress, approved May 5, 1892, as amended by an act approved Nov. 3, 1893, required all Chinese laborers lawfully within the limits of the United States before the passage of the first named act to be registered as in said acts provided, with a view of affording them better protection, the Chinese

Government will not object to the enforcement of such acts, and reciprocally the Government of the United States recognizes the right of the Government of China to enact and enforce similar laws or regulations for the registration, free of charge, of all laborers, skilled or unskilled, (not merchants as defined by said acts of Congress,) citizens of the United States in China, whether residing within or without the treaty ports. And the Government of the United States agrees that within twelve months from the date of the exchange of the ratifications of this convention, and annually thereafter, it will furnish to the Government of China registers or reports showing the full name, age, occupation, and number or place of residence of all other citizens of the United States, including missionaries, residing both within and without the treaty ports of China, not including, however, diplomatic and other officers of the United States residing or traveling in China upon official business, together with their body and household servants.

Article VI This convention shall remain in force for a period of ten years, beginning with the date of the exchange of ratifications, and if six months before the expiration of the said period of ten years neither Government shall have formally given notice of its final termination to the other, it shall remain in full force for another like period of ten years.

14

◆

NEW SOUTH, OLD SOUTH

Following the Civil War, the South suffered two ordeals: racism and poverty. The problem of race touched all Southerners, from oppressed former slaves to anxious white farmers and city dwellers. Poverty, especially the bleak agricultural poverty characteristic of the South, intensified the already severe problem of race. These twin cauldrons finally boiled over in the 1890s, when more than one hundred and fifty blacks were lynched per year, and collapsing farm prices drove many thousands of families—black and white—into bankruptcy.

The Cotton States Exposition of Industry and the Arts, held in Atlanta in 1895, was designed to address the problem of poverty. Mainly the brainchild of Atlanta publishers and bankers, the exposition made much of the prospects for railroad expansion, iron and textile manu-facturing, and lumber and tobacco processing. It was hoped their success would reduce the South's unhappy dependence on agriculture and tie the region to the rest of industrial America. But the explosive issue of race also loomed. To address it, the exposition organizers, almost as an afterthought, invited Booker T. Washington, head of the Tuskegee Institute, a black vocational school in Tuskegee, Alabama, to speak to the mostly white exposition gathering. The exposition produced only a slight effect on Southern industrialization—manu-facturing did not become widespread there until the 1920s and in-dustrial prosperity has barely arrived even today. Washington's speech, however, was of major importance. His moderate message, accom-modating tone, and stress on business and hard work generally pleased his listeners, who marked him as a worthy spokesman for his race. His reputation soon spread to the white North and to blacks as well. Thus, almost overnight, Washington became a prominent figure whose message mattered to everyone, especially in the South.

Not everyone agreed with Washington's approach. Black intellec-tuals and reformers still found their inspiration in Frederick Douglass, the great abolitionist and stalwart of Radical Reconstruction and equal rights. In their eyes, Washington's acceptance of disfranchisement and segregation seemed a betrayal. They thought his refusal to condemn lynching was a surrender and viewed his influence as mostly negative. One of the most forceful of these critics was Ida B. Wells, a Chicago woman born to Mississippi slaves. Well's *A Red Record,* excerpted below, told the gruesome story of antiblack violence in the South in persuasive, compelling terms. It thus formed an important counterpoint to Washington's conservative views.

Booker T. Washington was born a slave in Virginia in 1856, and he worked from the age of nine in West Virginia salt furnaces and coal mines. He later worked his way through Hampton Institute, a black school in Virginia, established by philanthropists following the Civil War. After graduating in 1875, he briefly attended a theological seminary in Washington, D.C. In 1881, he accepted the headship of Tuskegee Institute, which he built up from two small buildings and 40 pupils to one hundred buildings, 1,500 students, and a $1 million endowment a quarter-century later. Washington was successful at attracting funds from Northern tycoons and was at least tolerated by Southern politicians. His years of greatest fame came after the Atlanta speech and especially after President Theodore Roosevelt's invitation to dine at the White House in 1901. It was in these years that Washington developed what detractors called a "Tuskegee machine," based on the support of Tuskegee graduates and black businessmen and the willingness of Northern charities and politicians to seek his advice on donations and appointments. His well-known autobiography, *Up From Slavery,* appeared in 1901. He died, exhausted from overwork, in Tuskegee, Alabama, in 1915.

Ida B. Wells was born a slave in Holly Springs, Mississippi, in 1862. She was educated in a freedmen's school, became a teacher herself, and eventually moved to Memphis, Tennessee, where she taught school and attended Fisk University. She turned to journalism in 1891 after losing her teaching post for refusing to give up her seat in a "whites-only" railroad car. When she wrote against antiblack violence, whites retaliated by burning her newspaper office. She left the South in 1892, in time marrying Ferdinand Barnett, a prominent black Chicagoan. A tireless writer and speaker for both women's and black rights, Wells encouraged the Niagara Movement, a 1909 initiative of W.E.B. Du Bois and other militants opposed to the Tuskegee Machine. She refused to support its successor organization, the National Association for the Advancement of Colored People (NAACP), on the grounds that it was too moderate. She died in Chicago in 1931.

Questions to Consider. In reading Washington's Atlanta speech, consider especially the time in which it was delivered. Was Washington, as Wells and others accused, trading black rights for black work? Or was he attempting to use the leverage of black labor to achieve something even more precious—black safety—in the turbulent 1890s? Why might 1895 have seemed an especially good time to move whites in this way? When Washington said, "Cast down your bucket where you are," was he speaking mainly to whites or to blacks? Were there population movements in the 1890s that might have prompted him to address both groups?

Why did Ida B. Wells go to such enormous pains in *A Red Record* to establish the record, from white sources, of antiblack atrocities in the post-Civil War South? For whom does she appear to have been writing? Were there models elsewhere in American society for this kind of "exposé" journalism? In this excerpt, she also takes care to refute the arguments given by white Southerners to justify the violence. Do these passages constitute an attack on paternalism—male chauvinism—as well as on racism? If Wells wrote, as she said, "in no spirit of vindictiveness," why did whites burn her newspaper office for printing similar stories? Was vindictiveness inherent in the material, bound inevitably to provoke outrage and assault? What strategies did Wells devise to avoid this?

♦

Atlanta Exposition Address (1895)

BOOKER T. WASHINGTON

Mr. President and Gentlemen of the Board of Directors and Citizens: One-third of the population of the South is of the Negro race. No enterprise seeking the material, civil, or moral welfare of this section can disregard this element of our population and reach the highest success. I but convey to you, Mr. President and Directors, the sentiment of the masses of my race when I say that in no way have the value and manhood of the American Negro been more fittingly and generously recognized than by the managers of this magnificent Exposition at every stage of its progress. It is a recognition that will do more to cement the friendship of the two races than any occurrence since the dawn of our freedom.

Not only this, but the opportunity here afforded will awaken among us a new era of industrial progress. Ignorant and inexperienced, it is not strange that in the first years of our new life we began at the top instead of at the bottom; that a seat in Congress or the state legislature was more sought than real estate or industrial skill; that the political convention or stump speaking had more attractions than starting a dairy farm or truck garden.

A ship lost at sea for many days suddenly sighted a friendly vessel. From the mast of the unfortunate vessel was seen a signal, "Water, water;

From Booker T. Washington, *Up from Slavery: A Biography* (Doubleday, Page and Co., New York, 1901), 218–225.

we die of thirst!" The answer from the friendly vessel at once came back, "Cast down your bucket where you are." A second time the signal, "Water, water; send us water!" ran up from the distressed vessel, and was answered, "Cast down your bucket where you are." And a third and fourth signal for water was answered, "Cast down your bucket where you are." The captain of the distressed vessel, at last heeding the injunction, cast down his bucket, and it came up full of fresh, sparkling water from the mouth of the Amazon River. To those of my race who depend on bettering their condition in a foreign land or who underestimate the importance of cultivating friendly relations with the Southern white man, who is their next-door neighbour, I would say: "Cast down your bucket where you are"—cast it down in making friends in every manly way of the people of all races by whom we are surrounded.

Cast it down in agriculture, mechanics, in commerce, in domestic service, and in the professions. And in this connection it is well to bear in mind that whatever other sins the South may be called to bear, when it comes to business, pure and simple, it is in the South that the Negro is given a man's chance in the commercial world, and in nothing is this Exposition more eloquent than in emphasizing this chance. Our greatest danger is that in the great leap from slavery to freedom we may overlook the fact that the masses of us are to live by the productions of our hands, and fail to keep in mind that we shall prosper in proportion as we learn to dignify and glorify common labour, and put brains and skill into the common occupations of life; shall prosper in proportion as we learn to draw the line between the superficial and the substantial, the ornamental gewgaws of life and the useful. No race can prosper till it learns that there is as much dignity in tilling a field as in writing a poem. It is at the bottom of life we must begin, and not at the top. Nor should we permit our grievances to overshadow our opportunities.

To those of the white race who look to the incoming of those of foreign birth and strange tongue and habits for the prosperity of the South, were I permitted I would repeat what I say to my own race, "Cast down your bucket where your are." Cast it down among the eight millions of Negroes whose habits you know, whose fidelity and love you have tested in days when to have proved treacherous meant the ruin of your firesides. Cast down your bucket among these people who have, without strikes and labour wars, tilled your fields, cleared your forests, builded your railroads and cities, and brought forth treasures from the bowels of the earth, and helped make possible this magnificent representation of the progress of the South. Casting down your bucket among my people, helping and encouraging them as you are doing on these grounds, and to education of head, hand, and heart, you will find that they will buy your surplus land, make blossom the waste places in your fields, and run your factories. While doing this, you can be sure in the future, as in the past, that you and your families will be surrounded by the most patient, faithful, law-abiding, and unresentful people that the world has seen. As we have proved our loyalty to you in the past, in nursing your children, watching by the sick-bed of your mothers and fathers, and often following them with tear-dimmed eyes to their graves, so in the future, in our humble way, we shall stand by you with a devotion that no foreigner can approach, ready to lay down our lives, if need be, in defense of yours, interlacing our industrial, commercial, civil, and religious life with yours in a way that shall make the interests of both races one. In all things that are purely social we can be as separate as the fingers, yet one as the hand in all things essential to mutual progress.

There is no defense or security for any of us except in the highest intelligence and development of all. If anywhere there are efforts tending to curtail the fullest growth of the Negro, let these efforts be turned into stimulating, encouraging, and making him the most useful and intelligent citizen. Effort or means so invested will pay a thousand per cent interest. These efforts will be twice blessed—"blessing him that gives and him that takes."

There is no escape through law of man or God from the inevitable:—

> *"The laws of changeless justice bind*
> *Oppressor with oppressed;*
> *And close as sin and suffering joined*
> *We march to fate abreast."*

Nearly sixteen millions of hands will aid you in pulling the load upward, or they will pull against you the load downward. We shall constitute one-third and more of the ignorance and crime of the South, or one-third its intelligence and progress; we shall contribute one-third to the business and industrial prosperity of the South, or we shall prove a veritable body of death, stagnating, depressing, retarding every effort to advance the body politic.

Gentlemen of the Exposition, as we present to you our humble effort at an exhibition of our progress, you must not expect overmuch. Starting thirty years ago with ownership here and there in a few quilts and pump-kins and chickens (gathered from miscellaneous sources), remember the path that has led from these to the inventions and production of agricultural implements, buggies, steam-engines, newspapers, books, statuary, carv-ing, paintings, the management of drug stores and banks, has not been trodden without contact with thorns and thistles. While we take pride in what we exhibit as a result of our independent efforts, we do not for a moment forget that our part in this exhibition would fall far short of your expectations but for the constant help that has come to our educational life, not only from the Southern states, but especially from Northern phi-lanthropists, who have made their gifts a constant stream of blessing and encouragement.

The wisest among my race understand that the agitation of questions of social equality is the extremest folly, and that progress in the enjoyment of all the privileges that will come to us must be the result of severe and constant struggle rather than of artificial forcing. No race that has anything to contribute to the markets of the world is long in any degree ostracized. It is important and right that all privileges of the law be ours, but it is vastly more important that we be prepared for the exercise of these privileges. The opportunity to earn a dollar in a factory just now is worth infinitely more than the opportunity to spend a dollar in an opera-house.

In conclusion, may I repeat that nothing in thirty years has given us more hope and encouragement, and drawn us so near to you of the white race, as this opportunity offered by the Exposition; and here bending, as it were, over the altar that represents the results of the struggles of your race and mine, both starting practically empty-handed three decades ago, I pledge that in your effort to work out the great and intricate problem which God has laid at the doors of the South, you shall have at all times the patient, sympathetic help of my race; only let this be constantly in mind, that, while from representations in these buildings of the product of field, of forest, of mine, of factory, letters, and art, much good will come, yet far above and beyond material benefits will be that higher good, that, let us pray God, will come, in a blotting out of sectional differences and racial animosities and suspicions, in a determination to administer absolute justice, in a willing obedience among all classes to the mandates of law. This, coupled with our material prosperity, will bring into our beloved South a new heaven and a new earth.

◆

A Red Record (1895)

IDA B. WELLS

Not all nor nearly all of the murders done by white men, during the past thirty years in the South, have come to light, but the statistics as gathered and preserved by white men, and which have not been questioned, show that during these years more than ten thousand Negroes have been killed in cold blood, without the formality of judicial trial and legal execution. And yet, as evidence of the absolute impunity with which the white man dares to kill a Negro, the same record shows that during all these years, and for all these murders only three white men have been tried, convicted, and executed. As no white man has been lynched for the murder of colored

Ida B. Wells, *A Red Record. Tabulated Statistics and Alleged Causes of Lynchings in the United States, 1892–1893–1894* (Chicago, n.d.), pp.9–15, 20, 43, 45–48.

people, these three executions are the only instances of the death penalty being visited upon white men for murdering Negroes.

Naturally enough the commission of these crimes began to tell upon the public conscience, and the Southern white man, as a tribute to the nineteenth century civilization, was in a manner compelled to give excuses for his barbarism.

The first excuse given to the civilized world for the murder of unoffending Negroes was the necessity of the white man to repress and stamp out alleged "race riots." For years immediately succeeding the war there was an appalling slaughter of colored people, and the wires usually conveyed to northern people and the world the intelligence, first, that an insurrection was being planned by Negroes, which, a few hours later, would prove to have been vigorously resisted by white men, and controlled with a resulting loss of several killed and wounded. It was always a remarkable feature in these insurrections and riots that only Negroes were killed during the rioting, and that all the white men escaped unharmed. . . .

Then came the second excuse, which had its birth during the turbulent times of reconstruction. By an amendment to the Constitution the Negro was given the right of franchise, and, theoretically at least, his ballot became his invaluable emblem of citizenship. In a government "of the people, for the people, and by the people," the Negro's vote became an important factor in all matters of state and national politics. But this did not last long. The southern white man would not consider that the Negro had any right which a white man was bound to respect, and the idea of a republican form of government in the southern states grew into general contempt.

The white man's victory soon became complete by fraud, violence, intimidation and murder. The franchise vouchsafed to the Negro grew to be a "barren ideality," and regardless of numbers, the colored people found themselves voiceless in the councils of those whose duty it was to rule. With no longer the fear of "Negro Domination" before their eyes, the white man's second excuse became valueless. With the Southern governments all subverted and the Negro actually eliminated from all participation in state and national elections, there could be no longer an excuse for killing Negroes to prevent "Negro Domination."

Brutality still continued; Negroes were whipped, scourged, exiled, shot and hung whenever and wherever it pleased the white man so to treat them, and as the civilized world with increasing persistency held the white people of the South to account for its outlawry, the murderers invented the third excuse—that Negroes had to be killed to avenge their assaults upon women. There could be framed no possible excuse more harmful to the Negro and more unanswerable if true in its sufficiency for the white man.

Humanity abhors the assailant of womanhood, and this charge upon the Negro at once placed him beyond the pale of human sympathy. With such unanimity, earnestness, and apparent candor was this charge made and reiterated that the world has accepted the story that the Negro is a monster which the Southern white man has painted him. . . .

A word as to the charge itself. In considering the third reason assigned by the Southern white people for the butchery of blacks, the question must be asked, what the white man means when he charges the black man with rape. Does he mean the crime which the statutes of the civilized states describe as such? Not by any means. With the Southern white man, any mésalliance existing between a white woman and a black man is a sufficient foundation for the charge of rape. The Southern white man says that it is impossible for a voluntary alliance to exist between a white woman and a colored man, and therefore, the fact of an alliance is a proof of force. In numerous instances where colored men have been lynched on the charge of rape, it was positively known at the time of lynching, and indisputably proven after the victim's death, that the relationship sustained between the man and woman was voluntary and clandestine, and that in no court of law could even the charge of assault have been successfully maintained.

It was for the assertion of this fact, in the defense of her own race, that the writer hereof became an exile; her property destroyed and her return to her home forbidden under penalty of death. . . .

But threats cannot suppress the truth, and while the Negro suffers the soul deformity, resultant from two and a half centuries of slavery, he is no more guilty of this vilest of all vile charges than the white man who would blacken his name.

During all the years of slavery, no such charge was ever made, not even during the dark days of the rebellion, when the white man, following the fortunes of war went to do battle for the maintenance of slavery. While the master was away fighting to forge the fetters upon the slave, he left his wife and children with no protectors save the Negroes themselves. And yet during those years of trust and peril, no Negro proved recreant to his trust and no white man returned to a home that had been dispoiled.

Likewise during the period of alleged "insurrection," and alarming "race riots," it never occurred to the white man, that his wife and children were in danger of assault. Nor in the Reconstruction era, when the hue and cry was against "Negro Domination," was there ever a thought that the domination would ever contaminate a fireside or strike to death the virtue of womanhood. . . .

In his remarkable apology for lynching, Bishop Haygood, of Georgia, says: "No race, not the most savage, tolerates the rape of woman, but it may be said without reflection upon any other people that the Southern people are now and always have been most sensitive concerning the honor of their women—their mothers, wives, sisters and daughters." It is not the purpose of this defense to say one word against the white women of the South. Such need not be said, but it is their misfortune that the chivalrous white men of that section, in order to escape the deserved execration of the civilized world, should shield themselves by their cowardly and infamously false excuse, and call into question that very honor about which their distinguished priestly apologist claims they are most sensitive. To justify their own barbarism they assume a chivalry which they do not possess. . . .

When emancipation came to the Negroes, there arose in the northern part of the United States an almost divine sentiment among the noblest, purest and best white women of the North, who felt called to a mission to educate and Christianize the millions of southern ex-slaves. From every nook and corner of the North, brave young white women answered that call and left their cultured homes, their happy associations and their lives of ease, and with heroic determination went to the South to carry light and truth to the benighted blacks. It was a heroism no less than that which calls for volunteers for India, Africa, and the Isles of the sea. To educate their unfortunate charges; to teach them the Christian virtues and to inspire in them the moral sentiments manifest in their own lives, these young women braved dangers whose record reads more like fiction than fact. They became social outlaws in the South. The peculiar sensitiveness of the southern white men for women, never shed its protecting influence about them. No friendly word from their own race cheered them in their work; no hospitable doors gave them the companionship like that from which they had come. No chivalrous white man doffed his hat in honor or respect. They were "Nigger teachers" —unpardonable offenders in the social ethics of the South, and were insulted, persecuted and ostracized, not by Negroes, but by the white manhood which boasts of its chivalry toward women.

And yet these northern women worked on, year after year, unselfishly, with a heroism which amounted almost to martyrdom. Threading their way through dense forests, working in schoolhouse, in the cabin and in the church, thrown at all times and in all places among the unfortunate and lowly Negroes, whom they had come to find and to serve, these northern women, thousands and thousands of them, have spent more than a quarter of a century in giving to the colored people their splendid lessons for home and heart and soul. Without protection, save that which innocence gives to every good woman, they went about their work, fearing no assault and suffering none. . . . Before the world adjudges the Negro a moral monster, a vicious assailant of womanhood and a menace to the sacred precincts of home, the colored people ask the consideration of the silent record of gratitude, respect, protection, and devotion of the millions of the race in the South, to the thousands of northern white women who have served as teachers and missionaries since the war. . . .

These pages are written in no spirit of vindictiveness, for all who give the subject consideration must concede that far too serious is the condition of that civilized government in which the spirit of unrestrained outlawry constantly increases in violence, and casts its blight over a continually growing area of territory. We plead not for the colored people alone, but for all victims of the terrible injustice which puts men and women to death without form of law. During the year 1894, there were 132 persons executed in the United States by due form of law, while in the same year, 197 persons were put to death by mobs who gave the victims no opportunity to make a lawful defense. No comment need be made upon a condition of public sentiment responsible for such alarming results.

15

◆

THE SEGREGATED SOUTH

After the Dred Scott decision in 1857, the tide of federal decision making turned, becoming more favorable for blacks, at least through 1870 when the ratification of the Fifteenth Amendment to the Constitution guaranteed them the right to vote. But with President Rutherford B. Hayes's withdrawal of federal troops from the South in 1877, the current gradually shifted once more toward disfranchisement, exploitation, and increasingly, segregation. In the *Plessy* v. *Ferguson* case in 1896, the Supreme Court upheld a Louisiana law requiring separate railroad cars for blacks and whites.

Homer Plessy was one-eighth black; by sitting in the white section of a railway car en route from New Orleans to Covington, Louisiana, he violated a Louisiana "Jim Crow" (racial separation) law. He was arrested for refusing to move into a black section, and John H. Ferguson, the Louisiana judge who tried the case, found him guilty. Believing that the Jim Crow law violated the Fourteenth Amendment, Plessy appealed the decision. But the Supreme Court upheld the Louisiana law, stating that the Fourteenth Amendment, which forbids states to abridge the civil rights and liberties of citizens, requires only that separate facilities be equal.

This "separate but equal" doctrine allowed segregation not only of private commercial facilities like hotels, but also of public schools and even towns and cities. In practice it permitted the creation of facilities that were surely separate but hardly equal. The decision stood until 1954, when it was overturned by the Supreme Court in the landmark decision in *Brown* v. *The Board of Education of Topeka*.

Henry Billings Brown, the author of the Plessy decision, was born to wealthy parents in Massachusetts in 1836. He attended Yale College and set up a law practice in Detroit. Appointed to the Supreme Court by President Benjamin Harrison in 1890, Brown retired from the Court in 1906 and lived in New York until his death in 1913. His chief opinion besides Plessy was a concurrence in the decision in *Dawson* v. *Bidwell* (1901) that inhabitants of annexed territories, such as Puerto Rico, had no constitutional rights.

Questions to Consider. Several aspects of the Plessy opinion merit special attention. Note, for example, the dual themes of racism and growth. Did Henry Billings Brown believe his decision would segregate facilities in the South? Was it not, in fact, Southern industrial progress— new railroads, streetcars, hotels, and schools—and its effect on race relations that had brought the issue before the Court in the first place? Brown stated that although all citizens have a kind of "property" interest in their reputations because these can affect their future, seg- regation will not harm blacks' reputations unless they allow it to hurt their self-esteem. Whites in a minority position, said Brown, would not suffer diminished self-esteem; neither should blacks. What evi- dence is cited for this opinion? Note Brown's narrow view of the scope of the law. Law, he argued, can neither equalize nor unify society. In its Plessy decision, therefore, the Supreme Court declared actual racial experience—slavery, terrorism, and exploitation—to be irrelevant to the legal consideration of race relations. Do you agree with this reasoning?

◆

Plessy v. *Ferguson* **(1896)**

This case turns upon the constitutionality of an act of the general assembly of the state of Louisiana, passed in 1890, providing for separate railway carriages for the white and colored races. . . .

The constitutionality of this act is attacked upon the ground that it conflicts both with the 13th Amendment of the Constitution, abolishing slavery, and the 14th Amendment, which prohibits certain restrictive leg- islation on the part of the states.

That it does not conflict with the 13th Amendment, which abolished slavery and involuntary servitude, except as a punishment for crime, is too clear for argument. . . .

The object of the [14th] amendment was undoubtedly to enforce the absolute equality of the two races before the law, but in the nature of things it could not have been intended to abolish distinctions based upon color, or to enforce social, as distinguished from political, equality, or a com- mingling of the two races upon terms unsatisfactory to either. Laws per- mitting, and even requiring their separation in places where they are liable to be brought into contact do not necessarily imply the inferiority of either race to the other, and have been generally, if not universally, recognized

Plessy v. *Ferguson*, 163 U.S. 537 (1896).

as within the competency of the state legislatures in the exercise of their police power. The most common instance of this is connected with the establishment of separate schools for white and colored children, which have been held to be a valid exercise of the legislative power even by courts of states where the political rights of the colored race have been longest and most earnestly enforced. . . .

It is claimed by the plaintiff in error that, in any mixed community, the reputation of belonging to the dominant race, in this instance the white race, is property, in the same sense that a right of action, or of inheritance, is property. Conceding this to be so, for the purposes of this case, we are unable to see how this statute deprives him of, or in any way affects his right to, such property. If he be a white man and assigned to a colored coach, he may have his action for damages against the company for being deprived of his so-called property. Upon the other hand, if he be a colored man and be so assigned, he has been deprived of no property, since he is not lawfully entitled to the reputation of being a white man. . . .

So far, then, as a conflict with the 14th Amendment is concerned, the case reduces itself to the question whether the statute of Louisiana is a reasonable regulation, and with respect to this there must necessarily be a large discretion on the part of the legislature. In determining the question of reasonableness it is at liberty to act with reference to the established usages, customs, and traditions of the people, and with a view to the promotion of their comfort, and the preservation of the public peace and good order. Gauged by this standard, we cannot say that a law which authorizes or even requires the separation of the two races in public conveyances is unreasonable or more obnoxious to the 14th Amendment than the acts of Congress requiring separate schools for colored children in the District of Columbia, the constitutionality of which does not seem to have been questioned, or the corresponding acts of state legislatures.

We consider the underlying fallacy of the plaintiff's argument to consist in the assumption that the enforced separation of the two races stamps the colored race with a badge of inferiority. If this be so, it is not by reason of anything found in the act, but solely because the colored race chooses to put that construction upon it. The argument necessarily assumes that if, as has been more than once the case, and is not unlikely to be so again, the colored race should become the dominant power in the state legislature, and should enact a law in precisely similar terms, it would thereby relegate the white race to an inferior position. We imagine that the white race, at least, would not acquiesce in this assumption. The argument also assumes that social prejudice may be overcome by legislation, and that equal rights cannot be secured to the Negro except by an enforced commingling of the two races. We cannot accept this proposition. If the two races are to meet on terms of social equality, it must be the result of natural affinities, a mutual appreciation of each other's merits and a voluntary consent of individuals. . . .

Legislation is powerless to eradicate racial instincts or to abolish distinctions based upon physical differences, and the attempt to do so can only result in accentuating the difficulties of the present situation. If the civil and political right of both races be equal, one cannot be inferior to the other civilly or politically. If one race be inferior to the other socially, the Constitution of the United States cannot put them upon the same plane.

16

◆

BEARING GIFTS

Nativist bigotry was widespread in turn-of-the-century America, at-taching itself with special force to immigrants from Eastern or Catholic Europe and perhaps most venomously to Jews. Anti-Semitism was a powerful current from czarist Russia to the democratic United States in the late nineteenth century, intensifying in the United States with the beginning of large-scale Jewish immigration in the 1880s. There-after, anti-Semitism emerged in all regions, classes, and parties. Resort hotels and exclusive men's clubs barred Jewish businessmen, and upper-class colleges established quota systems. Small-town Midwes-terners and Southern farmers criticized not just Wall Street bankers but international Jewish bankers. Radical writers like Jack London cast a racist net that snared Jews as well as blacks. Even urban Catholic immigrants, who themselves experienced religious and nativist dis-crimination, harassed the "Christ-killers" and "Shylocks" who shared their ethnic slums.

Spokespersons for the various immigrant groups labored hard to counter nativist bigotry. They challenged stereotypes where they could, chiefly by publicizing their group's successes, including successful examples of Americanization. They also tried to portray the group's distinctive characteristics in positive terms, stressing how the country would benefit from Italian musical genius, for example, or Polish re-ligious fervor. The Jewish community had no finer advocate than Mary Antin, a young writer and political activist whose speech before a New York convention of the General Federation of Women's Clubs is ex-cerpted below.

Mary Antin was born in Russia in 1881 and emigrated with her parents to the United States in 1894. When she was still a teenager, Antin wrote her first book—in Yiddish—about the Jewish immigrant experience. After studying at Teachers College and Barnard College in New York City, she published *The Promised Land* (1912), perhaps our most beautiful version of the immigrant saga. An ardent socialist and union supporter, Antin continued to write and lecture on the subject of immigration; she was a notable opponent of congressional efforts to pass restrictive immigration laws. She died in Suffern, New York, on May 15, 1949.

Questions to Consider. Why didn't Mary Antin argue for the value of Jewish immigration by offering case studies, as immigrant defenders sometimes did, of successful individual Jews? What point was she trying to make by implicitly reinforcing a stereotype about Jews—that as a group they produced a disproportionate number of scholars, lawyers, and debaters? How did she attempt to connect the discussion about Jews and the law with her discussion later about the organization of the clothing industry? Was she right to argue that the passion for justice was fundamental to being a Jew, so that Jews were, in a sense, heirs to the "Spirit of '76" and therefore naturally American? What were the "false gods" Antin referred to in her final sentence?

◆

Russian Jews (1916)

MARY ANTIN

On the whole the Russian immigrant in this country is the Jewish immigrant, since we are the most numerous group out of Russia. But to speak for the Jews—the most misunderstood people in the whole of history—ten minutes, in which to clear away 2,000 years of misunderstanding! Your President has probably in this instance, as in other instances, been guided by some inspiration, the source of which none of us may know. I was called by name long before your President notified me that she would call me to this assembly. I was called by name to say what does the Jew bring to America—by a lady from Philadelphia. Miss Repplier, not long ago, in an article in her inimitable fashion, called things by their name, and sometimes miscalled them, spoke of "the Jew in America who has received from us so much and has given us so little." This comment was called down by something that I had said about certain things in American life that did not come up to the American standard. "The Jew who has given so little." Tonight I am the Jew—you are the Americans. Let us look over these things.

What do we bring you besides our poverty and our rags? Men, women, and children—the stuff that nations are built of. What sort of men and women? I shall not seek to tire you with a list of shining names of Jewish notables. If you want to know who's who among the Jews, I refer you to your biographical dictionary. You are as familiar as I am with the name of Jews who shine in the professions, who have done notable service to the state, in politics, in diplomacy, and where you will. . . .

From General Federation of Women's Clubs, *Thirteenth Biennial Convention* (New York, 1916).

You know as well as I what numbers of Jewish youth are always taking high ranks, high honors in the schools, colleges and universities. You know as well as I do in what numbers our people crowd your lecture halls and your civic centers, in all those places where the spiritual wine of life may be added to our daily bread. These are things that you know. I don't want you to be thinking of any list of Jewish notables.

A very characteristic thing of Jewish life is the democracy of virtue that you find in every Jewish community. We Jews have never depended for our salvation on the supreme constellations of any chosen ones. . . . Our shining ones were to us always examples by means of which the whole community was to be disciplined to what was Jewish virtue.

Take a group of Jews anywhere, and you will have the essence of their Jewishness, though there be not present one single shining luminary. The average Jew presents the average of whatsoever there is of Jewish virtue, talent or capacity.

What is this peculiar Jewish genius? If I must sum it up in a word, I will say that the Jewish genius is a love for living out the things that they believe. What do we believe? We Jews believe that the world is a world of law. Law is another name for our God, and the quest after the law, the formulation of it, has always permeated our schools, and the incorporation of the laws of life, as our scholars noted it down, has been the chief business of the Jewish masses. No wonder that when we come to America, a nation founded as was our ancient nation, a nation founded on law and principle, on an ideal—no wonder that we so quickly find ourselves at home, that presently we fall into the regulation habit of speaking of America as our own country, until Miss Repplier reproves us, and then we do it no more. I used formerly when speaking of American sins, tribulations, etc., I used to speak of them as "ours"; no more—your sins. I have been corrected.

Why then, now that we have come here, to this nation builded on the same principle as was our nation, no wonder that we so quickly seize on the fundamentals. We make no virtue of the fact—it is the Jewishness in us—that has been our peculiar characteristics, our habit. We need no one from outside of our ranks to remind us of the goodly things we have found and taken from your hands. We have been as eloquent as any that has spoken in appreciation of what we have found here, of liberty, justice, and a square deal. We give thanks. We have rendered thanks, we Jews, some of you are witnesses. We know the value of the gifts that we have found here.

Who shall know the flavor of bread if not they that have gone hungry, and we, who have been for centuries without the bread of justice, we know the full flavor of American justice, liberty, and equality.

To formulate and again formulate, and criticise the law,—what do our Rabbis in the Ghetto besides the study of law? To them used to come our lawyers, to our Rabbis, not to find the way how to get around the law, but to be sure that we were walking straight in the path indicated by the law. So today in America we are busy in the same fashion.

The Jewish virtues, such as they are, are widespread throughout the Jewish masses. Here in New York City is congregated the largest Jewish community in the whole world, and what is true of the Jews of New York, is true of the Jews of America, and the Jews of the world. If I speak of the characteristics of Jewish life on the East side, one of the great characteristics is its restlessness in physical form, due to the oppression of city life, and the greater restlessness, due to the unquenchable, turbulent quest for the truth, and more truth. You know that the East side of New York is a very spawning ground for debate, and debating clubs. There are more boys and girls in debating clubs than in boys' basket ball teams, or baseball teams. I believe in boys playing baseball, but I also believe in that peculiar enthusiasm of our Jewish people for studying the American law, just as they used to study their own law, to see whether any of the American principles find incorporation in American institutions and habits. We are the critics. We are never satisfied with things as they are. Go out and hear the boys and girls. They like to go to school and learn the names of liberty, and equality and justice, and after school they gather in their debating circles and discuss what might be the meaning of these names, and what is their application to life. That is the reason there is so much stirring, rebellion, and protest that comes out of the East side.

In the great labor movement, it is the effort of the people to arrive at a program of economic justice that shall parallel the political justice. Consider for a moment the present condition of the garment-making trade. That is a Jewish trade. Ages ago when the lords of the nations, among whom we lived, were preventing us from engaging in other occupations, they thrust into the hands of our people the needle, and the needle was our tool, why through the needle we have still thought to give expression to the Jewish genius in our life.

This immense clothing industry—a Jewish industry primarily—is today in a better condition as regards unionization, is further on the road to economic justice than any other great industry that you could name. Mind you, the sweatshop we found here when we came here. We took it just as it was, but the barring of the sweatshop and the organization of the clothing industry in such fashion that it is further in advance, more nearly on a basis that affords just treatment to all concerned—that has been the contribution of our tailor men and tailor women. We have done this thing. . . . The Protocol[1] is a piece of machinery for bringing about justice in this great industry. We have invented that thing, we Jews. We are putting

---

1. **The Protocol:** A labor-management agreement recognizing union rights and providing for improved working conditions in the garment industry.

it in operation, we are fighting for its perpetuation. Whatsoever good comes from it, we have done it. . . .

Consider us, if you will, in the most barbarous sense, but I point to this as our great contribution, we are always protesting, and if you want to know the value of that contribution, I remind you that the formulae of the rights of men, which was a criticism of things as they used to be, and a formularizing of things as they ought to be, was at least as efficient as all the armies of the continent put together in the revolutionary war. The Spirit of '76 is the spirit of criticism. We Jews in America are busy at our ancient business of pulling down false gods.

17

✦

CLOSING THE DOORS

For a half-century after the Civil War the United States maintained a relatively unrestrictive policy toward immigration from Europe. Yet the coming of so many millions of immigrants, particularly so many who were neither Protestant nor northern Europeans, caused growing alarm among "old-stock" Americans, who associated the newcomers with saloons, political corruption, and other "ills" of urban society. Labor leaders feared such floods of uncontrollable cheap labor; upper-class spokesmen were concerned about the possible "mongrelization" of the country.

The first broad effort to restrict immigration was the Literacy Test of 1917, which actually had little effect because most immigrants could in fact read and write. In 1921, Congress limited immigration from any country to 3 percent of that country's proportion of the American population as of 1910. By 1924 the public favored even more restrictive measures. The sweeping National Origins Act, excerpted below, brought the tradition of unrestricted entry by Europeans to a definitive close. Only people from the Western Hemisphere could come freely now. (A separate Oriental Exclusion Act later banned Asians altogether.) The national-origins standard, though modified, persisted until 1965, when the emphasis shifted from national origin to refugees, relatives, and occupational skills.

Questions to Consider. The Immigration Act of 1924 shows how American society rated the different nationalities at that time. According to the quotas listed in the act, for example, a Czech was worth thirty Chinese, a Swiss equaled twenty Syrians, and an Irishman ten Italians. Is this a fair interpretation of the act? Of course, the act was not purely racial legislation. Not even at this peak of feverish nationalism did the U.S. government discriminate arbitrarily between nationalities or allot immigration space on a random basis. With the notable exception of Asians, national quotas were figured on a percentage basis: limiting Armenians also meant limiting Austrians. Most of the Western Hemisphere, moreover, was exempt from the act. Nevertheless, by basing quotas on the 1890 rather than the 1910 census, the act did embody clear racial preferences. Why, then, was such care taken to employ percentages rather than absolute numbers? Ironically, it was the Republicans, not the Southern-dominated Democrats (Woodrow Wilson, a well-known segregationist, twice vetoed immigrant literacy legislation) who perceived mass immigration as a grave national danger. What accounted for this anomaly?

◆

The Immigration Act of 1924

It will be remembered that the quota limit act of May 1921, provided that the number of aliens of any nationality admissible to the United States in any fiscal year should be limited to 3 per cent of the number of persons of such nationality who were resident in the United States according to the census of 1910, it being also provided that not more than 20 per cent of any annual quota could be admitted in any one month. Under the act of 1924 the number of each nationality who may be admitted annually is limited to 2 per cent of the population of such nationality resident in the United States according to the census of 1890, and not more than 10 per cent of any annual quota may be admitted in any month except in cases where such quota is less than 300 for the entire year.

Under the act of May, 1921, the quota area was limited to Europe, the Near East, Africa, and Australasia. The countries of North and South America, with adjacent islands, and countries immigration from which was otherwise regulated, such as China, Japan, and countries within the Asiatic barred zone, were not within the scope of the quota law. Under the new act, however, immigration from the entire world, with the exception of the Dominion of Canada, Newfoundland, the Republic of Mexico, the Republic of Cuba, the Republic of Haiti, the Dominican Republic, the Canal Zone, and independent countries of Central and South America, is subject to quota limitations. The various quotas established under the new law are shown in the . . . proclamation of the President, issued on the last day of the present fiscal year: . . .

Country or Area of Birth	Quota 1924–1925
Afghanistan	100
Albania	100
Andorra	100
Arabian peninsula	100
Armenia	124

From the *Annual Report of the Commissioner-General of Immigration* (Government Printing Office, Washington, D.C., 1924).

"The Only Way to Handle It."   This 1921 cartoon from the *Providence Evening Bulletin* urged support for measures to restrict immigration according to the size of resident nationality groups. New England Yankees, such as the readers of the *Bulletin,* helped lead the restrictionist movement, with considerable assistance from Midwesterners and Californians. Restrictionists felt especially threatened by the renewal of mass European migration to America following the end of World War I. (Library of Congress)

Country or Area of Birth	Quota 1924–1925
Australia, including Papua, Tasmania, and all islands appertaining to Australia	121
Austria	785
Belgium	512
Bhutan	100
Bulgaria	100
Cameroon (proposed British mandate)	100
Cameroon (French mandate)	100
China	100
Czechoslovakia	3,073
Danzig, Free City of	228
Denmark	2,789
Egypt	100
Estonia	124
Ethiopia (Abyssinia)	100
Finland	170
France	3,954
Germany	51,227
Great Britain and Northern Ireland	34,007
Greece	100
Hungary	473
Iceland	100
India	100
Iraq (Mesopotamia)	100
Irish Free State	28,567
Italy, including Rhodes, Dodekanesia, and Castellorizzo	3,845
Japan	100
Latvia	142
Liberia	100
Liechtenstein	100
Lithuania	344
Luxemburg	100
Monaco	100
Morocco (French and Spanish Zones and Tangier)	100
Muscat (Oman)	100
Nauru (Proposed British mandate)	100
Nepal	100
Netherlands	1,648
New Zealand (including appertaining islands)	100
Norway	6,453
New Guinea, and other Pacific Islands under proposed Australian mandate	100
Palestine (with Trans-Jordan, proposed British mandate)	100
Persia	100
Poland	5,982
Portugal	503
Ruanda and Urundi (Belgium mandate)	100

Country or Area of Birth	Quota 1924–1925
Rumania	603
Russia, European and Asiatic	2,248
Samoa, Western (proposed mandate of New Zealand)	100
San Marino	100
Siam	100
South Africa, Union of	100
South West Africa (proposed mandate of Union of South Africa)	100
Spain	131
Sweden	9,561
Switzerland	2,081
Syria and The Lebanon (French mandate)	100
Tanganyika (proposed British mandate)	100
Togoland (proposed British mandate)	100
Togoland (French mandate)	100
Turkey	100
Yap and other Pacific islands (under Japanese mandate)	100
Yugoslavia	671

Triumphant return. Men of New York City's 165th Infantry Regiment arriving back home after the Great War—"the war to end all wars." (UPI/Bettmann Newsphotos)

CHAPTER FOUR

◆

Empire and Uplift

18

◆

THE LURE OF THE EAST

The United States went to war with Spain over Cuba in 1898. But the U.S. victory in the brief war brought acquisitions in the Pacific (the Philippines and Guam) as well as in the Caribbean (Puerto Rico): at this time the United States also got control of the Hawaiian Islands and Wake Island. In part these acquisitions represented the resumption of a long tradition of westward territorial expansion that had been abandoned since the purchase of Alaska in 1867. In part they represented America's desire for "great power" status at a time when the European nations were winning colonies in Asia and Africa. But powerful economic forces were at work, too, as they had been in the formulation of the recent Open Door policy or, for that matter, in President James Monroe's assertion of his famous Doctrine in 1823.

At the beginning of the war, President William McKinley was unsure himself whether or not the United States should take over the Philippines, and if it did, whether its forces would take only Manila, or the whole island of Luzon, or the entire archipelago. Not until December 1898 did the president finally announce that the United States would pursue a policy of "benevolent assimilation" toward the whole territory. This decision gave rise to a small but vocal anti-imperialist movement at home and, more important, a strong Filipino resistance struggle against the American occupation.

At this point, however, forceful advocates of imperialism rose to defend the president in the most vigorous terms. Of these none was more forceful or more important than Senator Albert J. Beveridge. His Senate speech of January 1900 in support of a (successful) resolution urging colonial status for the Philippines, excerpted below, provided the broadest possible grounds for the president's policy. With the fight thus in hand at home, McKinley turned to winning the fight abroad. Having made his decision, moreover, he stuck doggedly with it. In fact, the Americans overcame the insurgents only after another year's hard fighting and the death of more than a hundred thousand Filipinos.

President McKinley's ally and fellow Ohioan, Albert Beveridge, was only thirty-seven at the time of his imperialist speech of 1900, but he was already known as a proponent of military strength and Anglo-Saxon supremacy. This speech further enhanced his standing in Republican circles. Beveridge left the Senate in 1912 to devote himself to writing. In 1919, eight years before his death in Indiana, his *Life of John Marshall* was awarded the Pulitzer Prize for historical biography.

Questions to Consider. Beveridge's speech makes enormous claims for the strategic importance of the Philippines. On what grounds did Beveridge make these claims? Has history borne out Beveridge's predictions about the Pacific Ocean and world commerce? Did Beveridge think acquiring the Philippines would increase or reduce the chances of war? How did he seem to view the Declaration of Independence and the Constitution? Was Beveridge's main concern economics or race?

◆

America's Destiny (1900)

ALBERT BEVERIDGE

Mr. President, the times call for candor. The Philippines are ours forever, "territory belonging to the United States," as the Constitution calls them. And just beyond the Philippines are China's illimitable markets. We will not retreat from either. We will not repudiate our duty in the archipelago. We will not abandon our opportunity in the Orient. We will not renounce our part in the mission of our race, trustee, under God, of the civilization of the world. And we will move forward to our work, not howling out regrets like slaves whipped to their burdens, but with gratitude for a task worthy of our strength, and thanksgiving to Almighty God that He has marked us as His chosen people, henceforth to lead in the regeneration of the world.

This island empire is the last land left in all the oceans. If it should prove a mistake to abandon it, the blunder once made would be irretrievable. If it proves a mistake to hold it, the error can be corrected when we will. Every other progressive nation stands ready to relieve us.

But to hold it will be no mistake. Our largest trade henceforth must be with Asia. The Pacific is our ocean. More and more Europe will manufacture the most it needs, secure from its colonies the most it consumes. Where shall we turn for consumers of our surplus? Geography answers the question. China is our natural customer. She is nearer to us than to England, Germany, or Russia, the commercial powers of the present and the future. They have moved nearer to China by securing permanent bases on her borders. The Philippines give us a base at the door of all the East.

From the *Congressional Record*, 56th Congress, 1st session, 704–712.

Lines of navigation from our ports to the Orient and Australia; from the Isthmian Canal to Asia; from all Oriental ports to Australia, converge at and separate from the Philippines. They are a self-supporting, dividend-paying fleet, permanently anchored at a spot selected by the strategy of Providence, commanding the Pacific. And the Pacific is the ocean of the commerce of the future. Most future wars will be conflicts for commerce. The power that rules the Pacific, therefore, is the power that rules the world. And, with the Philippines, that power is and will forever be the American Republic. . . .

Nothing is so natural as trade with one's neighbors. The Philippines make us the nearest neighbors of all the East. Nothing is more natural than to trade with those you know. This is the philosophy of all advertising. The Philippines bring us permanently face to face with the most sought-for customers of the world. National prestige, national propinquity, these and commercial activity are the elements of commercial success. The Philippines give the first; the character of the American people supply the last. It is a providential conjunction of all the elements of trade, of duty, and of power. If we are willing to go to war rather than let England have a few feet of frozen Alaska, which affords no market and commands none, what should we not do rather than let England, Germany, Russia, or Japan have all the Philippines? And no man on the spot can fail to see that this would be their fate if we retired. . . .

Here, then, Senators, is the situation. Two years ago there was no land in all the world which we could occupy for any purpose. Our commerce was daily turning toward the Orient, and geography and trade developments made necessary our commercial empire over the Pacific. And in that ocean we had no commercial, naval, or military base. Today we have one of the three great ocean possessions of the globe, located at the most commanding commercial, naval, and military points in the eastern seas, within hail of India, shoulder to shoulder with China, richer in its own resources than any equal body of land on the entire globe, and peopled by a race which civilization demands shall be improved. Shall we abandon it? That man little knows the common people of the Republic, little understands the instincts of our race, who thinks we will not hold it fast and hold it forever, administering just government by simplest methods. We may trick up devices to shift our burden and lessen our opportunity; they will avail us nothing but delay. We may tangle conditions by applying academic arrangements of self-government to a crude situation; their failure will drive us to our duty in the end. . . .

But, Senators, it would be better to abandon this combined garden and Gibraltar of the Pacific, and count our blood and treasure already spent a profitable loss, than to apply any academic arrangement of self-government to these children. They are not capable of self-government. How could they be? They are not of a self-governing race. They are Orientals, Malays, instructed by Spaniards in the latter's worst estate.

They know nothing of practical government except as they have witnessed the weak, corrupt, cruel, and capricious rule of Spain. What magic will anyone employ to dissolve in their minds and characters those impressions of governors and governed which three centuries of misrule have created? What alchemy will change the oriental quality of their blood and set the self-governing currents of the American pouring through their Malay veins? How shall they, in the twinkling of an eye, be exalted to the heights of self-governing peoples which required a thousand years for us to reach, Anglo-Saxon though we are . . . ?

The Declaration of Independence does not forbid us to do our part in the regeneration of the world. If it did, the Declaration would be wrong, just as the Articles of Confederation, drafted by the very same men who signed the Declaration, was found to be wrong. The Declaration has no application to the present situation. It was written by self-governing men for self-governing men. . . .

Senators in opposition are stopped from denying our constitutional power to govern the Philippines as circumstances may demand, for such power is admitted in the case of Florida, Louisiana, Alaska. How, then, is it denied in the Philippines? Is there a geographical interpretation to the Constitution? Do degrees of longitude fix constitutional limitations? Does a thousand miles of ocean diminish constitutional power more than a thousand miles of land . . . ?

No; the oceans are not limitations of the power which the Constitution expressly gives Congress to govern all territory the nation may acquire. The Constitution declares that "Congress shall have power to dispose of and make all needful rules and regulations respecting the territory belonging to the United States." . . .

Mr. President, this question is deeper than any question of party politics; deeper than any question of the isolated policy of our country even; deeper even than any question of constitutional power. It is elemental. It is racial. God has not been preparing the English-speaking and Teutonic peoples for a thousand years for nothing but vain and idle self-contemplation and self-admiration. No! He has made us the master organizers of the world to establish system where chaos reigns. He has given us the spirit of progress to overwhelm the forces of reaction throughout the earth. He has made us adepts in government that we may administer government among savage and senile peoples. Were it not for such a force as this the world would relapse into barbarism and night. And of all our race He has marked the American people as His chosen nation to finally lead in the regeneration of the world. This is the divine mission of America, and it holds for us all the profit, all the glory, all the happiness possible to man. We are trustees of the world's progress, guardians of its righteous peace. The judgment of the Master is upon us: "Ye have been faithful over a few things; I will make you ruler over many things."

What shall history say of us? Shall it say that we renounced that holy trust, left the savage to his base condition, the wilderness to the reign of waste, deserted duty, abandoned glory, forgot our sordid profit even, because we feared our strength and read the charter of our powers with the doubter's eye and the quibbler's mind? Shall it say that, called by events to captain and command the proudest, ablest, purest race of history in history's noblest work, we declined that great commission? Our fathers would not have had it so. No! They founded no paralytic government, incapable of the simplest acts of administration. They planted no sluggard people, passive while the world's work calls them. They established no reactionary nation. They unfurled no retreating flag. . . .

Mr. President and Senators, adopt the resolution offered, that peace may quickly come and that we may begin our saving, regenerating, and uplifting work. . . . Reject it, and the world, history, and the American people will know where to forever fix the awful responsibility for the consequences that will surely follow such failure to do our manifest duty. . . .

19

◆

GUNBOAT DIPLOMACY

Although the Monroe Doctrine of 1823 had proclaimed a special interest in Latin American affairs, it was neither militaristic nor especially interventionist in spirit. But the Spanish-American War signaled a new military and economic aggressiveness in Washington and a new determination to assert the country's diplomatic ambitions. It was perhaps inevitable, therefore, that President Theodore Roosevelt should modify the Monroe Doctrine to provide a rationale for direct intervention by armed force on behalf of "progress" and "responsible government."

A hero of the U.S. Army's recent Cuban campaign against Spain and an admirer of Admiral George Dewey, victor in the Battle of Manila, Roosevelt urged a policy of expanding the country's military might. Advising the United States to "speak softly and carry a big stick," Roosevelt believed the United States should act as the policeman of Central America and the Caribbean. This role was especially necessary, he explained in the following 1905 message to Congress on the Dominican Republic, in cases where European powers might intervene to protect investments. Roosevelt seems to have won his argument. During the first twenty-five years of the twentieth century, the United States sent troops into Latin American countries on sixteen different occasions (including twice to the Dominican Republic).

Theodore Roosevelt, who inaugurated this era of "gunboat diplomacy," was born to well-to-do parents in New York City in 1858. After college he juggled politics, writing, ranching, and hunting, until McKinley appointed him assistant secretary of the navy in 1897. He resigned in 1898 to lead a cavalry unit called the Rough Riders in Cuba, but he returned to win the governorship of New York in 1899 and 1900. He moved on to the vice-presidency in 1901 and, in that same year, to the presidency when McKinley was assassinated. Over the next ten years Roosevelt promised a "square deal" and a "new nationalism," both embodying his notions of social and military progress. In 1912 he bolted the Republican party to head a Progressive ticket that lost to Woodrow Wilson, a Democrat whose internationalism Roosevelt relentlessly castigated until his death in 1919.

Questions to Consider. In what ways did Roosevelt's justification of U.S. intervention in the Caribbean differ from Senator Albert Beveridge's argument for seizing the Philippines? What role did Europe play in shaping U.S. policy in the area? What impression of Central America and the Caribbean did Roosevelt convey in this message? Did he establish any limits on the right of the United States to intervene in Latin American affairs? Who would decide when intervention was warranted or would cease? Given the likely increase in U.S. investment in the area in future years, was U.S. intervention also likely to increase?

◆

Message on the Caribbean (1905)

THEODORE ROOSEVELT

The conditions in the Republic of Santo Domingo [Dominican Republic] have been growing steadily worse for many years. There have been many disturbances and revolutions, and debts have been contracted beyond the power of the Republic to pay. Some of these debts were properly contracted and are held by those who have a legitimate right to their money. Others are without question improper or exorbitant, constituting claims which should never be paid in full and perhaps only to the extent of a very small portion of their nominal value.

Certain foreign countries have long felt themselves aggrieved because of the nonpayment of debts due their citizens. The only way by which foreign creditors could ever obtain from the Republic itself any guaranty of payment would be either by the acquisition of territory outright or temporarily, or else by taking possession of the custom-houses, which would of course in itself, in effect, be taking possession of a certain amount of territory.

It has for some time been obvious that those who profit by the Monroe Doctrine must accept certain responsibilities along with the rights which it confers; and that the same statement applies to those who uphold the doctrine. It can not be too often and too emphatically asserted that the United States has not the slightest desire for territorial aggrandizement at the expense of any of its southern neighbors, and will not treat the Monroe Doctrine as an excuse for such aggrandizement on its part. We do not propose to take any part of Santo Domingo, or exercise any other control over the island save what is necessary to its financial rehabilitation in

From Theodore Roosevelt, *Presidential Addresses and State Papers* (New York, 1910) III: 241–260.

Theodore Roosevelt. Roosevelt inspects the construction of the Panama Canal, a critical feature of TR's vision of the United States as a Great Power and a dominant commercial and military force in the Caribbean, Central America, and the Pacific. (Brown Brothers)

connection with the collection of revenue, part of which will be turned over to the Government to meet the necessary expense of running it, and part of which will be distributed pro rata among the creditors of the Republic upon a basis of absolute equity. The justification for the United States taking this burden and incurring this responsibility is to be found in the fact that it is incompatible with international equity for the United States to refuse to allow other powers to take the only means at their disposal of satisfying the claims of their creditors and yet to refuse, itself, to take any such steps.

An aggrieved nation can without interfering with the Monroe Doctrine take what action it sees fit in the adjustment of its disputes with American States, provided that action does not take the shape of interference with their form of government or of the despoilment of their territory under any disguise. But, short of this, when the question is one of a money claim, the only way which remains, finally, to collect it is a blockade, or bombardment, or the seizure of the custom-houses, and this means, as has been said above, what is in effect a possession, even though only a temporary possession, of territory. The United States then becomes a party in interest, because under the Monroe Doctrine it can not see any European power seize and permanently occupy the territory of one of these Republics; and yet such seizure of territory, disguised or undisguised, may eventually offer the only way in which the power in question can collect any debts, unless there is interference on the part of the United States.

One of the difficult and increasingly complicated problems, which often arise in Santo Domingo, grows out of the violations of contracts and concessions, sometimes improvidently granted, with valuable privileges and exemptions stipulated for upon grossly inadequate considerations which were burdensome to the State, and which are not infrequently disregarded and violated by the governing authorities. . . . There are Governments which do sometimes take energetic action for the protection of their subjects in the enforcement of merely contractual claims, and thereupon American concessionaires, supported by powerful influences, make loud appeal to the United States Government in similar cases for similar action. They complain that in the actual posture of affairs their valuable properties are practically confiscated, that American enterprise is paralyzed, and that unless they are fully protected even by the enforcement of their merely contractual rights, it means the abandonment to the subjects of other Governments of the interests of American trade and commerce through the sacrifice of their investments. . . .

The conditions in the Dominican Republic not only constitute a menace to our relations with other foreign nations, but they also concern the prosperity of the people of the island, as well as the security of American interests, and they are intimately associated with the interests of the South Atlantic and Gulf States, the normal expansion of whose commerce lies in that direction. At one time, and that only a year ago, three revolutions were in progress in the island at the same time. . . .

If the United States Government declines to take action and other foreign Governments resort to action to secure payment of their claims, the latter would be entitled . . . to the preferential payment of their claims; and this would absorb all the Dominican revenues and would be a virtual sacrifice of American claims and interests in the island. If moreover, any such action should be taken by them, the only method to enable them to secure the payment of their claims would be to take possession of the custom-houses, and considering the state of the Dominican finances this would mean a definite and very possibly permanent occupation of Dominican territory. . . .

The United States Government could not interfere to prevent such seizure and occupation of Dominican territory without either itself proposing some feasible alternative in the way of action, or else virtually saying to European Governments that they would not be allowed to collect their claims. This would be an unfortunate attitude for the Government of the United States to be forced to maintain at present. It can not with propriety say that it will protect its own citizens and interests, on the one hand, and yet on the other hand refuse to allow other Governments to protect their citizens and interests. . . .

The ordinary resources of diplomacy and international arbitration are absolutely impotent to deal wisely and effectively with the situation in the Dominican Republic. . . . Either we must abandon our duty under our traditional policy toward the Dominican people, who aspire to a republican form of government while they are actually drifting into a condition of permanent anarchy, in which case we must permit some other Government to adopt its own measures in order to safeguard its own interests, or else we must ourselves take seasonable and appropriate action. . . .

I call attention to the urgent need of prompt action on this matter. We now have a great opportunity to secure peace and stability in the island, without friction or bloodshed, by acting in accordance with the cordial invitation of the governmental authorities themselves. It will be unfortunate from every standpoint if we fail to grasp this opportunity; for such failure will probably mean increasing revolutionary violence in Santo Domingo, and very possibly embarrassing foreign complications in addition. This protocol affords a practical test of the efficiency of the United States Government in maintaining the Monroe Doctrine.

20

✦

CITY LIGHTS

Progressivism was a powerful force in turn-of-the century America. Progressives believed in efficiency, so they fought to reform the civil service and to make government as effective and accountable as private business. They believed that capital, labor, and government should work together, so they urged the mediation of labor conflicts and the regulation of giant corporations. Believing in citizen participation, Progressives pioneered woman suffrage, the secret ballot, and the removal from office of corrupt officials by popular vote. Concerned with the suffering poor, Progressives promoted charity work, better public schools, university extension service, and better housing. They thought saloons and liquor caused trouble, so they struggled for prohibition. Most Progressives were educated, middle-class, native-born Protestants who felt uneasy around corporate greed and slum violence; they could be both self-righteous and narrow-minded. But they cared about the country. They were confident they could change things, and tried energetically to do just that. As President Theodore Roosevelt once cried on their behalf, "We stand at Armageddon and do battle for the Lord."

Settlement houses were quintessential Progressive institutions. Established throughout urban America between 1880 and 1920, settlement houses—largely the handiwork of women reformers—arose to serve the vast swarm of newcomers to the country's great cities. These new "settlers" were European immigrants for the most part, but they also included recent arrivals, black and white, from the rural South. The settlement houses provided meeting halls. The staffs sponsored lectures, encouraged political participation and sometimes union activity, taught English classes, agitated for tighter health codes, and held citizenship and naturalization classes. These early social workers paid special attention to the problems of poor women and inevitably, therefore, to the problems of immigrant families.

Urban youth were a particular concern of the settlements. Settlement workers labored ceaselessly for child labor laws, more playgrounds, better schools. They worked to heal the generation gap between immigrant parents clinging to older ways and children rejecting everything old and old-fashioned, including the parents. The social workers tried to explain the new land to these children and to give them a smattering of self-improvement and urban survival skills. The following excerpt was written by Jane Addams, founder of Chicago's Hull House and in 1909 probably the country's most illustrious woman—almost certainly its most famous reformer. She did settlement work to benefit local Chicagoans. She then used local Chicagoans as case studies to demonstrate how badly the industrial system was damaging urban youth and how the system might be counteracted. This approach understandably brought great credit to the settlement houses and also great prestige to the reformers. Eventually their influence spread from neighborhood to city to state to, at last, nation.

Jane Addams was born in 1860 into a small-town middle-class Illinois family. After her graduation from college in 1881, Addams visited Europe, where she became inspired by a pioneer English settlement house that worked with the London poor. By 1889 she had founded a similar house in a ramshackle Chicago mansion. Addams attracted numerous bright, dedicated young women to work with her, including Florence Kelley, later an Illinois factory inspector, and Mary Kenny, a labor organizer. Together the three made Hull House famous. Addams's writings and speeches helped spread its reputation. *The Spirit of Youth and the City Streets* alone sold twenty thousand copies, and Addams's autobiography far more. She received the Nobel Peace Prize in 1931, four years before her death.

Questions to Consider. Why did Addams see the theater as a serious urban problem, and how did she propose to combat it? Does her distinction between baseball and theater seem valid? How did she account for the popularity of saloons among youth? What would she offer as a substitute? What role did factory labor play in the lives of the urban youth described by Addams? How did factory labor affect their behavior? Did she propose fundamental changes? Do her alternatives seem realistic? Would the problems of the theater, the saloon, and the factory have affected small-town youth, too?

◆

The Spirit of Youth (1909)

JANE ADDAMS

This spring a group of young girls accustomed to the life of a five-cent theater, reluctantly refused an invitation to go to the country for a day's outing because the return on a late train would compel them to miss one

From Jane Addams, *The Spirit of Youth and the City Streets* (The Macmillan Company, New York, 1909).

Jane Addams. Addams's first concern was the immigrants and their accultur-ation in the United States. From this starting point she moved in a logical progression to the problems of industrial workers and urban youth. She never used the words "adolescent" or "teenager." She thought the first too dry and academic; the second was slang. Still, this was the age group that most con-cerned her, as indeed it worried many other adults of that period. But they often wanted to pound delinquency out of the young by finger-wagging, con-finement, and force. "Saint Jane" hoped to bury the bad tendencies of young people by giving their good ones a fighting chance. (Photograph by Wallace Kirkland, Jane Addams Memorial Collection, University of Illinois at Chicago Library)

evening's performance. They found it impossible to tear themselves away not only from the excitements of the theater itself but from the gaiety of the crowd of young men and girls invariably gathered outside discussing the sensational posters.

A steady English shopkeeper lately complained that unless he provided his four daughters with the money for the five-cent theaters every evening they would steal it from his till, and he feared that they might be driven to procure it in even more illicit ways. Because his entire family life had been thus disrupted he gloomily asserted that "this cheap show had ruined his 'ome and was the curse of America." This father was able to formulate the anxiety of many immigrant parents who are absolutely bewildered by the keen absorption of their children in the cheap theater. This anxiety is not, indeed, without foundation. An eminent alienist[1] of Chicago states that he has had a number of patients among neurotic children whose emotional natures have been so over-wrought by the crude appeal to which they had been so constantly subjected in the theaters, that they have become victims of hallucination and mental disorder. . . .

This testimony of a physician that the conditions are actually pathological, may at last induce us to bestir ourselves in regard to procuring a more wholesome form of public recreation. Many efforts in social amelioration have been undertaken only after such exposures; in the meantime, while the occasional child is driven distraught, a hundred children permanently injure their eyes watching the moving films, and hundreds more seriously model their conduct upon the standards set before them on this mimic stage.

Three boys, aged nine, eleven, and thirteen years, who had recently seen depicted the adventures of frontier life including the holding up of a stage coach and the lassoing of the driver, spent weeks planning to lasso, murder, and rob a neighborhood milkman, who started on his route at four o'clock in the morning. They made their headquarters in a barn and saved enough money to buy a revolver, adopting as their watchword the phrase "Dead Men Tell no Tales." . . . Fortunately for him, as the lariat was thrown the horse shied, and, although the shot was appropriately fired, the milkman's life was saved. Such a direct influence of the theater is by no means rare, even among older boys. Thirteen young lads were brought into the Municipal Court in Chicago during the first week that "Raffles, the Amateur Cracksman" was upon the stage, each one with an outfit of burglar's tools in his possession, and each one shamefacedly admitting that the gentlemanly burglar in the play had suggested to him a career of similar adventure.

In so far as the illusions of the theater succeed in giving youth the rest and recreation which comes from following a more primitive code of morality, it has a close relation to the function performed by public games. It

---

1. **Alienist:** psychiatrist

is, of course, less valuable because the sense of participation is largely confined to the emotions and the imagination, and does not involve the entire nature. . . .

Well considered public games easily carried out in a park or athletic field, might both fill the mind with the imaginative material constantly supplied by the theater, and also afford the activity which the cramped muscles of the town dweller so sorely need. Even the unquestioned ability which the theater possesses to bring men together into a common mood and to afford them a mutual topic of conversation, is better accomplished with the one national game which we already possess, and might be infinitely extended through the organization of other public games.

The theater even now by no means competes with the baseball league games which are attended by thousands of men and boys who, during the entire summer, discuss the respective standing of each nine and the relative merits of every player. During the noon hour all the employees of a city factory gather in the nearest vacant lot to cheer their own home team in its practice for the next game with the nine of a neighboring manufacturing establishment and on a Saturday afternoon the entire male population of the city betakes itself to the baseball field; the ordinary means of transportation are supplemented by gay stage-coaches and huge automobiles, noisy with blowing horns and decked with gay pennants. The enormous crowd of cheering men and boys are talkative, good-natured, full of the holiday spirit, and absolutely released from the grind of life. They are lifted out of their individual affairs and so fused together that a man cannot tell whether it is his own shout or another's that fills his ears; whether it is his own coat or another's that he is wildly waving to celebrate a victory. He does not call the stranger who sits next to him his "brother" but he unconsciously embraces him in an overwhelming outburst of kindly feeling when the favorite player makes a home run. Does not this contain a suggestion of the undoubted power of public recreation to bring together all classes of a community in the modern city unhappily so full of devices for keeping men apart? . . .

We are only beginning to understand what might be done through the festival, the street procession, the band of marching musicians, orchestral music in public squares or parks, with the magic power they all possess to formulate the sense of companionship and solidarity. . . .

As it is possible to establish a connection between the lack of public reaction and the vicious excitements and trivial amusements which become their substitutes, so it may be illuminating to trace the connection between the monotony and dullness of factory work and the petty immoralities which are often the youth's protest against them.

There are many city neighborhoods in which practically every young person who has attained the age of fourteen years enters a factory. When the work itself offers nothing of interest, and when no public provision is made for recreation, the situation becomes almost insupportable to the youth whose ancestors have been rough-working and hard-playing peasants.

In such neighborhoods the joy of youth is well nigh extinguished; and in that long procession of factory workers, each morning and evening, the young walk almost as wearily and listlessly as the old. Young people working in modern factories situated in cities still dominated by the ideals of Puritanism face a combination which tends almost irresistibly to overwhelm the spirit of youth. When the Puritan repression of pleasure was in the ascendant in America the people it dealt with lived on farms and villages where, although youthful pleasures might be frowned upon and crushed out, the young people still had a chance to find self-expression in their work. Plowing the field and spinning the flax could be carried on with a certain joyousness and vigor which the organization of modern industry too often precludes. Present industry based upon the inventions of the nineteenth century has little connection with the old patterns in which men have worked for generations. The modern factory calls for an expenditure of nervous energy almost more than it demands muscular effort, or at least machinery so far performs the work of the massive muscles, that greater stress is laid upon fine and exact movements necessarily involving nervous strain. But these movements are exactly of the type to which the muscles of a growing boy least readily respond, quite as the admonition to be accurate and faithful is that which appeals the least to his big primitive emotions. . . .

In vast regions of the city which are completely dominated by the factory, it is as if the development of industry had outrun all the educational and social arrangements.

The revolt of youth against uniformity and the necessity of following careful directions laid down by some one else, many times results in such nervous irritability that the youth, in spite of all sorts of prudential reasons, "throws up his job," if only to get outside the factory walls into the freer street, just as the narrowness of the school inclosure induces many a boy to jump the fence.

When the boy is on the street, however, and is "standing around on the corner" with the gang to which he mysteriously attaches himself, he finds the difficulties of direct untrammeled action almost as great there as they were in the factory, but for an entirely different set of reasons. The necessity so strongly felt in the factory for an outlet to his sudden and furious bursts of energy, his overmastering desire to prove that he could do things "without being bossed all the time," finds little chance for expression, for he discovers that in whatever really active pursuit he tries to engage, he is promptly suppressed by the police. . . .

The unjustifiable lack of educational supervision during the first years of factory work makes it quite impossible for the modern educator to offer any real assistance to young people during that trying transitional period between school and industry. The young people themselves who fail to conform can do little but rebel against the entire situation.

There are many touching stories by which this might be illustrated. One of them comes from a large steel mill of a boy of fifteen whose business it was to throw a lever when a small tank became filled with molten metal. During the few moments when the tank was filling it was his foolish custom to catch the reflection of the metal upon a piece of looking-glass, and to throw the bit of light into the eyes of his fellow workmen. Although an exasperated foreman had twice dispossessed him of his mirror, with a third fragment he was one day flicking the gloom of the shop when the neglected tank overflowed, almost instantly burning off both his legs. Boys working in the stock yards, during their moments of wrestling and rough play, often slash each other painfully with the short knives which they use in their work, but in spite of this the play impulse is too irrepressible to be denied. . . .

The discovery of the labor power of youth was to our age like the discovery of a new natural resource, although it was merely incidental to the invention of modern machinery and the consequent subdivision of labor. In utilizing it thus ruthlessly we are not only in danger of quenching the divine fire of youth, but we are imperiling industry itself when we venture to ignore these very sources of beauty, of variety and of suggestion.

21

◆

THE WAR FOR DEMOCRACY

Woodrow Wilson won the presidency in 1912 on behalf of a "new freedom," a program involving lower tariffs, banking reform, antitrust legislation, and, in foreign policy, the repudiation of Theodore Roosevelt's gunboat diplomacy. Even after sending troops to various Caribbean countries and to Mexico, Wilson claimed that his main concern was to promote peach and democracy in the world. When World War I erupted in Europe, Wilson saw the war as the result of imperialistic rivalries ("a war with which we have nothing to do") and urged, despite personal sympathy with Great Britain, that the United States stay neutral so as to influence the peace negotiations. Wilson won reelection in 1916 largely on a promise to keep the country out of war. But a combination of pro-British propaganda in American newspapers and German submarine attacks on American ships proved formidable, and in April 1917, Wilson finally requested a declaration of war in the following address to Congress. The sweeping, visionary arguments of this remarkable speech shaped not only America's expectations about the war itself but also attitudes about the proper U.S. role in international affairs for years to come.

Born in 1856 in Virginia, Woodrow Wilson grew up in the South; his father was a Presbyterian minister. He attended Princeton and Johns Hopkins, where he earned a doctorate, and began to write and teach in the field of constitutional government and politics. He gained national stature while president of Princeton from 1902 until 1910; he became the Democratic governor of New Jersey in 1911 and, two years later, president of the United States. Wilson's main objective at the peace conference after World War I was to create a League of Nations to help keep the peace. In 1919 during an intensive speech-making campaign to arouse public support for the League, Wilson suffered a debilitating stroke. He died in Washington, D.C., in 1924.

Questions to Consider. Note, in reading the following message, that although Woodrow Wilson believed in the unique and superior character of American institutions, he was willing to enter into alliances with European powers. What were the four principal grounds on which Wilson was willing to reverse the American diplomatic tradition? Which of these did he seem to take most seriously? Were there other American interests that he might have stressed but did not? What reasons might Wilson have had for stressing so strongly America's attachment to Germany's people as opposed to its government? Might Wilson's arguments and rhetoric have served to prolong rather than to shorten the war?

◆

Address to Congress (1917)

WOODROW WILSON

I have called the Congress into extraordinary session because there are serious, very serious choices of policy to be made, and made immediately, which it was neither right nor constitutionally permissible that I should assume the responsibility of making.

On the third of February last I officially laid before you the extraordinary announcement of the Imperial German Government that on and after the first day of February it was its purpose to put aside all restraints of law or of humanity and use its submarines to sink every vessel that sought to approach either the ports of Great Britain and Ireland or the western coasts of Europe or any of the ports controlled by the enemies of Germany within the Mediterranean. . . .

I was for a little while unable to believe that such things would in fact be done by any government that had hitherto subscribed to the humane practices of civilized nations. International law had its origin in the attempt to set up some law which would be respected and observed upon the seas, where no nation had right of dominion and where lay the free highways of the world. . . . This minimum of right the German Government has swept aside under the plea of retaliation and necessity and because it had no weapons which it could use at sea except these which it is impossible to employ as it is employing them without throwing to the winds all scruples of humanity or of respect for all understandings that were supposed to underlie the intercourse of the world. I am not now thinking of the loss of property involved, immense and serious as that is, but only of the wanton and wholesale destruction of the lives of non-combatants, men, women, and children, engaged in pursuits which have always, even in the darkest periods of modern history, been deemed innocent and legitimate. Property can be paid for; the lives of peaceful and innocent people cannot be. The present German submarine warfare against commerce is a warfare against mankind.

From *The New York Times*, April 3, 1917.

It is a war against all nations. American ships have been sunk, American lives taken, in ways which it has stirred us very deeply to learn of, but the ships and people of other neutral and friendly nations have been sunk and overwhelmed in the waters in the way. There has been no discrimination. The challenge is to all mankind. Each nation must decide for itself how it will meet it. The choice we make for ourselves must be made with a moderation of counsel and a temperateness of judgement befitting our character and our motives as a nation. We must put excited feeling away. Our motive will not be revenge or the victorious assertion of the physical might of the nation, but only the vindication of right, of human right, of which we are only a single champion. . . .

With a profound sense of the solemn and even tragical character of the step I am taking and of the grave responsibilities which it involves, but in unhesitating obedience to what I deem my constitutional duty, I advise that the Congress declare the recent course of the Imperial German Government to be in fact nothing less than war against the government and people of the United States; that it formally accept the status of belligerent which has thus been thrust upon it; and that it take immediate steps not only to put the country in a more thorough state of defense but also to exert all its power and employ all its resources to bring the Government of the German Empire to terms and end the war. . . .

We have no quarrel with the German people. We have no feeling towards them but one of sympathy and friendship. It was not upon their impulse that their government acted in entering this war. It was not with their previous knowledge or approval. It was a war determined upon as wars used to be determined upon in the old, unhappy days when peoples were nowhere consulted by their rulers and wars were provoked and waged in the interest of dynasties or of little groups of ambitious men who were accustomed to use their fellow men as pawns and tools. . . .

We are accepting this challenge of hostile purpose because we know that in such a Government, following such methods, we can never have a friend; and that in the presence of its organized power, always lying in wait to accomplish we know not what purpose, there can be no assured security for the democratic Governments of the world. We are now about to accept gauge of battle with this natural foe to liberty and shall, if necessary, spend the whole force of the nation to check and nullify its pretensions and its power. We are glad, now that we see the facts with no veil of false pretense about them, to fight thus for the ultimate peace of the world and for the liberation of its peoples, the German peoples included: for the rights of nations great and small and the privilege of men everywhere to choose their way of life and of obedience. The world must be made safe for democracy. Its peace must be planted upon the tested foundations of political liberty. We have no selfish ends to serve. We desire no conquest, no dominion. We seek no indemnities for ourselves, no material compensation for the sacrifices we shall freely make. We are but one of the champions of the rights of mankind. We shall be satisfied when those rights have been made as secure as the faith and the freedom of nations can make them. . . .

It will be all the easier for us to conduct ourselves as belligerents in a high spirit of right and fairness because we act without animus, not in enmity towards a people or with the desire to bring any injury or disadvantage upon them, but only in armed opposition to an irresponsible government which has thrown aside all considerations of humanity and of right and is running amuck. We are, let me say again, the sincere friends of the German people, and shall desire nothing so much as the early reestablishment of intimate relations of mutual advantage between us,—however hard it may be for them, for the time being, to believe that this is spoken from our hearts. We have borne with their present Government through all these bitter months because of that friendship,—exercising a patience and forbearance which would otherwise have been impossible. We shall, happily, still have an opportunity to prove that friendship in our daily attitude and actions towards the millions of men and women of German birth and native sympathy who live amongst us and share our life, and we shall be proud to prove it towards all who are in fact loyal to their neighbors and to the Government in the hour of test. They are, most of them, as true and loyal Americans as if they had never known any other fealty of allegiance. They will be prompt to stand with us in rebuking and restraining the few who may be of a different mind and purpose. If there should be disloyalty, it will be dealt with with a firm hand of stern repression; but, if it lifts its head at all, it will lift it only here and there and without countenance except from a lawless and malignant few.

It is a distressing and oppressive duty, Gentlemen of the Congress, which I have performed in thus addressing you. There are, it may be, many months of fiery trial and sacrifice ahead of us. It is a fearful thing to lead this great peaceful people into war, into the most terrible and disastrous of all wars, civilization itself seeming to be in the balance. But the right is more precious than peace, and we shall fight for the things which we have always carried nearest our hearts,—for democracy, for the right of those who submit to authority to have a voice in their own Governments, for the rights and liberties of small nations, for a universal dominion of right by such a concert of free peoples as shall bring peace and safety to all nations and make the world itself at last free. To such a task we can dedicate our lives and our fortunes, everything that we have, with the pride of those who know that the day has come when America is privileged to spend her blood and her might for the principles that gave her birth and happiness and the peace which she has treasured. God helping her, she can do no other.

22

◆

SKEPTICS

Many Americans found great glory in World War I. After all, the doughboys, as the American infantrymen were called, had turned the tide against Germany, and John ("Black Jack") Pershing, commander of the U.S. forces, emerged from the conflict a national hero. But the human price had been stiff: 100,000 Americans dead and 200,000 wounded. American casualties in World War I were low compared with European casualties (almost 2 million Germans and 1 million British died) or with U.S. losses in the Civil War (600,000) or in World War II (400,000). But the American losses were hardly insignificant, particularly since the country was in the war for only eighteen months and mobilized only about 4 million men. Much of the dying occurred in the appalling conditions of the Argonne Forest, where years of trenching and shelling had created a veritable wasteland of death.

Justifying such remarkable carnage would have taken remarkable results—something on the order of the new international order that Woodrow Wilson had promised. But this, of course, the president had not been able to deliver, not even his own country's membership in the League of Nations. So the skepticism that had attended U.S. entry into the war persisted, engendering a somber, even cynical mood beneath the boisterous patriotic surface. One source of this dark mood was the *Chicago Tribune,* which was the most influential newspaper in the Midwest and contained persistent editorials criticizing Wilsonian interventionism. The *Tribune* editorial of November 13, 1921, reprinted below, is in response to a wave of recrimination, social unrest, and small-scale military skirmishes in Europe and also the growing European calls for U.S. financial aid. This editorial is an expression of characteristic midwestern Republican views on the foolishness of idealism, the evils of European politics, and the folly of war.

A variant of these views also pervaded the major fiction of the period. Many writers of the early twentieth century were probably predisposed to skepticism about the war effort because they felt alienated and estranged from "bourgeois" America, with its perpetual striving for status and possessions, and some had pacifist leanings even before the United States entered World War I in 1917. Actual participation in the war confirmed the pacifist inclinations of several writers.

Such books as E.E. Cummings's *The Enormous Room,* John Dos Passos's *Three Soldiers,* William Faulkner's *Soldier's Pay,* and Ernest Hemingway's *A Farewell to Arms* depicted the war as murderous and meaningless. Hemingway worked the war most deeply into his fiction. The excerpts below come from *In Our Time,* a collection of stories both about the war and about life in upstate Michigan strung together with brief mood-setting paragraphs; all the paragraphs reprinted here are this kind of paragraph, each with its own characters and locale. Hemingway wrote in a spare, detached style that was widely imitated in the postwar years and won him almost as much acclaim as his plots and characters. The disillusionment that pervaded his work was imitated, too, so much so that finally it seemed almost incredible that the United States could have participated in the war. Americans who sought an explanation for U.S. entry in World War I increasingly found some mixture of self-righteousness, bumbling stupidity, and the machinations of the arms dealers, and resolved never to go to war again—and did not until Pearl Harbor.

The editor and publisher of the *Chicago Tribune* when the editorial below was published was Robert R. McCormick, a graduate of Yale University and Northwestern University's law school and nephew of Cyrus H. McCormick of mechanical reaper fame. Forty-one years old in 1921, Robert McCormick had already held political office in Chicago and served as both a *Tribune* war correspondent and an artillery officer in France. Under McCormick's direction the *Tribune* company had a fivefold increase in newspaper circulation and also had acquired vast nonnewspaper business holdings. McCormick died in Illinois in 1955, with his formidable suspicions of idealists and Europeans still intact. His fellow Chicagoan, Ernest Hemingway, was born in 1899 into a middle-class family. Having skipped college to become a newspaper reporter, he spent the war years with a volunteer ambulance unit in Italy and after the war joined the growing colony of expatriate Americans in Paris. Hemingway received the Nobel Prize for Literature in 1954. He died at his home in Ketchum, Idaho, in 1961.

Questions to Consider. The 1921 *Tribune* editorial painted a gloomy picture of European conditions three years after the end of the war. Does the editorial seem to express surprise at this state of affairs? What or whom did the writer hold most responsible? Had the war, then, been utterly futile and valueless? What actions did the writer advise the United States to take, or not to take? With whom was the editorial arguing? In the Hemingway paragraphs, does the dominant mood seem to be anger, pity, or sarcasm? Are there any common features in these Hemingway scenes? Why might people of the 1920s have found them startling, even shocking? Do they still have shock power?

◆

Unregenerate Europe (1921)

THE CHICAGO TRIBUNE

It is natural that pacifists and excited humanitarians should stress the evil consequences of the world war at this time. It is equally natural that foreign statesmen and public agencies should join them in keeping this phase of the European situation [of famine and insurrections] before us. It gives a tremendous momentum to the pacifist propaganda, and it relieves the governments and peoples of Europe of a large part of their responsibility for the present condition of their affairs.

But the American mind should clear itself on this point. No one will deny that the war is responsible directly for a vast wastage of life and property. But what needs recognition and emphasis at this moment . . . is that had common sense and self-control governed the policies of the governments and the sentiments of the peoples of Europe their affairs would not be tottering now on the rim of chaos.

On the contrary, were there wisdom and courage in the statesmanship of Europe, were there the same selfless devotion in chancelleries and parliaments as was exhibited on the battlefield, Europe would have been today well on the way to recovery.

The expenditures of the war and the intensification of long existing animosities and jealousies undoubtedly have complicated the problems of statecraft and of government. Undoubtedly the temporary depletion of man power and the temporary exhaustion of body and spirit among the war worn peoples were a burden which recovery has had to assume. Undoubtedly the wastage of wealth and diversion of productive agencies were a handicap to expeditious restoration.

But that these are chiefly responsible for the present state of Europe we do not admit and the future judgment of history, we are confident, will deny.

It is chiefly the folly which has been persistently demonstrated by governments and people since the war that is responsible for Europe's condition today. It is because the moment hostilities ceased and the enemy was disarmed, victors and vanquished turned their backs on the healing and constructive principles they had solemnly asserted from time to time when matters were going against them at the battle front, that the European nations almost without exception have been going down hill. There never in history has been a more perfect illustration of the ancient sarcasm: "When the devil is sick, the devil a monk would be; when the devil is well, the devil a monk is he."

If we wish to know why Europe is in the present state, we cannot do better than to draw a parallel between the assertions of purpose and principle of the allies and "associated" powers in 1916, '17, and '18, and what has actually happened since Nov. 11, 1918.

The war was a gigantic folly and waste. No one will deny that. But it was not so foolish nor so wasteful as the peace which has followed it. The European governments, those who come at our invitation and those who remain away, would have us believe they are mere victims of the war. They say nothing of what the war did for them. We might remind them that they profited as well as lost by the war. Many of them were freed from age long tyranny. They got rid of kaisers and saber clattering aristocracies. They were given freedom, and their present state shows how little they have known how to profit by it. They have been given new territories and new resources, and they have shown how little they deserve their good fortune. The last three years in Europe have been given not to sane efforts to heal wounds, remove hostilities, develop cooperation for the common economic restoration which is essential to the life of each. On the contrary, they have been marked by new wars and destruction, by new animosities and rivalries, by a refusal to face facts, make necessary sacrifices and compromises for financial and economic recovery, by greedy grabbing of territory and new adventures in the very imperialism which brought about the war.

It is well for Americans and their representatives to keep this in mind. The appeal to America's disinterestedness is unfairly fortified by the assumption that Europe is the innocent victim of one egotist's or one nation's ruthless ambition. We can take due account of the disastrous effects of the Prussian effort at dominance, but that should not overshadow the stubborn errors which began over again on the very threshold of peace, and which have made the peace more destructive than the war. When the European governments and peoples are ready to make a real peace, which cannot arrive until they give over the policies and attitudes that produced the world war, America will then not fail to give generous aid. But America would be foolish to contribute to the support of present methods or give any encouragement to the spirit which now prevails in the old world.

◆

In Our Time (1925)

ERNEST HEMINGWAY

Minarets stuck up in the rain out of Adrianople [Turkey] across the mud flats. The carts were jammed for thirty miles along the Karagatch road. Water buffalo and cattle were hauling carts through the mud. There was no end and no beginning. Just carts loaded with everything they owned. The old men and women, soaked through, walked along keeping the cattle moving. The Maritza [River] was running yellow almost up to the bridge. Carts were jammed solid on the bridge with camels bobbing along through them. Greek cavalry herded along the procession. The women and children were in the carts, crouched with mattresses, mirrors, sewing machines, bundles. There was a woman having a baby with a young girl holding a blanket over her and crying. Scared sick looking at it. It rained all through the evacuation. . . .

*

We were in a garden in Mons [Belgium]. Young Buckley came in with his patrol from across the river. The first German I saw climbed up over the garden wall. We waited till he got one leg over and then potted him. He had so much equipment on and looked awfully surprised and fell down into the garden. Then three more came over further down the wall. We shot them. They all came just like that. . . .

*

It was a frightfully hot day. We'd jammed an absolutely perfect barricade across the bridge. It was simply priceless. A big old wrought-iron grating from the front of a house. Too heavy to lift and you could shoot through it and they would have to climb over it. It was absolutely topping. They tried to get over it, and we potted them from forty yards. They rushed it, and officers came out alone and worked on it. It was an absolutely perfect obstacle. Their officers were very fine. We were frightfully put out when we heard the flank had gone, and we had to fall back. . . .

*

They shot the six cabinet ministers at half-past six in the morning against the wall of a hospital. There were pools of water in the courtyard. There were wet dead leaves on the paving of the courtyard. It rained hard. All the shutters of the hospital were nailed shut. One of the ministers was

On the western front. American machine gunners searching out pockets of resistance in the German defenses during the costly U.S. offensive of summer 1918. (Bilderdienst Suddeutscher Verlag)

sick with typhoid. Two soldiers carried him downstairs and out into the rain. They tried to hold him up against the wall but he sat down in a puddle of water. The other five stood very quietly against the wall. Finally the officer told the soldiers it was no good trying to make him stand up. When they fired the first volley he was sitting down in the water with his head on his knees.

*

Nick sat against the wall of the church where they had dragged him to be clear of machine gun fire in the street. Both legs stuck out awkwardly. He had been hit in the spine. His face was sweaty and dirty. The sun shone on his face. The day was very hot. Rinaldi, big backed, his equipment sprawling, lay face downward against the wall. Nick looked straight ahead brilliantly. The pink wall of the house opposite had fallen out from the roof, and an iron bedstead hung twisted toward the street. Two Austrian dead lay in the rubble in the shade of the house. Up the street were other dead. Things were getting forward in the town. It was going well. Stretcher bearers would be along any time now. Nick turned his head and looked down at Rinaldi. "Senta Rinaldi; Senta. You and me we've made a separate peace." Rinaldi lay still in the sun, breathing with difficulty. "We're not patriots." Nick turned his head away, smiling sweatily. Rinaldi was a disappointing audience. . . .

*

While the bombardment was knocking the trench to pieces at Fossalta [Italy], he lay very flat and sweated and prayed, "Oh Jesus Christ get me out of here. Dear Jesus, please get me out. Christ, please, please, please, Christ. If you'll only keep me from getting killed I'll do anything you say. I believe in you and I'll tell everybody in the world that you are the only thing that matters. Please, please, dear Jesus." The shelling moved further up the line. We went to work on the trench and in the morning the sun came up and the day was hot and muggy and cheerful and quiet. The next night back at Mestre he did not tell the girl he went upstairs with at the Villa Rossa about Jesus. And he never told anybody.

23

◆

A Progressive Spirit

The campaign for women's rights, which had begun before the Civil War, made painfully slow progress after the war. Most Americans continued to hold fast to the idea that a woman is weaker than a man and that her place is in the home caring for her husband and children. Age-old handicaps persisted: educational deprivation, legal discrimination, economic exploitation, and political disfranchisement. But veteran women's rights leaders like Elizabeth Cady Stanton carried on the struggle for equal rights undaunted, and energetic new reformers like Anna Howard Shaw joined their ranks. There was some progress in education: women's colleges appeared and the new state universities opened their doors to women. There was also some improvement in the legal status of married women. Yet the inequalities remained great. The number of women entering professions like law and medicine remained minuscule, and whenever women did obtain work outside the home they were vastly underpaid.

Some feminists argued that, with the ballot in their hands, American women would have a powerful weapon with which to fight for all their other rights. The suffragists sought action at both the federal and the state levels. Congress began considering suffrage proposals as early as 1868 but failed to adopt any of them. The states did somewhat better. In 1890 Wyoming entered the Union with woman suffrage, and a few years later Colorado, Utah, and Idaho followed suit. By 1914, eleven states, all but one in the West, had given women the right to vote, and in 1916 Montana sent the first woman, Jeannette Rankin, to Congress. By this time, Carrie Chapman Catt, successor to Susan B. Anthony as president of the National Woman Suffrage Association, and other suffragists had renewed their struggle for federal action. In 1919, at long last, Congress passed an amendment to the Constitution stating that the right of citizens to vote could not "be denied or abridged by the United States or by any state on account of sex." Ratification of the Nineteenth Amendment by the states was complete by August 1920, and American women were able to vote in the presidential election that November.

Meanwhile, the struggle for women's economic and social, as well as political, rights continued. The General Federation of Women's

Clubs, founded in 1889, devoted considerable energy toward improving working conditions for women and children in industry. At the same time radical feminists like Margaret H. Sanger and Emma Goldman began sponsoring unrestricted dissemination of birth-control information. The birth-control advocates at first stressed economics: the gradual reduction in the size of the working class by means of birth control, they insisted, would increase labor's ability to bargain with the capitalists. But the birth-control movement took root among middle-class rather than working-class women and centered on individual self-fulfillment rather than social reconstruction. It would, they realized, liberate them from many restrictions of the traditional American home. But it was not until after the adoption of the Nineteenth Amendment that feminists began devoting major energies to the birth-control crusade.

From almost the crusade's beginning, the name of Margaret Sanger and the cause of birth control were synonymous. Sanger and her friends, in fact, invented the term *birth control*. Sanger was not the first advocate of planned parenthood, nor was she the only influential leader in the movement. But her effectiveness, both as speaker and writer, soon won her fame both in the United States and abroad.

Margaret Sanger, the sixth of eleven children, was born in Corning, New York, in 1883. She studied nursing as a young woman and became a maternity nurse serving in New York City's crowded Lower East Side. There she became aware of the poverty, misery, illness, and even death produced by involuntary pregnancies and self-induced abortions. She gave up nursing in 1912 to devote her full attention to the cause of birth control. In 1914 she founded the National Birth Control League and began publishing a magazine called *Woman Rebel*, which had the slogan "No Gods, No Masters" on the masthead. In 1915 she was indicted for sending birth-control literature through the mails and in 1916 arrested for operating a birth-control clinic in Brooklyn. During her brief prison stay she started a new magazine called the *Birth Control Review*, which was dedicated to the scientific control of human reproduction. After World War I, with the relaxation of laws forbidding doctors to prescribe contraceptives and give instruction in birth-control methods, she was able to open a birth-control clinic in Manhattan and to encourage the formation of similar clinics in other cities. She sponsored numerous national and international birth-control conferences and published many articles and books on birth control and sex education. She died in Tucson, Arizona, in 1966.

Questions to Consider. Among Sanger's many writings was a book entitled *Happiness in Marriage*, published in 1926 and centered on transforming marriage into a voluntary association. In the excerpt from the book reprinted below, Sanger expanded on the ways in which "premature parenthood" could wreck marriage. How did she think the "position of womanhood" had changed in the past few years? What did she mean by saying that social equality complicates as well as ennobles the marriage relationship? What objectives did she seek for American women, and why did she think birth control would help them achieve those objectives? How convincing do you think her argument was for people (and there were still many in the early twentieth century) who thought birth-control literature was obscene? Sanger was considered a radical in her day. Would she be called one today?

◆

Happiness in Marriage (1926)

MARGARET H. SANGER

We must recognize that the whole position of womanhood has changed today. Not so many years ago it was assumed to be a just and natural state of affairs that marriage was considered as nothing but a preliminary to motherhood. A girl passed from the guardianship of her father or nearest male relative to that of her husband. She had no will, no wishes of her own. Hers not to question why, but merely to fulfil duties imposed upon her by the man into whose care she was given.

Marriage was synonymous with maternity. But the pain, the suffering, the wrecked lives of women and children that such a system caused, show us that it did not work successfully. Like all other professions, motherhood must serve its period of apprenticeship.

Today women are on the whole much more individual. They possess as strong likes and dislikes as men. They live more and more on the plane of social equality with men. They are better companions. We should be glad that there is more enjoyable companionship and real friendship between men and women.

This very fact, it is true, complicates the marriage relation, and at the same time ennobles it. Marriage no longer means the slavish subservience of the woman to the will of the man. It means, instead, the union of two strong and highly individualized natures. Their first problem is to find out just what the terms of this partnership are to be. Understanding full and complete cannot come all at once, in one revealing flash. It takes time to arrive at a full and sympathetic understanding of each other, and mutually to arrange lives to increase this understanding. Out of the mutual adjustments, harmony must grow and discords gradually disappear.

From Margaret Sanger, *Happiness in Marriage* (Blue Ribbon Books, New York, 1926), 83–97. Reprinted by permission.

Margaret Sanger. Activists like Margaret Sanger provided a major impetus to social reform between 1900 and 1925. In these years, government spending on education and welfare at all levels rose by 1,000 percent to approximately $5 billion. The biggest increase came at the local level, and of this local increase, the bulk went for schooling. The number of child workers shrank drastically. So, too, did the burglary rate and the consumption of alcohol. Contraceptive use spread most rapidly among America's middle classes, whose symbol of the liberated woman became not the social activist but the flapper. This photograph shows Margaret Sanger (left) at the booth of the National Committee on Federal Legislation for Birth Control. (Library of Congress)

These results cannot be obtained if the problem of parenthood is thrust upon the young husband and wife before they are spiritually and economically prepared to meet it. For naturally the coming of the first baby means that all other problems must be thrust aside. That baby is a great fact, a reality that must be met. Preparations must be made for its coming. The layette must be prepared. The doctor must be consulted. The health of the wife may need consideration. The young mother will probably prefer to go to the hospital. All of these preparations are small compared to the regime after the coming of the infant.

Now there is a proper moment for every human activity, a proper season for every step in self-development. The period for cementing the bond of love is no exception to this great truth. For only by the full and glorious living through these years of early marriage are the foundations of an enduring and happy married life rendered possible. By this period the woman attains a spiritual freedom. Her womanhood has a chance to bloom. She wins a mastery over her destiny; she acquires self-reliance, poise, strength, a youthful maturity. She abolishes fear. Incidentally, few of us realize, since the world keeps no record of this fact, how many human beings are conceived in fear and even in repugnance by young mothers who are the victims of undesired maternity. Nor has science yet determined the possibilities of a generation conceived and born of conscious desire.

In the wife who has lived through a happy marriage, for whom the bonds of passionate love have been fully cemented, maternal desire is intensified and matured. Motherhood becomes for such a woman not a penalty or a punishment, but the road by which she travels onward toward completely rounded self-development. Motherhood thus helps her toward the unfolding and realization of her higher nature.

Her children are not mere accidents, the outcome of chance. When motherhood is a mere accident, as so often it is in the early years of careless or reckless marriages, a constant fear of pregnancy may poison the days and nights of the young mother. Her marriage is thus converted into a tragedy. Motherhood becomes for her a horror instead of a joyfully fulfilled function.

Millions of marriages have been blighted, not because of any lack of love between the young husband and wife, but because children have come too soon. Often these brides become mothers before they have reached even physical maturity, before they have completed the period of adolescence. This period in our race is as a rule complete around the age of twenty-three. Motherhood is possible after the first menstruation. But what is physically possible is very often from every other point of view inadvisable. A young woman should be fully matured from every point of view—physically, mentally and psychically—before maternity is thrust upon her.

Those who advise early maternity neglect the spiritual foundation upon which marriage must inevitably be built. This takes time. They also ignore the financial responsibility a family brings.

The young couple begin to build a home. They may have just enough to get along together. The young wife, as in so many cases of early marriage these days, decides to continue her work. They are partners in every way—a commendable thing. The young man is just beginning his career—his salary is probably small. Nevertheless, they manage to get along, their hardships are amusing, and are looked upon as fun. Then suddenly one day, the young wife announces her pregnancy. The situation changes immediately. There are added expenses. The wife must give up her work. The husband must go into debt to pay the expenses of the new and joyfully received arrival. The novelty lasts for some time. The young wife assumes the household duties and the ever growing care of the infant. For a time the child seems to bring the couple closer together. But more often there ensues a concealed resentment on the part of the immature mother at the constant drudgery and slavery to the unfortunate child who has arrived too early upon the scene, which has interfered with her love life.

Two brothers I know married practically at the same time. They were both carpenters, living in the same neighborhood. The wife of the one gave birth to six children in a period of ten years. In spite of the efforts of the man to sustain the family, they were forced at the end of ten years to accept outside charity. The wife became a household drudge, nervous, broken, spiritless, neglected by her husband, despised by her children. The wife of the other brother did not become a mother until three years after marriage. This man remained throughout the ten years of my observation, clean, alert, honest, kind to his wife and two children. The wife kept up neat, tidy looks and was able to help her husband and children to advance themselves. Yet at the time of marriage both girls were equally attractive and intelligent. . . .

For the unthinking husband, the "proud papa," the blushing bride is converted at once into the "mother of my children." It is not an unusual occurrence to find that three months after the birth of the baby, the parents are thinking and speaking to each other as "mumsy" and "daddy." The lover and sweetheart relation has disappeared forever and the "mama-papa" relation has taken its place.

Instead of being a self-determined and self-directing love, everything is henceforward determined by the sweet tyranny of the child. I have known of several young mothers, despite a great love for the child, to rebel against this intolerable situation. Vaguely feeling that this new maternity has rendered them unattractive to their husbands, slaves to a deadly routine of bottles, baths and washing, they have revolted. I know of innumerable marriages which have been wrecked by premature parenthood. . . .

For these reasons, in order that harmonious and happy marriage may be established as the foundation for happy homes and the advent of healthy and desired children, premature parenthood must be avoided. Birth Control is the instrument by which this universal problem may be solved.

Down and out in Newark. Unemployed men seeking federal jobs at the Newark, New Jersey, armory in 1933, the worst year of the Great Depression. (Courtesy Newark Public Library)

CHAPTER FIVE

◆

Crisis and Hope

24

◆

AMERICAN EARTHQUAKE

American industrialization meant not only surging production but also periodic business "busts"—in the 1870s, the 1890s, 1907, and 1919–21. In each of these cases, prices, profits, and employment all plunged and remained low until the economy's basic strength pushed them again to higher levels. But no previous bust matched the Great Depression, which descended on the nation in the early 1930s. From 1929, when Herbert Hoover became the third consecutive Republican president since World War I, until 1933, when Franklin D. Roosevelt, a Democrat, succeeded him, the economy all but collapsed. Stocks and bonds lost three-fourths of their value, bank failures increased from five hundred to four thousand a year, farm income fell by half, and unemployment rose from 4 percent to almost 25 percent.

It was this last figure that most stunned and terrified ordinary Americans. There had been unemployment before, but never so much or for so long. And this joblessness was not limited to minorities or factory workers, as so often had been the case. The ranks of the destitute now included hundreds of thousands of white-collar workers, small businesspeople, and sharecroppers. Most disturbing of all, millions of women were now jobless and impoverished; many were homeless, with nowhere to turn. The country found it disquieting in the extreme.

People were aware of the massive human suffering of the Great Depression both because it was so widespread and because it was reported with such immediacy and attention to stark detail. Great fiction appeared, from Jack Conroy's *The Disinherited* at the beginning of the period to *The Grapes of Wrath,* John Steinbeck's epic of displaced Okies, at its end. Gripping photography and murals and innovative drama and poetry, glittering with unprecedented concreteness of detail, all depicted facets of the American ordeal. Journalism followed a similar path. Meridel LeSueur's article on Minnesota women, excerpted below, appeared in *New Masses,* a lively, irreverent Communist Party literary journal that attracted and published much excellent social writing. In this case, the editors—staunch Stalinists—praised LeSueur's writing but also reproached her for defeatism and lack of "true revolutionary spirit."

Meridel LeSueur was born in 1900 in Iowa. Her grandfather was a

Protestant fundamentalist temperance zealot; her father helped found the Industrial Workers of the World. After high school LeSueur attended the American Academy of Dramatic Art and worked in Hollywood as an actress and stuntwoman in the 1920s. During the 1930s she lived with her two children in Minneapolis while writing what a critic called "luminous short stories" as well as articles on farmers and the un-employed, especially women. Hailed in the 1930s as a major writer, she was blacklisted during the 1940s as a Communist sympathizer and lived by writing children's books and women's articles under a pseu-donym. One of the first writers to examine the lives of poor women, her literary career revived during the 1970s with the emergence of feminism. Between 1971 and 1985 twelve of her books, new and old, appeared. She is currently working on three more—"my best writing, the most living images, and a real chorale of my whole life and my time."

Questions to Consider.   Who were the poor women LeSueur described in "Women on the Breadlines"? What did they have in common besides their poverty? Were they equally poor? Were their aspirations the same? How did their gender affect their condition and behavior during the Great Depression? How did they relate to one another, to authority figures, and to men? In later years conservatives would attack LeSueur for her radicalism. Can the reasons for these attacks be seen in this article? When Stalinists of the 1930s attacked her for being too negative and defeatist, were the attacks justified?

◆

Women on the Breadlines (1932)

MERIDEL LESUEUR

I am sitting in the city free employment bureau. It's the woman's section. We have been sitting here now for four hours. We sit here every day, waiting for a job. There are no jobs. Most of us have had no breakfast. Some have had scant rations for over a year. Hunger makes a human being lapse into a state of lethargy, especially city hunger. Is there any place else in the world where a human being is supposed to go hungry amidst plenty without an outcry, without protest, where only the boldest steal or kill for bread, and the timid crawl the streets, hunger like the beak of a terrible bird at the vitals?

From *New Masses* (January 1932), 5–7.

Homeless during the Great Depression. Unable to pay rent, the jobless were often evicted into the street with all their belongings, as in this Chicago scene. (Chicago Historical Society)

We sit looking at the floor. No one dares think of the coming winter. There are only a few more days of summer. Everyone is anxious to get work to lay up something for that long siege of bitter cold. But there is no work. Sitting in the room we all know it. That is why we don't talk much. We look at the floor dreading to see that knowledge in each other's eyes. There is a kind of humiliation in it. We look away from each other. We look at the floor. It's too terrible to see this animal terror in each other's eyes.

So we sit hour after hour, day after day, waiting for a job to come in. There are many women for a single job. A thin sharp woman sits inside the wire cage looking at a book. For four hours we have watched her looking at that book. She has a hard little eye. In the small bare room there are half a dozen women sitting on the benches waiting. Many come and go. Our faces are all familiar to each other, for we wait here everyday.

This is a domestic employment bureau. Most of the women who come here are middle-aged, some have families, some have raised their families and are now alone, some have men who are out of work. Hard times and the man leaves to hunt for work. He doesn't find it. He drifts on. The woman probably doesn't hear from him for a long time. She expects it. She isn't surprised. She struggles alone to feed the many mouths. Sometimes she gets help from the charities. If she's clever she can get herself a good living from the charities, if she's naturally a lick-spittle, naturally a little docile and cunning. If she's proud then she starves silently, leaving her children to find work, coming home after a day's searching to wrestle with her house, her children.

Some such story is written on the faces of all these women. There are young girls too, fresh from the country. Some are made brazen too soon by the city. There is a great exodus of girls from the farms into the city now. Thousands of farms have been vacated completely in Minnesota. The girls are trying to get work. The prettier ones can get jobs in the stores when there are any, or waiting on table, but these jobs are only for the attractive and the adroit, the others, the real peasants, have a more difficult time. . . .

A young girl who went around with Ellen [a poor, attractive young woman] tells about seeing her last evening back of a cafe downtown outside the kitchen door, kicking, showing her legs so that the cook came out and gave her some food and some men gathered in the alley and threw small coin on the ground for a look at her legs. And the girl says enviously that Ellen had a swell breakfast and treated her to one too, that cost two dollars.

A scrub woman whose hips are bent forward from stooping with hands gnarled like water soaked branches clicks her tongue in disgust. No one saves their money, she says, a little money and these foolish young things buy a hat, a dollar for breakfast, a bright scarf. And they do. If you've ever been without money, or food, something very strange happens when you get a bit of money, a kind of madness. You don't care. You can't remember that you had no money before, that the money will be gone. You can remember nothing but that there is the money for which you have been suffering. Now here it is. A lust takes hold of you. You see food in the windows. In imagination you eat hugely; you taste a thousand meals. You look in windows. Colours are brighter; you buy something to dress up in. An excitement takes hold of you. You know it is suicide but you can't help it. You must have food, dainty, splendid food and a bright hat so once again you feel blithe, rid of that ratty gnawing shame.

"I guess she'll go on the street now," a thin woman says faintly and no one takes the trouble to comment further. Like every commodity now the body is difficult to sell and the girls say you're lucky if you get fifty cents. . . .

It's one of the great mysteries of the city where women go when they are out of work and hungry. There are not many women in the bread line. There are no flop houses for women as there are for men, where a bed can be had for a quarter or less. You don't see women lying on the floor at the mission in the free flops. They obviously don't sleep in the jungle or under newspapers in the park. There is no law I suppose against their being in these places but the fact is they rarely are.

Yet there must be as many women out of jobs in cities and suffering extreme poverty as there are men. What happens to them? Where do they go? Try to get into the Y.W. without any money or looking down at heel. Charities take care of very few and only those that are called "deserving." The lone girl is under suspicion by the virgin women who dispense charity.

I've lived in cities for many months broke, without help, too timid to get in bread lines. I've known many women to live like this until they simply faint on the street from privations, without saying a word to anyone. A woman will shut herself up in a room until it is taken away from her, and eat a cracker a day and be as quiet as a mouse so there are no social statistics concerning her. . . .

Sometimes a girl facing the night without shelter will approach a man for lodging. A woman always asks a man for help. Rarely another woman. I have known girls to sleep in men's rooms for the night, on a pallet without molestation, and given breakfast in the morning. . . .

Mrs. Grey, sitting across from me is a living spokesman for the futility of labour. She is a warning. Her hands are scarred with labour. Her body is a great puckered scar. She has given birth to six children, buried three, supported them all alive and dead, bearing them, burying them, feeding them. Bred in hunger they have been spare, susceptible to disease. For seven years she tried to save her boy's arm from amputation, diseased from tuberculosis of the bone. It is almost too suffocating to think of that long close horror of years of child bearing, child feeding, rearing, with the bare suffering of providing a meal and shelter.

Now she is fifty. Her children, economically insecure, are drifters. She never hears of them. She doesn't know if they are alive. She doesn't know if she is alive. Such subtleties of suffering are not for her. For her the brutality of hunger and cold, the bare bone of life. That is enough. These will occupy a life. Not until these are done away with can those subtle feelings that make a human being be indulged.

She is lucky to have five dollars ahead of her. That is her security. She has a tumour that she will die of. She is thin as a worn dime with her tumour sticking out of her side. She is brittle and bitter. Her face is not the face of a human being. She has born more than it is possible for a human being to bear. She is reduced to the least possible denominator of human feelings.

It is terrible to see her little bloodshot eyes like a beaten hound's, fearful in terror.

We cannot meet her eyes. When she looks at any of us we look away. She is like a woman drowning and we turn away. . . .

The young ones know though. I don't want to marry. I don't want any children. So they all say. No children. No marriage. They arm themselves alone, keep up alone. The man is helpless now. He cannot provide. If he propagates he cannot take care of his young. The means are not in his hands. So they live alone. Get what fun they can. The life risk is too horrible now. Defeat is too clearly written on it.

It is appalling to think that these women sitting so listless in the room may work as hard as it is possible for a human being to work, may labour night and day, like Mrs. Gray wash street cars from midnight to dawn and offices in the early evening, scrubbing for fourteen and fifteen hours a day, sleeping only five hours or so, doing this their whole lives, and never earn one day of security, having always before them the pit of the future. The endless labour, the bending back, the water soaked hands, earning never more than a week's wages, never having in their hands more life than that.

25

✦

The Politics of Upheaval

There are cycles in American presidential politics. Of the first nine presidential elections, for instance, Jefferson's Democratic-Republicans won seven, the Federalists two. The Democrats also won six of the next nine elections. Then a new cycle began in which the Republicans won seven of nine elections from 1860 to 1892 (versus just two for the once-mighty Democrats) and also won seven of the next nine, with their only setbacks coming at the hands of Woodrow Wilson in 1912 and 1916. At this point, the cataclysm of the Great Depression and the charisma of Franklin D. Roosevelt returned the Democrats to dominance. They won, often by landslide margins, every election from 1932 to 1964, except for two losses to Dwight Eisenhower in the 1950s. Since then, however, they have reverted to their post-Civil War form, enabling the Nixon-Reagan-Bush GOP to post a five-to-one score through 1988.

Given the magnitude of the Great Depression and Franklin D. Roosevelt's role in triggering so massive a political realignment, his inaugural address in 1933 might appear moderate. It calls for confidence, honest labor, the protection of agriculture and land, organized relief, and a bit of economic planning. Only Roosevelt's castigation of the "money changers" and his plea for executive authority to meet the crisis seemed to prefigure the sweeping liberalism that many observers instinctively associate with the Roosevelt years. Nevertheless, the address was charged with emotion and a sense of mission. Its moderation reflected both the confusion of the times, when few people understood the nation's problems and still fewer had solutions, and the personal conservatism of the speaker, who was ultimately American capitalism's savior as well as its reformer.

Franklin Delano Roosevelt, a distant cousin of Theodore Roosevelt, was born in 1882 to a wealthy New York family. He attended exclusive schools and colleges and practiced law in New York City. He married his cousin Eleanor in 1905, entered Democratic politics—serving in the state senate from 1910 to 1913—and became assistant secretary of the navy in 1913. After running (and losing) as the Democrats' vice-presidential candidate in 1920, he contracted polio, which left him permanently crippled. Remaining active in politics, he served as governor of New York from 1928 to 1932, when he defeated Hoover for the presidency. During the 1932 campaign Roosevelt criticized Hoover for excessive government spending and an unbalanced budget. Nevertheless, after entering the White House, Roosevelt also was obliged to adopt a spending policy to help those who were starving, put people to work, and revive the economy. His New Deal stressed economic recovery as well as relief and reform. Roosevelt's programs, backed by the great Democratic majorities that he forged, mitigated many of the effects of the Great Depression, though the slump never actually ended until the advent of World War II. Roosevelt achieved reelection in 1936, 1940, and 1944, a record unequaled then and unconstitutional since 1951. He died in office in Warm Springs, Georgia, in 1945.

Questions to Consider. Why, in his first inaugural address, did Roosevelt place great emphasis on candor, honesty, and truth. Did he display these qualities himself in discussing the crisis? In what ways did he try to reassure the American people? What reasons did he give for the Great Depression? What values did he think were important for sustaining the nation in a time of trouble? What solutions did he propose for meeting the economic crisis? How did he regard his authority to act under the Constitution? How would you have reacted to his address if you had been an unemployed worker, a hard-pressed farmer, or a middle-class citizen who had lost a home through foreclosure?

◆

First Inaugural Address (1933)

FRANKLIN D. ROOSEVELT

This is a day of national consecration, and I am certain that my fellow-Americans expect that on my induction into the Presidency I will address them with a candor and a decision which the present situation of our nation impels. This is pre-eminently the time to speak the truth, the whole truth, frankly and boldly. Nor need we shrink from honestly facing conditions in our country today. This great nation will endure as it has endured, will revive and will prosper.

So first of all let me assert my firm belief that the only thing we have to fear is fear itself—nameless, unreasoning, unjustified terror which paralyzes needed efforts to convert retreat into advance. In every dark hour

From *The New York Times*, March 5, 1933.

F.D.R. Franklin D. Roosevelt, the "happy warrior," with his wife, Eleanor, and their daughter Anna, en route from the railroad to the family cottage in Warm Springs, Georgia, a favorite spot for family rest and recreation. (Franklin D. Roosevelt Library)

of our national life a leadership of frankness and vigor has met with that understanding and support of the people themselves which is essential to victory. I am convinced that you will again give that support to leadership in these critical days.

In such a spirit on my part and on yours we face our common difficulties. They concern, thank God, only material things. Values have shrunken to fantastic levels; taxes have risen; our ability to pay has fallen; government of all kinds is faced by serious curtailment of income; the means of exchange are frozen in the currents of trade; the withered leaves of industrial enterprise lie on every side; farmers find no markets for their produce; the savings of many years in thousands of families are gone.

More important, a host of unemployed citizens face the grim problem of existence, and an equally great number toil with little return. Only a foolish optimist can deny the dark realities of the moment.

Yet our distress comes from no failure of substance. We are stricken by no plague of locusts. Compared with the perils which our forefathers conquered because they believed and were not afraid, we have still much to be thankful for. Nature still offers her bounty and human efforts have multiplied it. Plenty is at our doorstep, but a generous use of it languishes in the very sight of the supply. Primarily, this is because the rulers of the exchange of mankind's goods have failed through their own stubbornness and their own incompetence, have admitted their failure and abdicated. Practices of the unscrupulous money changers stand indicted in the court of public opinion, rejected by the hearts and minds of men.

True, they have tried, but their efforts have been cast in the pattern of an outworn tradition. Faced by failure of credit, they have proposed only the lending of more money. Stripped of the lure of profit by which to induce our people to follow their false leadership, they have resorted to exhortations, pleading tearfully for restored confidence. They know only the rules of a generation of self-seekers. They have no vision, and when there is no vision the people perish.

The money changers have fled from their high seats in the temple of our civilization. We may now restore that temple to the ancient truths. The measure of the restoration lies in the extent to which we apply social values more noble than mere monetary profit.

Happiness lies not in the mere possession of money; it lies in the joy of achievement, in the thrill of creative effort. The joy and moral stimulation of work no longer must be forgotten in the mad chase of evanescent profits. These dark days will be worth all they cost us if they teach us that our true destiny is not to be ministered unto but to minister to ourselves and to our fellow-men.

Recognition of the falsity of material wealth as the standard of success goes hand in hand with the abandonment of the false belief that public office and high political position are to be valued only by the standards of pride of place and personal profit; and there must be an end to a conduct in banking and in business which too often has given to a sacred trust the likeness of callous and selfish wrongdoing. Small wonder that confidence languishes, for it thrives only on honesty, on honor, on the sacredness of obligations, on faithful protection, on unselfish performance. Without them it cannot live.

Restoration calls, however, not for changes in ethics alone. This nation asks for action, and action now.

Our greatest primary task is to put people to work. This is no unsolvable problem if we face it wisely and courageously. It can be accomplished in part by direct recruiting by the Government itself, treating the task as we would treat the emergency of war, but at the same time, through this employment, accomplishing greatly needed projects to stimulate and re-organize the use of our natural resources.

Hand in hand with this, we must frankly recognize the overbalance of population in our industrial centers and, by engaging on a national scale in the redistribution, endeavor to provide a better use of the land for those best fitted for the land. The task can be helped by definite efforts to raise the values of agricultural products and with this the power to purchase the output of our cities. It can be helped by preventing realistically the tragedy of the growing loss, through foreclosure, of our small homes and our farms. It can be helped by insistence that the Federal, State and local governments act forthwith on the demand that their cost be drastically reduced. It can be helped by the unifying of relief activities which today are often scattered, uneconomical and unequal. It can be helped by national planning for a supervision of all forms of transportation and of communications and other utilities which have a definitely public character. There are many ways in which it can be helped, but it can never be helped merely by talking about it. We must act, and act quickly. . . .

This I propose to offer, pledging that the larger purposes will bind upon us all as a sacred obligation with a unity of duty hitherto evoked only in the time of armed strife.

With this pledge taken, I assume unhesitatingly the leadership of this great army of our people, dedicated to a disciplined attack upon our common problems.

Action in this image and to this end is feasible under the form of government which we have inherited from our ancestors. Our Constitution is so simple and practical that it is possible always to meet extraordinary needs by changes in emphasis and arrangement without loss of essential form. That is why our constitutional system has proved itself the most superbly enduring political mechanism the modern world has produced. It has met every stress of vast expansion of territory, of foreign wars, of bitter internal strife, of world relations.

It is to be hoped that the normal balance of executive and legislative authority may be wholly adequate to meet the unprecedented task before us. But it may be that an unprecedented demand and need for undelayed action may call for temporary departure from that normal balance of public procedure.

I am prepared under my constitutional duty to recommend the measures that a stricken nation in the midst of a stricken world may require. These measures, or such other measures as the Congress may build out of its experience and wisdom, I shall seek, within my constitutional authority, to bring to speedy adoption.

But in the event that the Congress shall fail to take one of these two courses, and in the event that the national emergency is still critical, I shall not evade the clear course of duty that will then confront me. I shall ask the Congress for the one remaining instrument to meet the crisis—broad Executive power to wage a war against the emergency as great as the power that would be given me if we were in fact invaded by a foreign foe.

For the trust reposed in me I will return the courage and the devotion that befit the time. I can do no less. . . .

26

◆

ORGANIZING THE MASSES

Economic conditions in the 1930s had a tremendous impact on American labor. The Great Depression wreaked havoc with the lives of working people. By 1932, New York had a million jobless and Chicago another 600,000; 50 percent of Cleveland's workforce was unemployed, as was 60 percent of Akron's and 80 percent of Toledo's. Even those who still had jobs saw their wages and hours decline dramatically, and things did not greatly improve as the decade wore on.

The New Deal gave labor unions an opportunity to replenish their membership, which had plummeted to half of its World War I strength. The chief piece of legislation affecting unions was the Labor Relations Act of 1935, which established a national board to keep employers from interfering with labor organizers or union members and to supervise union elections. Thus encouraged, leaders of several large unions bolted the conservative American Federation of Labor (AFL) to form the Committee for Industrial Organization, which soon became the Congress of Industrial Organizations (CIO). The AFL emphasized craft unions (which were made up of workers in a given trade); the CIO insisted that industrial unions (which included all industrial workers, skilled and unskilled, in an industry) were essential in the great mass-production industries in which labor previously had been unorganized. In 1936 and 1937 the CIO, led by John L. Lewis, president of the United Mine Workers, mounted successful, though bloody, organizing campaigns to establish unions in the steel, rubber, electrical, automobile, and other basic industries. The AFL soon responded with organizing drives of its own. Thus, total union membership had tripled by 1940. The New Deal facilitated the rise of Big Labor as it did the welfare state, all the while preserving the country's basic economic system.

John L. Lewis, the forceful CIO leader, was born near Lucas, Iowa, in 1880 to a Welsh immigrant family. Leaving school after the seventh grade, Lewis worked briefly with his father in the coal fields and then wandered across the West for several years before returning to the mines in about 1905. He soon became active in union affairs and in 1920 was elected president of the United Mine Workers. Although he was originally associated with the AFL, Lewis spearheaded the formation of the CIO after the passage of the Labor Relations Act of 1935 and presided vigorously and dramatically for the next few years over the violent struggle for industrial unionism. In the 1940s he repeatedly quarreled with leaders of the CIO, the AFL, and the federal government, called several bitter coal strikes, and was twice held in contempt of court for ignoring antistrike injunctions. He nonetheless remained a revered labor spokesman. He was president of the United Mine Workers until 1960 and chairman of its retirement fund until his death in Washington, D.C., in 1969.

Questions to Consider. John L. Lewis had great gifts as an orator. ("He can use his voice like a policeman's billy," said one commentator, "or like a monk at orisons"). His physical appearance was also striking— he had a mass of reddish hair, bushy eyebrows, and piercing blue eyes. But his effectiveness as a speaker depended on his choice of words. In the 1936 radio speech reprinted below, he was trying to justify the CIO to an American public still not particularly friendly to organized labor. Do you think his style of speech was likely to win the understanding and sympathy of middle-class Americans? How "radical" was the position taken in his speech? How did he link the CIO to traditional American values and institutions? How extensive, according to Lewis, was resistance to the CIO's organizing drive in the big unorganized industries of the country? How did he implicate the federal government in this resistance? In what ways did he distinguish the CIO's philosophy from that of "alien" doctrines like Communism? What did he have to say about politics?

———————◆———————

The Steelworkers Organization Campaign (1936)

JOHN L. LEWIS

Out of the agony and travail of economic America, the Committee for Industrial Organization was born. To millions of Americans, exploited without stint by corporate industry and socially debased beyond the understanding of the fortunate, its coming was as welcome as the dawn to the night watcher. To a lesser group of Americans, infinitely more fortunately situated, blessed with larger quantities of the world's goods and

From *John L. Lewis and the International Union, United Mine Workers of America: The Story from 1917 to 1952* (United Mine Workers of America, Washington, D.C., 1952), 43–49. Reprinted by permission of the United Mine Workers of America.

Strike pickets. During the winter of 1936–1937 the Congress of Industrial Organizations climaxed its drive to unionize America's basic industries with a series of strikes that caused conflict in some communities and tensions in many others. In this artwork, workers picket for bargaining rights and higher wages in late 1937. A year later, total union membership had zoomed to almost 8 million. Workers were responding to CIO organizers who sang, "You'll win. What I mean. . . . Take it easy . . . but take it!" ("We Demand" by Joe Jones; The Butler Institute of American Art)

insolent in their assumption of privilege, its coming was heralded as a harbinger of ill, sinister of purpose, of unclean methods and nonvirtuous objectives.

The workers of the nation were tired of waiting for corporate industry to right their economic wrongs, to alleviate their social agony and to grant them their political rights. Despairing of fair treatment, they resolved to do something for themselves. They, therefore, have organized a new labor movement, conceived within the principles of the national Bill of Rights and committed to the proposition that the workers are free to assemble in their own forums, voice their own grievances, declare their own hopes, and contract on even terms with modern industry, for the sale of their only material possession—their labor.

The Committee for Industrial Organization has a numerical enrollment of 3,718,000 members. It has thirty-two affiliated national and international unions. Of this number, eleven unions account for 2,765,000 members. This group is organized in the textile, auto, garment, lumber, rubber, electrical manufacturing, power, steel, coal and transport industries. The remaining membership exists in the maritime, oil production and refining, shipbuilding, leather, chemical, retail, meat packing, vegetable canning, metalliferous mining, miscellaneous manufacturing, agricultural labor, and service and miscellaneous industries. Some 200 thousand workers are organized into 506 chartered local unions not yet attached to a national industrial union. Much of this progress was made in the face of violent and deadly opposition which reached its climax in the slaughter of workers paralleling the massacres of Ludlow [Colorado, 1914] and Homestead [Pennsylvania, 1892].

In the steel industry, the corporations generally have accepted collective bargaining and negotiated wage agreements with the Committee for Industrial Organization. Eighty-five per cent of the industry is thus under contract and a peaceful relationship exists between the management and the workers. Written wage contracts have been negotiated with 399 steel companies covering 510 thousand men. One thousand thirty-one local lodges in 700 communities have been organized.

Five of the corporations in the steel industry elected to resist collective bargaining and undertook to destroy the steel workers' union. These companies filled their plants with industrial spies, assembled depots of guns and gas bombs, established barricades, controlled their communities with armed thugs, leased the police power of cities and mobilized the military power of a state to guard them against the intrusion of collective bargaining within their plants.

During this strike, eighteen steel workers were either shot to death or had their brains clubbed out by police or armed thugs in the pay of the steel companies. In Chicago, Mayor [Edward V.] Kelly's police force was successful in killing ten strikers before they could escape the fury of the police, shooting eight of them in the back. One hundred sixty strikers were maimed and injured by police clubs, riot guns and gas bombs and were hospitalized. Hundreds of strikers were arrested, jailed, treated with brutality while incarcerated and harassed by succeeding litigation. None but strikers were murdered, gassed, injured, jailed or maltreated. No one had to die except the workers who were standing for the right guaranteed them by the Congress and written in the law.

The infamous Governor [Martin L.] Davey of Ohio, successful in the last election because of his reiterated promises of fair treatment to labor, used the military power of the commonwealth on the side of the Republic Steel Co. and the Youngstown Sheet and Tube Co. Nearly half of the staggering military expenditure incident to the crushing of this strike in Ohio was borne by the federal government through the allocation of financial aid to the military establishment of the state.

The steel workers have now buried their dead, while the widows weep and watch their orphaned children become objects of public charity. The murder of these unarmed men has never been publicly rebuked by any authoritative officer of the state or federal government. Some of them, in extenuation, plead lack of jurisdiction, but murder as a crime against the moral code can always be rebuked without regard to the niceties of legalistic jurisdiction by those who profess to be the keepers of the public conscience.

Shortly after Kelly's police force in Chicago had indulged in their bloody orgy, Kelly came to Washington looking for political patronage. That patronage was forthcoming and Kelly must believe that the killing of the strikers is no liability in partisan politics.

The men in the steel industry who sacrificed their all were not merely aiding their fellows at home but were adding strength to the cause of their comrades in all industry. Labor was marching toward the goal of industrial democracy and contributing constructively toward a more rational arrangement of our domestic economy.

Labor does not seek industrial strife. It wants peace, but a peace with justice. In the long struggle for labor's rights, it has been patient and forebearing. Sabotage and destructive syndicalism have had no part in the American labor movement. Workers have kept faith in American institutions. Most of the conflicts which have occurred have been when labor's right to live has been challenged and denied.

Fascist organizations have been launched and financed under the shabby pretext that the CIO movement is communistic. The real breeders of discontent and alien doctrines of government and philosophies subversive of good citizenship are such as these who take the law into their own hands.

No tin-hat brigade of goose-stepping vigilantes or Bible-babbling mob of blackguarding and corporation-paid scoundrels will prevent the onward march of labor, or divert its purpose to play its natural and rational part in the development of the economic, political and social life of our nation.

Unionization, as opposed to Communism, presupposes the relation of employment; it is based upon the wage system and it recognizes fully and unreservedly the institution of private property and the right to investment profit.

The organized workers of America, free in their industrial life, conscious partners in production, secure in their homes and enjoying a decent standard of living, will prove the finest bulwark against the intrusion of alien doctrines of government.

Do those who have hatched this foolish cry of Communism in the CIO fear the increased influence will be cast on the side of shorter hours, a better system of distributed employment, better homes for the underprivileged, social security for the aged, a fairer distribution of the national income?

Certainly labor wants a fairer share in the national income. Assuredly labor wants a larger participation in increased productivity efficiency. Obviously the population is entitled to participate in the fruits of the genius of our men of achievement in the field of the material sciences.

Under the banner of the Committee for Industrial Organization, American labor is on the march. Its objectives today are those it had in the beginning: to strive for the unionization of our unorganized millions of workers and for the acceptance of collective bargaining as a recognized American institution.

The objectives of this movement are not political in a partisan sense. Yet it is true that a political party which seeks the support of labor and makes pledges of good faith to labor must, in equity and good conscience, keep that faith and redeem those pledges.

The spectacle of august and dignified members of the Congress, servants of the people and agents of the republic, skulking in hallways and closets, hiding their faces in a party caucus to prevent a quorum from acting upon a labor measure, is one that emphasizes the perfidy of politicians and blasts the confidence of labor's millions in politicians' promises and statesmen's vows.

Labor next year cannot avoid the necessity of a political assay of the work and deeds of its so-called friends and its political beneficiaries. It must determine who are its friends in the arena of politics as elsewhere. It feels that its cause is just and that its friends should not view its struggle with neutral detachment or intone constant criticism of its activities.

Those who chant their praises of democracy, but who lose no chance to drive their knives into labor's defenseless back, must feel the weight of labor's woe even as its open adversaries must ever feel the thrust of labor's power.

Labor, like Israel, has many sorrows. Its women weep for their fallen and they lament for the future of the children of the race. It ill behooves one who has supped at labor's table and who has been sheltered in labor's house to curse with equal fervor and fine impartiality both labor and its adversaries when they become locked in deadly embrace.

27

◆

WAR AIMS

Circumstances change, said Franklin D. Roosevelt, and so did he as president, from (in other words) "Mr. New Deal" facing the dangers of the Great Depression in the 1930s to "Mr. Win-the-War" facing the dangers of the Axis Powers in the 1940s. Historians have sometimes seen the coming of war as a discontinuity in his administration.

But the break was not so sharp as it might have been. One thread providing continuity was that Roosevelt was never disinterested in world affairs, even during the most urgent days of the Depression. As the Nazi threat to France and England and the Japanese threat to China grew in the late 1930s, so did Roosevelt's determination to help—if he could do so without declaring war. Another thread was that Roosevelt perceived the looming conflict partly in ideological terms—as a struggle, with the forces of authoritarianism and social reaction pitted against the forces of democracy and social progress. To some extent, Roosevelt's view of the conflict resembled Woodrow Wilson's goal in the First World War of making the world "safe for democracy." It also followed logically from the nature of the enemy, which most people regarded as nothing but a coalition of racist, militaristic tyrants. Opposing such an enemy meant, by extension, opposing what the enemy stood for.

In his "Four Freedoms" address, delivered to Congress and broadcast to the public in January 1941—prior to America's formal entry into the war—Roosevelt went beyond Woodrow Wilson in his statement of war goals. In this speech, as in others he delivered over the next four years, the president made it clear that he considered this war to be not just about freedom of speech, press, and religion, as his predecessors might have it. This was also a war about freedom from want, the philosophy underlying many of the New Deal programs. And it was about freedom from fear, a sentiment that had filled his first inaugural address eight years before. At least in this 1941 statement, "Mr. Win-the-War" continued to be "Mr. New Deal."

Questions to Consider. Isolationist, antiwar feelings were still very strong in the country in early 1941. How did Roosevelt try at the beginning of his speech to neutralize antiwar sentiment? At what point in the address did he introduce what might be considered progressive political ideas of the kind that characterized the New Deal? According to Roosevelt, what were the foundations of "a healthy and strong democracy"? Would all Americans have agreed with his list of democratic "foundations"? Why did the president demand individual sacrifice and warn people not to try to get rich from his programs? Of the "four freedoms" Roosevelt eventually enumerated, which do you think would have been most popular in the 1940s?

♦

The Four Freedoms (1941)

FRANKLIN D. ROOSEVELT

I address you, the Members of the Seventy-seventh Congress, at a moment unprecedented in the history of the Union. I use the word "unprecedented," because at no previous time has American security been as seriously threatened from without as it is today. . . .

Every realist knows that the democratic way of life is at this moment being directly assailed in every part of the world—assailed either by arms, or by secret spreading of poisonous propaganda by those who seek to destroy unity and promote discord in nations still at peace.

During sixteen months this assault has blotted out the whole pattern of democratic life in an appalling number of independent nations, great and small. The assailants are still on the march, threatening other nations, great and small.

Therefore, as your President, performing my constitutional duty to "give to the Congress information on the state of the Union," I find it necessary to report that the future and the safety of our country and of our democracy are overwhelmingly involved in events far beyond our borders.

Armed defense of democratic existence is now being gallantly waged in four continents. If that defense fails, all the population and all the resources of Europe, Asia, Africa, and Australasia will be dominated by the conquerors. The total of those populations and their resources greatly exceeds the sum total of the population and resources of the whole of the Western Hemisphere—many times over. . . .

No realistic American can expect from a dictator's peace international generosity, or return of true independence, or world disarmament, or freedom of expression, or freedom of religion—or even good business.

From *The New York Times* January 7, 1941.

Such a peace would bring no security for us or for our neighbors. Those who would give up essential liberty to purchase a little temporary safety deserve neither liberty nor safety. . . .

There is much loose talk of our immunity from immediate and direct invasion from across the seas. Obviously, as long as the British Navy retains its power, no such danger exists. Even if there were no British Navy, it is not probable that any enemy would be stupid enough to attack us by landing troops in the United States from across thousands of miles of ocean, until it had acquired strategic bases from which to operate.

But we learn much from the lessons of the past years in Europe—particularly the lesson of Norway, whose essential seaports were captured by treachery and surprise built up over a series of years. . . .

As long as the aggressor nations maintain the offensive, they, not we, will choose the time and the place and the method of their attack. . . .

Let us say to the democracies, "We Americans are vitally concerned in your defense of freedom. We are putting forth our energies, our resources, and our organizing powers to give you the strength to regain and maintain a free world. We shall send you, in ever-increasing numbers, ships, planes, tanks, guns. This is our purpose and our pledge."

In fulfillment of this purpose we will not be intimidated by the threats of dictators that they will regard as a breach of international law and as an act of war our aid to the democracies which dare to resist their aggression. Such aid is not an act of war, even if a dictator should unilaterally proclaim it so to be.

When the dictators are ready to make war upon us, they will not wait for an act of war on our part. They did not wait for Norway or Belgium or The Netherlands to commit an act of war.

Their only interest is in a new one-way international law, which lacks mutuality in its observance and, therefore, becomes an instrument of oppression. . . .

As men do not live by bread alone, they do not fight by armaments alone. Those who man our defenses, and those behind them who build our defenses, must have the stamina and courage which come from an unshakable belief in the manner of life which they are defending. The mighty action which we are calling for cannot be based on a disregard of all things worth fighting for.

There is nothing mysterious about the foundations of a healthy and strong democracy. The basic things expected by our people of their political and economic systems are simple.

They are:

Equality of opportunity for youth and for others.
Jobs for those who can work.
Security for those who need it.
The ending of special privilege for the few.

The preservation of civil liberties for all.

The enjoyment of the fruits of scientific progress in a wider and constantly rising standard of living.

These are the simple and basic things that must never be lost sight of in the turmoil and unbelievable complexity of our modern world. The inner and abiding strength of our economic and political systems is dependent upon the degree to which they fulfill these expectations. . . .

I have called for personal sacrifice. I am assured of the willingness of almost all Americans to respond to that call.

A part of the sacrifice means the payment of more money in taxes. . . . No person should try, or be allowed to get rich out of this program. . . .

In the future days, which we seek to make secure, we look forward to a world founded upon four essential human freedoms.

The first is freedom of speech and expression, everywhere in the world.

The second is freedom of every person to worship God in his own way, everywhere in the world.

The third is freedom from want, which, translated into world terms, means economic understandings which will secure to every nation a healthy peacetime life for its inhabitants, everywhere in the world.

The fourth is freedom from fear—which, translated into world terms, means a worldwide reduction of armaments to such a point and in such a thorough fashion that no nation will be in a position to commit an act of physical aggression against any neighbor—anywhere in the world.

That is no vision of a distant millennium. It is a definite basis for a kind of world attainable in our own time and not the so-called new order of tyranny which the dictators seek to impose. That kind of world is the very antithesis of the kind created with the crash of a bomb.

To that new order we oppose the greater conception—the moral order. A good society is able to face schemes of world domination and foreign revolutions alike without fear.

Since the beginning of our American history we have been engaged in change—in a perpetual peaceful revolution—a revolution which goes on steadily, quietly adjusting itself to changing conditions—without the concentration camp or the quicklime in the ditch. The world order which we seek is the cooperation of free countries, working together in a friendly, civilized society.

This Nation has placed its destiny in the hands and heads and hearts of its millions of free men and women; and its faith in freedom under the guidance of God. Freedom means the supremacy of human rights everywhere. Our support goes to those who struggle to gain those rights or keep them. Our strength is in our unity of purpose.

To that high concept there can be no end save victory.

28

◆

DAY OF INFAMY

The United States did not completely isolate itself from other nations after the disillusionment of World War I. During the 1920s the U.S. government negotiated arms-limitations pacts, sought to preserve the Open Door in China, encouraged massive bank loans to a war-ravaged Europe, and maintained troops in Latin America. Yet throughout the 1920s and into the 1930s the United States held steady on two key matters. It refused to enter military or defense alliances with any nation and to spend heavily on armies and armaments. During the 1930s the American public was probably more opposed to war than at any other time in U.S. history.

The rise of aggressive governments in Nazi Germany, Fascist Italy and Imperial Japan gradually changed America's sense of detachment. But the shift to involvement was slow. Not until German forces subdued France in 1940 did President Franklin Roosevelt promise "everything short of war" to a beleaguered England. Roosevelt asked Congress for a declaration of war only when Japan, which saw America's presence in the Pacific as a threat to its own ambitions there, conducted devastating attacks on the American fleet and naval base at Pearl Harbor, Hawaii, and on the Philippines on December 7, 1941. The president's emphasis on the surprise element in this "day of infamy" and on the need henceforth to guard against "treachery" presaged not only the vast wartime military build-up to come but also the maintenance of a large military establishment after the war was over. Roosevelt's address in 1941 thus shaped America's perceptions of its international position just as Woodrow Wilson's had in 1917, though in a profoundly different direction.

Questions to Consider. Several questions arise from a reading of Roosevelt's announcement of war. How comparable was the sinking of American ships by Japanese airplanes in 1941 to the sinking of American ships by German submarines in 1917? Did this difference in the nature of the weaponry add to the impact of Roosevelt's announcement? Note, too, that Roosevelt did not attach a lengthy declaration of large goals for humanity to his message, as Wilson had done. Why not? Did the facts actually "speak for themselves," as Roosevelt stated?

How could the president assert that the American people had "already formed their opinion"? Did the notions of American exceptionalism and the redemption of humanity sneak into the message despite its brevity?

◆

Address to Congress (1941)

FRANKLIN D. ROOSEVELT

Yesterday, December 7, 1941—a date which will live in infamy—the United States of America was suddenly and deliberately attacked by naval and air forces of the Empire of Japan.

The United States was at peace with that nation and, at the solicitation of Japan, was still in conversation with its Government and its Emperor looking toward the maintenance of peace in the Pacific. Indeed, one hour after Japanese air squadrons had commenced bombing in Oahu, the Japanese Ambassador to the United States and his colleague delivered to the Secretary of State a formal reply to a recent American message. While this reply stated that it seemed useless to continue the existing diplomatic negotiations, it contained no threat or hint of war or armed attack.

It will be recorded that the distance of Hawaii from Japan makes it obvious that the attack was deliberately planned many days or even weeks ago. During the intervening time the Japanese Government has deliberately sought to deceive the United States by false statements and expressions of hope for continued peace.

The attack yesterday on the Hawaiian Islands has caused severe damage to American naval and military forces. Very many American lives have been lost. In addition American ships have been reported torpedoed on the high seas between San Francisco and Honolulu.

Yesterday the Japanese Government also launched an attack against Malaya. Last night Japanese forces attacked Hong Kong. Last night Japanese forces attacked Guam. Last night Japanese forces attacked the Philippine Islands. Last night the Japanese attacked Wake Island. This morning the Japanese attacked Midway Island.

Japan has, therefore, undertaken a surprise offensive extending throughout the Pacific area. The facts of yesterday speak for themselves. The people of the United States have already formed their opinions and well understand the implications to the very life and safety of our nation.

As Commander-in-Chief of the Army and Navy, I have directed that all measures be taken for our defense.

From *The New York Times*, December 9, 1941.

Pearl Harbor, December 1941. The Japanese attack on Pearl Harbor sank or damaged eighteen major warships, including these two destroyers and the lightly damaged battleship, the *Pennsylvania,* in the background. The raid also destroyed 180 aircraft and killed more than 2,000 Americans. Yet the assault left vital oil storage and repair facilities undamaged. (National Archives)

Always will we remember the character of the onslaught against us.

No matter how long it may take us to overcome this premeditated invasion, the American people in their righteous might will win through to absolute victory.

I believe I interpret the will of the Congress and of the people when I assert that we will not only defend ourselves to the uttermost but will make very certain that this form of treachery shall never endanger us again.

Hostilities exist. There is no blinking at the fact that our people, our territory and our interests are in grave danger.

With confidence in our armed forces—with the unbounded determination of our people—we will gain the inevitable triumph—so help us God.

I ask that the Congress declare that since the unprovoked and dastardly attack by Japan on Sunday, December seventh, a state of war has existed between the United States and the Japanese Empire.

29

◆

DESTROYER OF WORLDS

American strategy in the Pacific war was to "island-hop" toward Japan, occupying undefended atolls where possible and taking others by amphibious assault where necessary. This oceanic march began in 1942 with a painful, costly victory at Guadalcanal, northeast of Australia. It culminated in 1945 at Okinawa, off southern Japan, in a gruesome fight that produced 150,000 casualties. Meanwhile, the United States had proved its new air capability with the victory of its carrier-based planes at Midway in 1942 and with long-range bombing of the Japanese mainland after 1943. Finally, as American soldiers grouped to invade Japan in mid-1945, President Harry S Truman warned the Japanese that unless they surrendered by August 3 they would face "prompt and utter destruction." When they did not surrender, he ordered that an atomic bomb be dropped on Hiroshima on August 6 and another on Nagasaki on August 9.

The concept of the atomic bomb was brought to the United States by scientists fleeing Nazi Germany and Fascist Italy. In 1939, after suggestions from scientist Albert Einstein that the Germans might develop nuclear weapons, President Roosevelt authorized a National Defense Research Committee, which in turn led to the top-secret Manhattan Project for developing the bomb. By 1945, nuclear plants in Tennessee and Washington had produced enough fissionable material to construct a test bomb, which was exploded spectacularly in the New Mexico desert in July. One of the first decisions that President Truman faced upon succeeding Roosevelt in office concerned using the bomb against Japan. Why he ordered the use of the bomb continues to be debated. He claimed he did so to avoid a bloody land assault that would have cost many lives—American and Japanese. Some historians suggest he did so to demonstrate U.S. power to the Russians. Nevertheless, the effects of the bomb itself were soon clear. More than 100,000 Japanese died from the two blasts.

While on assignment in late 1945 and 1946, John Hersey, a journalist covering the Far East for major American periodicals, prepared an account of how the bomb affected individual Japanese. Though most Allied leaders regarded the atomic bomb as just another big bomb, the excerpts from Hersey's *Hiroshima* reprinted below make clear that in its capacity for devastation the bomb dwarfed all other weapons of war.

John Hersey was born in 1914 in Tientsin, China, to American missionary parents, and became a journalist in the late 1930s after study at Yale University and Cambridge University in England. His first major work was *Men on Bataan* (1942), based on a series of interviews. A stream of books based on interviews and news clippings soon followed, including *Into the Valley* (1943), about a company of marines on Guadalcanal, and *Hiroshima* (1946). Hersey won the Pulitzer Prize for *A Bell for Adano* (1944), a story about the American occupation of Italy.

Questions to Consider. *Hiroshima* probably continues to be the most widely read and influential study of the effects of the dropping of the bomb. What clues in the excerpts below help explain this popularity? Is it strictly a consequence of Hersey's strategy of focusing on individuals? Might his style of writing also be a factor? Why does Hersey tell us about the blind soldiers? Is it the blindness that moves us, or the fact that these blind are soldiers? Why did Hersey choose to make two of his six main characters, Dr. Fujii and Dr. Sasaki, medical men? Why is one of the six, Father Kleinsorge, not Japanese? Some U.S. officials were upset, even angry, that *Hiroshima* was so popular. What passage in the excerpts do you think might have caused such official distress?

◆

Hiroshima (1946)

JOHN HERSEY

The lot of Drs. Fujii, Kanda, and Machii right after the explosion—and, as these three were typical, that of the majority of the physicians and surgeons of Hiroshima—with their offices and hospitals destroyed, their equipment scattered, their own bodies incapacitated in varying degrees, explained why so many citizens who were hurt went untended and why so many who might have lived died. Of a hundred and fifty doctors in the city, sixty-five were already dead and most of the rest were wounded. Of 1,780 nurses, 1,654 were dead or too badly hurt to work. In the biggest hospital, that of the Red Cross, only six doctors out of thirty were able to function, and only ten nurses out of more than two hundred. The sole uninjured

Hiroshima. After three years and $2 billion of secret research, the United States exploded the first atomic bomb at Alamogordo, New Mexico, on the morning of July 16, 1945. A scientist who was there said it was as if the "earth had opened" and the "skies had split," or like the moment of creation when God said, "Let there be light." Although the catastrophic power of the weapon was clear, President Truman never really considered not using it against Japan. After the bloody battle of Okinawa in mid-1945, few Americans would have decided differently. (National Archives)

doctor on the Red Cross Hospital staff was Dr. Sasaki. After the explosion, he hurried to a storeroom to fetch bandages. This room, like everything he had seen as he ran through the hospital, was chaotic—bottles of medicines thrown off shelves and broken, salves spattered on the walls, instruments strewn everywhere. He grabbed up some bandages and an unbroken bottle of mercurochrome, hurried back to the chief surgeon, and bandaged his cuts. Then he went out into the corridor and began patching up the wounded patients and the doctors and nurses there. He blundered so without his glasses that he took a pair off the face of a wounded nurse, and although they only approximately compensated for the errors of his vision, they were better than nothing. (He was to depend on them for more than a month.)

Dr. Sasaki worked without method, taking those who were nearest him first, and he noticed soon that the corridor seemed to be getting more and more crowded. Mixed in with the abrasions and lacerations which most people in the hospital had suffered, he began to find dreadful burns. He realized then that casualties were pouring in from outdoors. There were so many that he began to pass up the lightly wounded; he decided that all he could hope to do was to stop people from bleeding to death. Before long, patients lay and crouched on the floors of the wards and the laboratories and all the other rooms, and in the corridors, and on the stairs, and in the front hall, and under the portecochère, and on the stone front steps, and in the driveway and courtyard, and for blocks each way in the streets outside. Wounded people supported maimed people; disfigured families leaned together. Many people were vomiting. A tremendous number of schoolgirls—some of those who had been taken from their classrooms to work outdoors, cleaning fire lanes—crept into the hospital. In a city of two hundred and forty-five thousand, nearly a hundred thousand people had been killed or doomed at one blow; a hundred thousand more were hurt. At least ten thousand of the wounded made their way to the best hospital in town, which was altogether unequal to such a trampling, since it had only six hundred beds, and they had all been occupied. The people in the suffocating crowd inside the hospital wept and cried, for Dr. Sasaki to hear, "*Sensei!* Doctor!" and the less seriously wounded came and pulled at his sleeve and begged him to go to the aid of the worse wounded. Tugged here and there in his stockinged feet, bewildered by the numbers, staggered by so much raw flesh, Dr. Sasaki lost all sense of the profession and stopped working as a skillful surgeon and a sympathetic man; he became an automaton, mechanically wiping, daubing, winding, wiping, daubing, winding. . . .

The morning, again, was hot. Father Kleinsorge went to fetch water for the wounded in a bottle and a teapot he had borrowed. He had heard that it was possible to get fresh tap water outside Asano Park. Going through the rock gardens, he had to climb over and crawl under the trunks of fallen pine trees; he found he was weak. There were many dead in the gardens. At a beautiful moon bridge, he passed a naked, living woman who seemed to have been burned from head to toe and was red all over. Near the entrance to the park, an Army doctor was working, but the only medicine he had was iodine, which he painted over cuts, bruises, slimy burns, everything—and by now everything he painted had pus on it. Outside the gate of the park, Father Kleinsorge found a faucet that still worked—part of the plumbing of a vanished house—and he filled his vessels and returned. When he had given the wounded the water, he made a second trip. This time, the woman by the bridge was dead. On his way back with the water, he got lost on a detour around a fallen tree, and as he looked for his way through the woods, he heard a voice ask from the underbrush,

"Have you anything to drink?" He saw a uniform. Thinking there was just one soldier, he approached with the water. When he had penetrated the bushes, he saw there were about twenty men, and they were all in exactly the same nightmarish state: their faces were wholly burned, their eye-sockets were hollow, the fluid from their melted eyes had run down their cheeks. (They must have had their faces upturned when the bomb went off; perhaps they were anti-aircraft personnel.) Their mouths were mere swollen, pus-covered wounds, which they could not bear to stretch enough to admit the spout of the teapot. So Father Kleinsorge got a large piece of grass and drew out the stem so as to make a straw, and gave them all water to drink that way. One of them said, "I can't see anything." Father Kleinsorge answered, as cheerfully as he could, "There's a doctor at the entrance to the park. He's busy now, but he'll come soon and fix your eyes, I hope." . . .

Early that day, August 7th, the Japanese radio broadcast for the first time a succinct announcement that very few, if any, of the people most concerned with its content, the survivors in Hiroshima, happened to hear: "Hiroshima suffered considerable damage as the result of an attack by a few B-29s. It is believed that a new type of bomb was used. The details are being investigated." Nor is it probable that any of the survivors happened to be tuned in on a short-wave rebroadcast of an extraordinary announcement by the president of the United States, which identified the new bomb as atomic: "That bomb had more power than twenty thousand tons of TNT. It had more than two thousand times the blast power of the British Grand Slam, which is the largest bomb ever yet used in the history of warfare." Those victims who were able to worry at all about what had happened thought of it and discussed it in more primitive, childish terms— gasoline sprinkled from an airplane, maybe, or some combustible gas, or a big cluster of incendiaries, or the work of parachutists; but, even if they had known the truth, most of them were too busy or too weary or too badly hurt to care that they were the objects of the first great experiment in the use of atomic power, which (as the voices on the short wave shouted) no country except the United States, with its industrial know-how, its willingness to throw two billion gold dollars into an important wartime gamble, could possibly have developed. . . .

Dr. Sasaki and his colleagues at the Red Cross Hospital watched the unprecedented disease unfold and at last evolved a theory about its nature. It had, they decided, three stages. The first stage had been all over before the doctors even knew they were dealing with a new sickness; it was the direct reaction to the bombardment of the body, at the moment when the bomb went off, by neutrons, beta particles, and gamma rays. The apparently uninjured people who had died so mysteriously in the first few hours or days had succumbed in this first stage. It killed ninety-five per cent of the people within a half-mile of the center, and many thousands who were farther away. The doctors realized in retrospect that even though most of these dead had also suffered from burns and blast effects, they had absorbed enough radiation to kill them. The rays simply destroyed body cells—caused their nuclei to degenerate and broke their walls. Many people who did not die right away came down with nausea, headache, diarrhea, malaise, and fever, which lasted several days. Doctors could not be certain whether some of these symptoms were the result of radiation or nervous shock. The second stage set in ten or fifteen days after the bombing. Its first symptom was falling hair. Diarrhea and fever, which in some cases went as high as 106, came next. Twenty-five to thirty days after the explosion, blood disorders appeared: gums bled, the white-blood-cell count dropped sharply, and *petechiae* [eruptions] appeared on the skin and mucous membranes. The drop in the number of white blood corpuscles reduced the patient's capacity to resist infection, so open wounds were unusually slow in healing and many of the sick developed sore throats and mouths. The two key symptoms, on which the doctors came to base their prognosis, were fever and the lowered white-corpuscle count. If fever remained steady and high, the patient's chances for survival were poor. The white count almost always dropped below four thousand; a patient whose count fell below one thousand had little hope of living. Toward the end of the second stage, if the patient survived, anemia, or a drop in the red blood count, also set in. The third stage was the reaction that came when the body struggled to compensate for its ills—when, for instance, the white count not only returned to normal but increased to much higher than normal levels. In this stage, many patients died of complications, such as infections in the chest cavity. Most burns healed with deep layers of pink, rubbery scar tissue, known as keloid tumors. The duration of the disease varied, depending on the patient's constitution and the amount of radiation he had received. Some victims recovered in a week; with others the disease dragged on for months.

As the symptoms revealed themselves, it became clear that many of them resembled the effects of overdoses of X-ray, and the doctors based their therapy on that likeness. They gave victims liver extract, blood transfusions, and vitimins, especially B_1. The shortage of supplies and instruments hampered them. Allied doctors who came in after the surrender found plasma and penicillin very effective. Since the blood disorders were, in the long run, the predominant factor in the disease, some of the Japanese doctors evolved a theory as to the seat of the delayed sickness. They thought that perhaps gamma rays, entering the body at the time of the explosion, made the phosphorus in the victims' bones radioactive, and that they in turn emitted beta particles, which, though they could not penetrate far through flesh, could enter the bone marrow, where blood is manufactured, and gradually tear it down. Whatever its source, the disease had some baffling quirks. Not all the patients exhibited all the main symptoms.

People who suffered flash burns were protected, to a considerable extent, from radiation sickness. Those who had lain quietly for days or even hours after the bombing were much less liable to get sick than those who had been active. Gray hair seldom fell out. And, as if nature were protecting man against his own ingenuity, the reproductive processes were affected for a time; men became sterile, women had miscarriages, menstruation stopped. . . .

A surprising number of the people of Hiroshima remained more or less indifferent about the ethics of using the bomb. Possibly they were too terrified by it to want to think about it at all. Many citizens of Hiroshima, however, continued to feel a hatred for Americans which nothing could possibly erase. "I see," Dr. Sasaki once said, "that they are holding a trial for war criminals in Tokyo just now. I think they ought to try the men who decided to use the bomb and they should hang them all."

Father Kleinsorge and the other German Jesuit priests, who as foreigners, could be expected to take a relatively detached view, often discussed the ethics of using the bomb. One of them, Father Siemes, who was out at Nagatsuka [Hiroshima suburb] at the time of the attack, wrote in a report to the Holy See in Rome: "Some of us consider the bomb in the same category as poison gas and were against its use on a civilian population. Others were of the opinion that in total war, as carried on in Japan, there was no difference between civilians and soldiers, and that the bomb itself was an effective force tending to end the bloodshed, warning Japan to surrender and thus to avoid total destruction. It seems logical that he who supports total war in principle cannot complain of a war against civilians. The crux of the matter is whether total war in its present form is justifiable, even when it serves a just purpose. Does it not have material and spiritual evil as its consequences which far exceed whatever good might result? When will our moralists give us a clear answer to this question?"

The Berlin Wall. A West German greets friends and family in East Germany across the Berlin Wall. Constructed in 1961, the Berlin Wall was built by East Germany to keep its inhabitants from escaping to the West. The construction of the Wall added fuel to the Cold War and heightened tensions between the United States and the Soviet Union. (© Rene Burri/Magnum Photos)

CHAPTER SIX

◆

Protracted Conflict

30

◆

CONTAINMENT

When Germany invaded Poland in September 1939, Britain and France came to Poland's aid, and World War II began. But the surrender of Germany in May 1945 did not mean a free and independent Poland. Instead, when the war ended, the Soviet Union took over most of eastern Europe, including Poland, and installed regimes of its own choosing, backed by military force. The Russians had suffered severely in both World War I and World War II from invasions from the West and were determined to surround themselves with a ring of friendly states after the war. But American policy makers, shocked by the ruthlessness with which the Russians had accomplished their purpose, interpreted Soviet policy as expansionist rather than defensive in nature and began to fear that the Soviet Union had designs on western Europe as well. The United States therefore sponsored economic aid (the Marshall Plan) as well as military aid (the Truman Doctrine) to nations in Europe that seemed threatened by Soviet aggression; it also persuaded the nations of western Europe to organize the North Atlantic Treaty Organization (NATO). Thus was born the cold war between the Soviet Union and the United States.

In July 1947 an article entitled "The Sources of Soviet Conduct" appeared in *Foreign Affairs,* an influential journal published in New York. The author, identified only as "X," was later revealed to be George F. Kennan, head of the policy-planning staff of the State Department, so the article may have reflected official American views on Soviet foreign policy. Pointing out that the Soviet Union based its policies on a firm belief in the "innate antagonism between capitalism and socialism," Kennan warned that the Russians were going to be difficult to deal with for a long time. He added that the Kremlin was "under no ideological compulsion to accomplish its purposes in a hurry" and that the only wise course for the United States to follow was that of "a long-term, patient but firm and vigilant containment of Russian expansionist tendencies." Kennan's article, which is excerpted below, shaped as well as reflected American policy.

George F. Kennan was born in Milwaukee, Wisconsin, in 1904. After graduating from Princeton University in 1925, he joined the foreign service, in which he specialized in Russian affairs while serving in minor European posts. In 1933, he went to Moscow when the United States extended diplomatic recognition to the Soviet Union and opened an embassy there. Kennan served elsewhere in the late 1930s, but he returned to the Soviet Union during World War II and was appointed U.S. ambassador there in 1952. Kennan continued to write extensively on Russian and American diplomacy even after leaving the foreign service in the late 1950s. He came to deplore the excessively military application of the containment doctrine he had outlined in 1947, and in his later books and articles he made various proposals for demilitarization and disengagement that might diminish cold war tensions and lessen the chances of nuclear war.

Questions to Consider. In assigning responsibility for the cold war to a combination of Marxist ideology, the Kremlin's desire for power, and the world Communist movement, Kennan was also arguing, of course, that the West was largely defensive and even innocent. What evidence from twentieth-century history might be introduced to counter this argument? Kennan argued, similarly, that the Soviet threat was likely to last, practically speaking, forever. Given his views on Soviet objectives, were social or political changes conceivable that might alter these objectives or the Soviet capacity to pursue them? Did changes of this type in fact occur? Again, Kennan's article outlined his notions of Soviet society clearly enough. What assumptions, according to the evidence of the article, was Kennan making about American society? Finally, Kennan wrote his essay to mold American policy. One can imagine, however, various policies flowing from this analysis: an effort to roll back Russian power in Europe, an armed "garrison" state in the United States, intense economic or propaganda competition, and even a pre-emptive nuclear strike. Which of these did Kennan himself hope to see?

◆

The Sources of Soviet Conduct (1947)

GEORGE F. KENNAN

The political personality of Soviet power as we know it today is the product of ideology and circumstances: ideology inherited by the present Soviet leaders from the movement in which they had their political origin, and circumstances of the power which they now have exercised for nearly three decades in Russia. . . .

From *Foreign Affairs* (July 1947), 25:566–582. Reprinted by permission of *Foreign Affairs,* July 1947. Copyright 1947 by the Council on Foreign Relations, Inc.

Berlin apartment block. The U.S. Congress approved the first $5 billion for the European Recovery Program (as the Marshall Plan was officially called) in 1948 with the stipulation that most of the funds would go to purchase American-made products. Goods began to arrive in Europe soon afterward. Much of the early aid went, in fact, for agricultural assistance and housing construction to stave off the malnutrition and homelessness that haunted Europe after World War I. (UPI/Bettmann Newsphoto)

Marxian ideology, in its Russian-Communist projection, has always been in process of subtle evolution. The materials on which it bases itself are extensive and complex. But the outstanding features of Communist thought as it existed in 1916 may perhaps be summarized as follows: (a) that the central factor in the life of man, the fact which determines the character of public life and the "physiognomy of society," is the system by which material goods are produced and exchanged; (b) that the capitalist system of production is a nefarious one which inevitably leads to the exploitation of the working class by the capital-owning class and is incapable of developing adequately the economic resources of society or of distributing fairly the material goods produced by human labor; (c) that capitalism contains the seeds of its own destruction and must, in view of the inability of the capital-owning class to adjust itself to economic change, result eventually and inescapably in a revolutionary transfer of power to the working class; and (d) that imperialism, the final phase of capitalism, leads directly to war and revolution.

The rest may be outlined in Lenin's own words: "Unevenness of economic and political development is the inflexible law of capitalism. It follows from this that the victory of Socialism may come originally in a few capitalist countries or even in a single capitalist country. The victorious proletariat of that country, having expropriated the capitalists and having organized Socialist production at home, would rise against the remaining capitalist world, drawing to itself in the process the oppressed classes of other countries." It must be noted that there was no assumption that capitalism would perish without proletarian revolution. A final push was needed from a revolutionary proletariat movement in order to tip over the tottering structure. But it was regarded as inevitable that sooner or later that push be given. . . .

Now the outstanding circumstance concerning the Soviet regime is that down to the present day this process of political consolidation has never been completed and the men in the Kremlin have continued to be predominantly absorbed with the struggle to secure and make absolute the power which they seized in November 1917. They have endeavored to secure it primarily against forces at home, within Soviet society itself. But they have also endeavored to secure it against the outside world. For ideology, as we have seen, taught them that the outside world was hostile and that it was their duty eventually to overthrow the political forces beyond their borders. The powerful hands of Russian history and tradition reached up to sustain them in this feeling. . . .

Now it lies in the nature of the mental world of the Soviet leaders, as well as in the character of their ideology, that no opposition to them can be officially recognized as having any merit or justification whatsoever. Such opposition can flow, in theory, only from the hostile and incorrigible forces of dying capitalism. As long as remnants of capitalism were officially recognized as existing in Russia, it was possible to place on them, as an internal element, part of the blame for the maintenance of a dictatorial form of society. But as these remnants were liquidated, little by little, this justification fell away; and when it was indicated officially that they had been finally destroyed, it disappeared altogether. And this fact created one of the most basic of the compulsions which came to act upon the Soviet regime: since capitalism no longer existed in Russia and since it could not be admitted that there could be serious or widespread opposition to the Kremlin springing spontaneously from the liberated masses under its authority, it became necessary to justify the retention of the dictatorship by stressing the menace of capitalism abroad. . . .

As things stand today, the rulers can no longer dream of parting with these organs and suppression. The quest for absolute power, pursued now for nearly three decades with a ruthlessness unparalleled (in scope at least) in modern times, has again produced internally as it did externally, its own reaction. The excesses of the police apparatus have fanned the potential opposition to the regime into something far greater and more dangerous than it could have been before those excesses began. . . .

So much for the historical background. What does it spell in terms of the political personality of Soviet power as we know it today?

Of the original ideology, nothing has been officially junked. Belief is maintained in the basic badness of capitalism, in the inevitability of its destruction, in the obligation of the proletariat to assist in that destruction and to take power into its own hands. But stress has come to be laid primarily on those concepts which relate most specifically to the Soviet regime itself: to its position as the sole truly Socialist regime in a dark and misguided world, and to the relationships of power within it.

The first of these concepts is that of the innate antagonism between capitalism and Socialism. . . . It means that there can never be on Moscow's side any sincere assumption of a community of aims between the Soviet Union and powers which are regarded as capitalism. It must invariably be assumed in Moscow that the aims of the capitalist world are antagonistic to the Soviet regime and, therefore, to the interests of the peoples it controls. If the Soviet Government occasionally sets its signature to documents which would indicate the contrary, this is to be regarded as a tactical maneuver permissible in dealing with the enemy (who is without honor) and should be taken in the spirit of *caveat emptor* [let the buyer beware]. Basically, the antagonism remains. It is postulated. And from it flow many of the phenomena which we find disturbing in the Kremlin's conduct of foreign policy: the secretiveness, the lack of frankness, the duplicity, the war suspiciousness, and the basic unfriendliness of purpose. These phenomena are there to stay, for the foreseeable future. . . .

This means that we are going to continue for a long time to find the Russians difficult to deal with. It does not mean that they should be considered as embarked upon a do-or-die program to overthrow our society by a given date. The theory of the inevitability of the eventual fall of capitalism has the fortunate connotation that there is no hurry about it. The forces of progress can take their time in preparing the final *coup de grace*. Meanwhile, what is vital is that the "Socialist fatherland"—that oasis of power which has been already won for Socialism in the person of the Soviet Union—should be cherished and defended by all good Communists at home and abroad, its fortunes promoted, its enemies badgered and confounded. The promotion of premature, "adventuristic" revolutionary projects abroad which might embarrass Soviet power in any way would be an inexcusable, even a counter-revolutionary act. The cause of Socialism is the support and promotion of Soviet power, as defined in Moscow.

This brings us to the second of the concepts important to contemporary Soviet outlook. This is the infallibility of the Kremlin. The Soviet concept of power, which permits no focal points of organization outside the Party itself, requires that the Party leadership remain in theory the sole repository of truth. For if truth were to be found elsewhere, there would be justification for its expression in organized activity. But it is precisely that which the Kremlin cannot and will not permit.

The leadership of the Communist Party is therefore always right, and has been always right ever since in 1929 Stalin formalized his personal power by announcing that decisions of the Politburo were being taken unanimously.

On the principle of infallibility there rests the iron discipline of the Communist Party. In fact, the two concepts are mutually self-supporting. Perfect discipline requires recognition of infallibility. Infallibility requires the observance of discipline. And the two together go far to determine the behaviorism of the entire Soviet apparatus of power. But their effect cannot be understood unless a third factor be taken into account: namely, the fact that the leadership is at liberty to put forward for tactical purposes any particular thesis which it finds useful to the cause at any particular moment and to require the faithful and unquestioning acceptance of that thesis by the members of the movement as a whole. This means that truth is not a constant but is actually created, for all intents and purposes, by the Soviet leaders themselves. It may vary from week to week, from month to month. It is nothing absolute and immutable—nothing which flows from objective reality. . . . Once a given party line has been laid down on a given issue of current policy, the whole Soviet governmental machine, including the mechanism of diplomacy, moves inexorably along the prescribed path, like a persistent toy automobile wound up and headed in a given direction, stopping only when it meets with some unanswerable force. The individuals who are the components of this machine are unamenable to argument or reason which comes to them from outside sources. . . . Since there can be no appeal to common purposes, there can be no appeal to common mental approaches. For this reason, facts speak louder than words to the ears of the Kremlin; and words carry the greatest weight when they have the ring of reflecting, or being backed up by, facts of unchallengeable validity.

But we have seen that the Kremlin is under no ideological compulsion to accomplish its purposes in a hurry. Like the Church, it is dealing in ideological concepts which are of long-term validity, and it can afford to be patient. It has no right to risk the existing achievements of the revolution for the sake of vain baubles of the future. The very teachings of Lenin himself require great caution and flexibility in the pursuit of Communist purposes. Again, these precepts are fortified by the lessons of Russian history: of centuries of obscure battles between nomadic forces over the stretches of a vast unfortified plain. Here caution, circumspection, flexibility and deception are the valuable qualities; and their value finds natural appreciation in the Russian or the oriental mind. Thus the Kremlin has no compunction about retreating in the face of superior force. And being under the compulsion of no timetable, it does not get panicky under the necessity for such a retreat. Its political action is a fluid stream which moves constantly, wherever it is permitted to move, toward a given goal. Its main concern is to make sure that it has filled every nook and cranny available to it in the basin of world power. But if it finds unassailable barriers in its path, it accepts these philosophically and accommodates itself to them. . . .

These considerations make Soviet diplomacy at once easier and more difficult to deal with than the diplomacy of individual aggressive leaders like Napoleon and Hitler. On the one hand it is more sensitive to contrary force, more ready to yield on individual sectors of the diplomatic front when that force is felt to be too strong, and thus more rational in the logic and rhetoric of power. On the other hand it cannot be easily defeated or discouraged by a single victory on the part of its opponents. And the patient persistence by which it is animated means that it can be effectively countered not by sporadic acts which represent the momentary whims of democratic opinion but only by intelligent long-range policies on the part of Russia's adversaries—policies no less steady in their purpose, and no less variegated and resourceful in their application, than those of the Soviet Union itself.

In these circumstances it is clear that the main element of any United States policy toward the Soviet Union must be that of a long-term, patient but firm and vigilant containment of Russian expansive tendencies. It is important to note, however, that such a policy has nothing to do with outward histrionics: with threats or blustering or superfluous gestures of outward "toughness." While the Kremlin is basically flexible in its reaction to political realities, it is by no means unamenable to considerations of prestige. Like almost any other government, it can be placed by tactless and threatening gestures in a position where it cannot afford to yield even though this might be dictated by its sense of realism. The Russian leaders are keen judges of human psychology, and as such they are highly conscious that loss of temper and of self-control is never a source of strength in political affairs. They are quick to exploit such evidence of weakness. For these reasons, it is a *sine qua non* of successful dealing with Russia that the foreign government in question should remain at all times cool and collected and that its demands on Russian policy should be put forward in such a manner as to leave the way open for a compliance not too detrimental to Russian prestige. . . .

It is clear that the United States cannot expect in the foreseeable future to enjoy political intimacy with the Soviet regime. It must continue to regard the Soviet Union as a rival, not a partner, in the political arena. It must continue to expect that Soviet policies will reflect no abstract love of peace and stability, no real faith in the possibility of a permanent happy coexistence of the Socialist and capitalist worlds, but rather a cautious, persistent pressure toward the disruption and weakening of all rival influence and rival power.

Balanced against this are the fact that Russia, as opposed to the Western world in general, is still by far the weaker party, that Soviet policy is highly flexible, and that Soviet society may well contain deficiencies which will eventually weaken its own total potential. This would of itself warrant the United States entering with reasonable confidence upon a policy of firm containment, designed to confront the Russians with unalterable counter-force at every point where they show signs of encroaching upon the interests of a peaceful and stable world.

But in actuality the possibilities for American policy are by no means limited to holding the line and hoping for the best. It is entirely possible for the United States to influence by its actions the internal developments, both within Russia and throughout the international Communist movement, by which Russian policy is largely determined. This is not only a question of the modest measure of informational activity which this government can conduct in the Soviet Union and elsewhere, although that, too, is important. It is rather a question of the degree to which the United States can create among the peoples of the world generally the impression of a country which knows what it wants, which is coping successfully with the problems of its internal life and with the responsibilities of a World Power, and which has a spiritual vitality capable of holding its own among the major ideological currents of the time. . . .

By the same token, exhibitions of indecision, disunity and internal disintegration within this country have an exhilarating effect on the whole Communist movement. At each evidence of these tendencies, a thrill of hope and excitement goes through the Communist world; a new jauntiness can be noted in the Moscow tread; now groups of foreign supporters climb on to what they can only view as the band wagon of international politics; and Russian pressure increases all along the line in international affairs.

It would be an exaggeration to say that American behavior unassisted and alone could exercise a power of life and death over the Communist movement and bring about the early fall of Soviet power in Russia. But the United States has it in its power to increase enormously the strains under which Soviet policy must operate, to force upon the Kremlin a far greater degree of moderation and circumspection than it has had to observe in recent years, and in this way to promote tendencies which must eventually find their outlet in either the breakup or the gradual mellowing of Soviet power. . . .

Thus the decision will really fall in large measure in this country itself. The issue of Soviet-American relations is in essence a test of the overall worth of the United States as a nation among nations. To avoid destruction the United States need only measure up to its own best traditions and prove itself worthy of preservation as a great nation.

Surely, there was never a fairer test of national quality than this. In the light of these circumstances, the thoughtful observer of Russian-American relations will find no cause for complaint in the Kremlin's challenge to American society. He will rather experience a certain gratitude to a Providence which, by providing the American people with this implacable challenge, has made their entire security as a nation dependent on their pulling themselves together and accepting the responsibilities of moral and political leadership that history plainly intended them to bear.

31

♦

SEEING REDS

In 1946 Joseph R. McCarthy defeated Progressive Senator Robert M. LaFollette, Jr., in the Republican primary in Wisconsin and went on to win election to the U.S. Senate that fall. During the primary contest he was supported by Wisconsin Communists who were infuriated by LaFollette's pre-Pearl Harbor anti-interventionism and by his criticisms of Soviet dictator Joseph Stalin. Asked about the support the Communists were giving him against LaFollette, McCarthy said airily, "The Communists have votes, too, don't they?" Four years later he became the leader of an impassioned crusade against Communism, and the word "McCarthyism" came to mean a reckless and demagogic assault on domestic dissent.

McCarthyism did not operate in a vacuum. Revelations of Communist spy activity in Canada, England, and the United States after World War II produced demands for counterespionage measures, and in 1947 President Truman inaugurated a loyalty program to ferret out Communists in government. Meanwhile, a series of "spy" cases hit the headlines: the trial and conviction of eleven Communist leaders under the Smith Act for conspiring to advocate the violent overthrow of the government; the conviction of former State Department official Alger Hiss, denounced as a Communist spy, for perjury; and the trial and execution of Julius and Ethel Rosenberg, government workers charged with passing atomic secrets to the Russians. For many Americans, the distinction between the expression of unpopular ideas and deliberate conspiratorial activity on behalf of a foreign power became increasingly blurred. In 1950, Senator McCarthy obliterated the distinction.

In a radio speech (excerpted below) given in Wheeling, West Virginia, in February 1950, McCarthy announced that he had in his hand a list of Communists in the State Department "known to the Secretary of State" and "still working and making policy." Overnight McCarthy became a national figure. Although he never showed anyone his famous "list" and was increasingly vague about the precise number of names it contained (205 or 81 or 57 or "a lot"), he came to exercise great influence in the U.S. Senate and in the nation. In July 1950, a Senate subcommittee headed by Maryland's Millard Tydings dismissed

McCarthy's charges as "a fraud and a hoax." But when Tydings, a conservative Democrat, ran for reelection that fall, McCarthy's insinuations that he was pro-Communist helped defeat him. Similar accusations helped defeat Connecticut Democrat William Benton in 1952.

Not every Republican admired Senator McCarthy or approved his tactics, even when they benefited Republican candidates. Margaret Chase Smith of Maine, the only woman in the U.S. Senate in 1950, had served with McCarthy on the Permanent Investigations Subcommittee of the Senate and had become perturbed by his lack of concern for the unfair damage the subcommittee might do to individuals' reputations. Smith became still more perturbed following McCarthy's West Virginia speech in February 1950 about Communists in the State Department. Conscious that she was a first-term senator and believing that the initial challenge to McCarthy should come from the Democrats (the majority party in the Senate), she delayed speaking her mind for some time. When the Democrats failed to rebut McCarthy's charges effectively, she determined to speak out and did so on June 1, 1950. Six other Republican senators endorsed Smith's "Declaration of Conscience," as it soon came to be called. But she was the one who made the speech, which became one of the most famous of its time.

It would take more than a statement by a handful of Senate Republicans to halt Joe McCarthy. In 1951 McCarthy charged that George C. Marshall, President Truman's former secretary of state and of defense, was part of "a conspiracy so immense and infamy so black as to dwarf any previous venture in the history of man." During the 1952 presidential campaign McCarthy talked ominously of "twenty years of treason" under the Democrats. His followers identified Roosevelt's New Deal, Truman's Fair Deal, and, indeed, all efforts for social reform since the Great Depression as Communist inspired. In 1953, as chairman of the Senate Committee on Government Operations, McCarthy launched a series of investigations of federal agencies, including the Voice of America, the International Information Agency, and the Army Signal Corps installation at Fort Monmouth, New Jersey. When the army decided to fight back, McCarthyism reached its climax in a series of televised Senate hearings in the spring of 1954. During these hearings, the Wisconsin senator's accusations and defamations of character gradually alienated all but his most devoted followers. On July 30, Republican Senator Ralph Flanders of Vermont, who had not endorsed Margaret Chase Smith's 1950 Declaration, introduced a resolution of censure. In December, the Senate voted, 67 to 32, to censure McCarthy for his behavior.

Joseph R. McCarthy was born in Grand Chute, Wisconsin, in 1908 to middle-class Roman Catholic parents. He graduated from Marquette University and entered the legal profession in Wisconsin in 1935. Originally a Democrat, he won his first political race (for a local judgeship) as a Republican in 1939. After serving as a Marine from 1942 to 1944, he became a state Republican power with his defeat of LaFollette in the 1946 senatorial race. McCarthy's strongest bases of support were Wisconsin's small business owners and voters of German heritage; they reelected him in 1952 and largely continued their support even after his fall from national popularity. He died at the Bethesda Naval Hospital in Maryland in 1957.

Margaret Chase was born in 1897 in Skowhegan, Maine, where, after graduating from high school, she taught school, worked for the telephone company, and was circulation manager for a local newspaper. In 1930 she married Clyde Harold Smith, who served in Congress from 1936 to 1940. When he died in 1940, Margaret Chase Smith was elected to fill his seat, and in 1949 she became the first woman ever elected to the U.S. Senate. Following her 1950 "Declaration of Conscience," she became a target of the McCarthyites, who in 1954 ran a "proxy" candidate against her in the Maine Republican primary. Smith won by a five-to-one margin and later lodged a successful million-dollar lawsuit against two reporters who had labeled her a Communist. Liberal on race and civil liberties issues, conservative in foreign policy, Smith was one of the most senior members of the U.S. Senate and the ranking Republican on the Armed Services Committee when she finally lost a reelection bid in 1972 at age 75.

Questions to Consider. Why did McCarthy launch his attack in 1950 rather than in 1949 or 1951? What area of the world most concerned him and what had happened there to give his message impact? Why did he attack from an out-of-the-way place (Wheeling, West Virginia) rather than from Washington or even his home state, Wisconsin, and why, moreover, on the radio? What reasons might McCarthy have had for singling out the State Department for attack, rather than, for example, the Department of Defense or the Department of Justice? In view of the fact that seven twentieth-century presidents and even more secretaries of state had attended just four private colleges (Yale, Harvard, Princeton, and Amherst) was there a certain logic in men such as McCarthy trying to link a Communist conspiracy with a conspiracy of "those who have had all the benefits"?

Margaret Chase Smith's Declaration began with a reference to "national suicide" and ineffectual legislative and executive leadership. Why did Smith begin a speech designed to thwart a Republican senator in this way? How did Smith define "Americanism"? Would most Americans have agreed with her in 1950? Why was it considered courageous for Smith to oppose the political tactics of "Fear, Ignorance, Bigotry, and Smear"? Did Smith believe that Communists might in fact be in the federal government? Did she believe they should remain there if discovered? What two reasons did she give for opposing McCarthy?

◆

Lincoln Day Address (1950)

JOSEPH R. MCCARTHY

Ladies and gentlemen, tonight as we celebrate the one hundred and forty-first birthday of one of the greatest men in American history, I would like to be able to talk about what a glorious day today is in the history of the world. As we celebrate the birth of this man who with his whole heart and soul hated war, I would like to be able to speak of peace in our time, of war being outlawed, and of worldwide disarmament. These would be truly appropriate things to be able to mention as we celebrate the birthday of Abraham Lincoln.

Five years after a world war has been won, men's hearts should anticipate a long peace, and men's minds should be free from the heavy weight that comes with war. But this is not such a period—for this is not a period of peace. This is a time of the "cold war." This is a time when all the world is split into two vast, increasingly hostile armed camps—a time of a great armaments race.

Today we are engaged in a final, all-out battle between Communistic atheism and Christianity. The modern champions of Communism have selected this as the time. And, ladies and gentlemen, the chips are down—they are truly down.

Six years ago, at the time of the first conference to map out the peace—Dumbarton Oaks—there was within the Soviet orbit 180 million people. Lined up on the antitotalitarian side there were in the world roughly 1,625 million people. Today, only six years later, there are 800 million people under the absolute domination of soviet Russia—an increase of over 400 percent. On our side, the figure has shrunk to around 500 million. In other words, in less than six years the odds have changed from 9 to 1 in our favor to 8 to 5 against us. This indicates the swiftness of the tempo of Communist victories and American defeats in the cold war. As one of our outstanding historical figures once said, "When a great democracy is destroyed, it will not be because of enemies from without, but rather because of enemies from within."

The truth of this statement is becoming terrifyingly clear as we see this country each day losing on every front. . . .

The reason why we find ourselves in a position of impotency is not because our only powerful potential enemy has sent men to invade our shores, but rather because of the traitorous actions of those who have been treated so well by this Nation. It has not been the less fortunate or members

From *The Congressional Record*, 81st Congress, v. 96, part 2 (February 20, 1950).

of minority groups who have been selling this Nation out, but rather those who have had all the benefits that the wealthiest nation on earth has had to offer—the finest homes, the finest college education, and the finest jobs in Government we can give.

This is glaringly true in the State Department. There the bright young men who are born with silver spoons in their mouths are the ones who have been worst. . . .

When Chiang Kai-shek was fighting our war, the State Department had in China a young man named John S. Service. His task, obviously, was not to work for the Communization of China. Strangely, however, he sent official reports back to the State Department urging that we torpedo our ally Chiang Kai-shek and stating, in effect, that Communism was the best hope for China.

Later, this man—John Service—was picked up by the Federal Bureau of Investigation for turning over to the Communists secret State Department information. Strangely, however, he was never prosecuted. However, Joseph Grew, the Under Secretary of State, who insisted on his prosecution, was forced to resign. Two days after Grew's successor, Dean Acheson, took over as Under Secretary of State, this man—John Service— who had been picked up by the FBI and who had previously urged that Communism was the best hope of China, was not only reinstated in the State Department but promoted. And finally, under Acheson, placed in charge of all placements and promotions.

Today, ladies and gentlemen, this man Service is on his way to represent the State Department and Acheson in Calcutta—by far and away the most important listening post in the Far East. . . .

This, ladies and gentlemen, gives you somewhat of a picture of the type of individuals who have been helping to shape our foreign policy. In my opinion the State Department, which is one of the most important government departments, is thoroughly infested with Communists.

I have in my hand 57 cases of individuals who would appear to be either card carrying members or certainly loyal to the Communist Party, but who nevertheless are still helping to shape our foreign policy.

One thing to remember in discussing the Communists in our Government is that we are not dealing with spies who get 30 pieces of silver to steal the blueprints of a new weapon. We are dealing with a far more sinister type of activity because it permits the enemy to guide and shape our policy. . . .

As you hear this story of high treason, I know that you are saying to yourself, "Well, why doesn't the Congress do something about it?" Actually, ladies and gentlemen, one of the important reasons for the graft, the corruption, the dishonesty, the disloyalty, the treason in high Government positions—one of the most important reasons why this continues is a lack of moral uprising on the part of the 140 million American people. In the light of history, however, this is not hard to explain.

It is the result of an emotional hangover and a temporary moral lapse which follows every war. It is the apathy to evil which people who have been subjected to the tremendous evils of war feel. As the people of the world see mass murder, the destruction of defenseless and innocent people, and all of the crime and lack of morals which go with war, they become numb and apathetic. It has always been thus after war.

However, the morals of our people have not been destroyed. They still exist. This cloak of numbness and apathy has only needed a spark to rekindle them. Happily, this spark has finally been supplied.

As you know, very recently the Secretary of State [Dean Acheson] proclaimed his loyalty to a man [Alger Hiss] guilty of what has always been considered as the most abominable of all crimes—of being a traitor to the people who gave him a position of great trust. The Secretary of State in attempting to justify his continued devotion to the man who sold out the Christian world to the atheistic world, referred to Christ's Sermon on the Mount as a justification and reason therefor, and the reaction of the American people to this would have made the heart of Abraham Lincoln happy.

When this pompous diplomat in striped pants, with a phony British accent, proclaimed to the American people that Christ on the Mount endorsed Communism, high treason, and betrayal of a sacred trust, the blasphemy was so great that it awakened the dormant indignation of the American people.

He has lighted the spark which is resulting in a moral uprising and will end only when the whole sorry mess of twisted, warped thinkers are swept from the national scene so that we may have a new birth of national honesty and decency in Government.

◆

Declaration of Conscience (1950)

MARGARET CHASE SMITH

I would like to speak briefly and simply about a serious national condition. It is a national feeling of fear and frustration that could result in national suicide and the end of everything that we Americans hold dear. It is a condition that comes from the lack of effective leadership in either the Legislative Branch or the Executive Branch of our Government.

That leadership is so lacking that serious and responsible proposals are being made that national advisory commissions be appointed to provide such critically needed leadership. . . .

I speak as a Republican. I speak as a woman. I speak as a United States Senator. I speak as an American. . . .

I think that it is high time that we remembered that we have sworn to uphold and defend the Constitution. I think that it is high time that we remembered that the Constitution, as amended, speaks not only of the freedom of speech but also of trial by jury instead of trial by accusation. . . .

Those of us who shout the loudest about Americanism in making character assassinations are all too frequently those who, by our own words and acts, ignore some of the basic principles of Americanism:

The right to criticize;
The right to hold unpopular beliefs;
The right to protest;
The right of independent thought.

The exercise of these rights should not cost one single American citizen his reputation or his right to a livelihood nor should he be in danger of losing his reputation or livelihood merely because he happens to know someone who holds unpopular beliefs. Who of us doesn't? Otherwise none of us could call our souls our own. Otherwise thought control would have set in.

The American people are sick and tired of being afraid to speak their minds lest they be politically smeared as "Communists" or "Fascists" by their opponents. Freedom of speech is not what it used to be in America. It has been so abused by some that it is not exercised by others. . . .

Today our country is being psychologically divided by the confusion and the suspicions that are bred in the United States Senate to spread like cancerous tentacles of "know nothing, suspect everything" attitudes. Today we have a Democratic Administration that has developed a mania for loose spending and loose programs. History is repeating itself—and the

From *The New York Times* June 2, 1950.

Republican Party again has the opportunity to emerge as the champion of unity and prudence.

The record of the present Democratic Administration has provided us with sufficient campaign issues without the necessity of resorting to political smears. America is rapidly losing its position as leader of the world simply because the Democratic Administration has pitifully failed to provide effective leadership. . . .

Yet to displace it with a Republican regime embracing a philosophy that lacks political integrity or intellectual honesty would prove equally disastrous to this nation. The nation sorely needs a Republican victory. But I don't want to see the Republican Party ride to political victory on the Four Horsemen of Calumny—Fear, Ignorance, Bigotry, and Smear.

I doubt if the Republican Party could—simply because I don't believe the American people will uphold any political party that puts political exploitation above national interest. Surely we Republicans aren't that desperate for victory. . . .

As a United States Senator, I am not proud of the way in which the Senate has been made a publicity platform for irresponsible sensationalism. I am not proud of the reckless abandon in which unproved charges have been hurled from this side of the aisle. I am not proud of the obviously staged, undignified countercharges that have been attempted in retaliation from the other side of the aisle.

I don't like the way the Senate has been made a rendezvous for vilification, for selfish political gain at the sacrifice of individual reputations and national unity. I am not proud of the way we smear outsiders from the Floor of the Senate and hide behind the cloak of congressional immunity and still place ourselves beyond criticism on the Floor of the Senate.

As an American, I am shocked at the way Republicans and Democrats alike are playing directly into the Communist design of "confuse, divide, and conquer." As an American, I don't want a Democratic Administration "whitewash" or "cover-up" any more than I want a Republican smear or witch hunt.

As an American, I condemn a Republican "Fascist" just as much as I condemn a Democrat "Communist." I condemn a Democrat "Fascist" just as much as I condemn a Republican "Communist." They are equally dangerous to you and me and to our country. As an American, I want to see our nation recapture the strength and unity it once had when we fought the enemy instead of ourselves.

It is with these thoughts that I have drafted what I call a "Declaration of Conscience." I am gratified that [six Republican senators] have concurred in that declaration and have authorized me to announce their concurrence.

32

◆

A QUESTION OF COMMAND

In 1950 the cold war between the United States and the Soviet Union turned suddenly hot in Korea, a peninsula abutting China near Japan. Korea had been freed from Japanese rule at the end of World War II, divided at the 38th parallel, and occupied by Russian troops in the north and American troops in the south. The Russians installed a friendly regime in North Korea and then withdrew; the United Nations, at U.S. urging, did the same in South Korea. On June 25, 1950, North Korean armies suddenly crossed the 38th parallel and launched a full-scale invasion of South Korea. President Truman, seeing the hand of China and therefore of the Soviet Union behind this move, promptly committed American troops to the defense of South Korea. He won the backing of the United Nations for his action and announced American determination to support anticommunist governments throughout East Asia. The Korean War lasted from June 1950 until the armistice of July 1953. Under United Nations auspices, sixteen nations participated in the conflict against North Korea. South Korea remained independent, but the Korean War cost the United States $22 billion and 34,000 dead.

The Korean War also prompted a major reassertion of the constitutional primacy of civilian rule in the U.S. government. The United Nations commander in the Korean theater was General Douglas MacArthur, one of the greatest U.S. heroes of World War II and the American proconsul in charge of transforming postwar Japanese society. Against the advice of the American joint chiefs of staff, MacArthur launched a brilliant amphibious landing behind Communist lines. He then recaptured the capital city of Seoul and moved far enough into North Korea to reach the border with China.

MacArthur had gambled that China would not commit troops to the conflict; President Truman's advisers feared it would. MacArthur was wrong. Massive Chinese forces poured across the border, pushing U.N. forces back down the peninsula. Embarrassed, MacArthur publicly called for President Truman to order massive air strikes on China. The President, fearing a long and costly land war with China, refused the general's request and asked him not to argue U.S. policy in the newspapers. MacArthur again called for air attacks on China, took a swipe at the American doctrine of limited (non-nuclear and geographically restricted) war, and implied that Truman was practicing appeasement. President Truman had had enough: On April 10, 1951, he fired MacArthur for insubordination. On April 11 he gave the following radio address to the American public. MacArthur returned home to an enormous ticker-tape parade, an invitation to address a joint session of Congress, and a brief flirtation with Republican party kingpins. But Matthew Ridgway now commanded U.N. forces in Korea, Harry Truman was still president and commander in chief—and the long-established constitutional subordination of military to civilian authority again held firm.

Harry S Truman was born on a farm near Independence, Missouri, in 1884. After graduating from high school, he worked as a farmer and a bank clerk and, during World War I, saw action in France as a captain in the field artillery. On his return from the war he entered the clothing business and in 1922 went into politics. After serving as county judge and presiding judge of Jackson County, Missouri, he was elected senator in 1934 and served in the Senate until his election as vice-president in 1944. As a senator he supported Roosevelt's New Deal policies and won a national reputation as an enemy of favoritism and waste in defense spending. His presidency from 1945 to 1953 was characterized by futile efforts to ram progressive Fair Deal legislation through a conservative Congress and, increasingly, by an anticommunist domestic and foreign policy. He is popularly remembered for his integrity, combativeness, and sense of responsibility—"The buck," he said, "stops here." Truman never made a more politically risky decision than to fire Douglas MacArthur. He died at his home in Independence, Missouri, in 1972.

Questions to Consider. Americans of Truman's era, it has been said, had two overwhelming fears: Communism and war. How did Truman attempt to balance these two fears in his 1950 address? On which side did he finally come down most strongly? American policy makers of the 1950s have been accused of exaggerating the scope and unity of international Communism. Did Truman fall into this habit? Did the confrontation with MacArthur perhaps drive Truman to overcompensate? Truman's action preserved the primacy of civilian control of war policy; why did he not defend his actions on these grounds?

Address on Korea and MacArthur (1951)

HARRY S TRUMAN

In the simplest terms, what we are doing in Korea is this:

We are trying to prevent a third world war.

I think most people in this country recognized that fact last June. And they warmly supported the decision of the Government to help the Republic of Korea against the Communist aggressors. Now, many persons, even some who applauded our decision to defend Korea, have forgotten the basic reason for our action. . . .

The aggression against Korea is the boldest and most dangerous move the Communists have yet made.

The attack on Korea was part of a greater plan for conquering all of Asia. . . .

They want to control all Asia from the Kremlin.

This plan of conquest is in flat contradiction to what we believe. We believe that Korea belongs to the Koreans. We believe that India belongs to the Indians. We believe that all the nations of Asia should be free to work out their affairs in their own way. This is the basis of peace in the Far East and it is the basis of peace everywhere else.

The whole Communist imperialism is back of the attack on peace in the Far East. It was the Soviet Union that trained and equipped the North Koreans for aggression. The Chinese Communists massed forty-four well-trained and well-equipped divisions on the Korean frontier. These were the troops they threw into battle when the North Korean Communists were beaten.

The question we have had to face is whether the Communist plan of conquest can be stopped without general war. Our Government and other countries associated with us in the United Nations believe that the best chance of stopping it without general war is to meet the attack in Korea and defeat it there.

That is what we have been doing. It is a difficult and bitter task.

But so far it has been successful.

So far, we have prevented World War III.

So far, by fighting a limited war in Korea, we have prevented aggression from succeeding, and bringing on a general war. And the ability of the whole free world to resist Communist aggression has been greatly improved. . . .

From *The New York Times*, April 12, 1951.

General Douglas MacArthur. On June 29, 1950, the American government ordered combat troops into Korea under the command of General MacArthur. Three months later, MacArthur's forces engineered a brilliant landing behind North Korean lines and quickly overran the northern half of the country. This position proved untenable because, contrary to MacArthur's prediction, Chinese troops entered the war and pushed the Americans far into the south—one of the the longest retreats in U.S. history. Here MacArthur, left, receives a decoration from President Harry S Truman—who would soon strip him of his command for insubordination. (UPI/Bettmann Newsphoto)

We do not want to see the conflict in Korea extended. We are trying to prevent a world war—not to start one. The best way to do that is to make it plain that we and the other free countries will continue to resist the attack.

But you may ask why can't we take other steps to punish the aggressor. Why don't we bomb Manchuria and China itself? Why don't we assist Chinese Nationalist troops to land on the mainland of China?

If we were to do these things we would be running a very grave risk of starting a general war. If that were to happen, we would have brought about the exact situation we are trying to prevent.

If we were to do these things, we would become entangled in a vast conflict on the continent of Asia and our task would become immeasurably more difficult all over the world.

What would suit the ambitions of the Kremlin better than for our military forces to be committed to a full-scale war with Red China?

It may well be that, in spite of our best efforts, the Communists may spread the war. But it would be wrong—tragically wrong—for us to take the initiative in extending the war.

The dangers are great. Make no mistake about it. Behind the North Koreans and Chinese Communists in the front lines stand additional millions of Chinese soldiers. And behind the Chinese stand the tanks, the planes, the submarines, the soldiers, and the scheming rulers of the Soviet Union.

Our aim is to avoid the spread of the conflict. . . .

If the Communist authorities realize that they cannot defeat us in Korea, if they realize it would be foolhardy to widen the hostilities beyond Korea, then they may recognize the folly of continuing their aggression. A peaceful settlement may then be possible. The door is always open.

Then we may achieve a settlement in Korea which will not compromise the principles and purposes of the United Nations.

I have thought long and hard about this question of extending the war in Asia. I have discussed it many times with the ablest military advisers in the country. I believe with all my heart that the course we are following is the best course.

I believe that we must try to limit the war to Korea for these vital reasons: To make sure that the precious lives of our fighting men are not wasted, to see that the security of our country and the free world is not needlessly jeopardized, and to prevent a third world war.

A number of events have made it evident that General MacArthur did not agree with that policy. I have, therefore, considered it essential to relieve General MacArthur so that there would be no doubt or confusion as to the real purpose and aim of our policy.

It was with the deepest personal regret that I found myself compelled to take this action. General MacArthur is one of our greatest military commanders. But the cause of world peace is more important than any individual.

The change in commands in the Far East means no change whatever in the policy of the United States. We will carry on the fight in Korea with vigor and determination in an effort to bring the war to a speedy and successful conclusion. . . .

Real peace can be achieved through a settlement based on the following factors:

One: The fighting must stop.

Two: Concrete steps must be taken to insure that the fighting will not break out again.

Three: There must be an end to the aggression.

A settlement founded upon these elements would open the way for the unification of Korea and the withdrawal of all foreign forces.

33

♦

THE MILITARY-INDUSTRIAL COMPLEX

During Dwight D. Eisenhower's eight years as president, the United States ended the Korean War and moved to replace expensive conventional armaments with "cheap" nuclear weapons. Moreover, though the Eisenhower administration landed troops briefly in Lebanon, sent military aid to Indochina, and helped overthrow radical governments in Iran and Guatemala, the United States managed to stay out of war in other parts of the world. There was intense cold war. But there was also peace.

Despite all the years of peace under Eisenhower, the United States in 1960 still kept 2,500,000 military personnel on active duty, poured $51 billion into the defense budget—10 percent of the entire gross national product—and threw every scientific resource into creating sophisticated weapons systems. So striking was this development that President Eisenhower, himself a former general and a probusiness Republican, felt compelled in his 1961 farewell address to warn the public against the rise of a "military-industrial complex" in the land. Since military spending never in fact receded after Eisenhower, the concept and the phrase entered permanently into the political vocabulary, thus becoming somewhat ironic Eisenhower legacies to the people.

Born in Texas in 1890, Dwight D. Eisenhower grew up in Kansas in modest circumstances. A West Point graduate of 1915, he served at various army posts in the United States and Asia and under General Douglas MacArthur during the 1930s; his abilities were also perceived by General George Marshall, and he won promotion to brigadier general in 1941. Commander of the Allied forces in western Europe, he oversaw Allied invasions of North Africa, Italy, and France during World War II, demonstrating impressive diplomatic and administrative skills, and returned to America in late 1945 as a five-star general and a vastly popular hero. It was largely these skills and this reputation, plus his disarming grin and the irresistible slogan "I like Ike," that propelled him to landslide presidential victories in 1952 and 1956. After 1961, Eisenhower eased quickly into retirement and discovered that, much like his nemesis Harry Truman, he had become one of America's beloved political figures. He died in Washington, D.C., in 1969.

Questions to Consider. Two aspects of President Eisenhower's striking address deserve special attention. First, Eisenhower was warning not only against the influence of the military and the arms industry, as represented by huge military budgets, but also against the rise of a scientific-technological elite, as symbolized by the growing control of scholarship by Washington. Of these two tendencies, which did he seem to see as the greater threat? Second, although Eisenhower said plainly that these forces—the military-industrial and the scientific-technological—represented a danger to our liberties and democratic processes, he was vague about how exactly the forces did endanger them and especially about what might, in a concrete way, be done to prevent such threats. Was Eisenhower, a former general, perhaps tacitly urging that soldiers and defense contractors be restricted in their political activities—in campaign contributions, for example, or lobbying efforts—or that defense budgets be scrutinized and slimmed down with special rigor? How realistic were these hints? What connection, if any, was he making at the end of his speech between disarmament and democracy?

————————◆————————

Farewell Address (1961)

DWIGHT D. EISENHOWER

A vital element in keeping the peace is our military establishment. Our arms must be mighty, ready for instant action, so that no potential aggressor may be tempted to risk his own destruction.

Our military organization today bears little relation to that known by any of my predecessors in peacetime, or indeed by the fighting men of World War II or Korea.

Until the latest of our world conflicts, the United States had no armaments industry. American makers of plowshares could, with time and as required, make swords as well. But now we can no longer risk emergency improvisation of national defense; we have been compelled to create a permanent armaments industry of vast proportions. Added to this, three and a half million men and women are directly engaged in the defense establishment. We annually spend on military security more than the net income of all United States corporations.

This conjunction of an immense military establishment and a large arms industry is new in the American experience. The total influence—economic, political, even spiritual—is felt in every city, every statehouse, every office of the federal government. We recognize the imperative need for

From *The New York Times*, January 18, 1961.

this development. Yet we must not fail to comprehend its grave implications. Our toil, resources, and livelihood are all involved; so is the very structure of our society.

In the councils of government, we must guard against the acquisition of unwarranted influence, whether sought or unsought, by the military-industrial complex. The potential for the disastrous rise of misplaced power exists and will persist.

We must never let the weight of this combination endanger our liberties or democratic processes. We should take nothing for granted. Only an alert and knowledgeable citizenry can compel the proper meshing of the huge industrial and military machinery of defense with our peaceful methods and goals, so that security and liberty may prosper together.

Akin to, and largely responsible for the sweeping changes in our industrial-military posture, has been the technological revolution during recent decades.

In this revolution, research has become central; it also becomes more formalized, complex, and costly. A steadily increasing share is conducted for, by, or at the discretion of, the federal government. . . .

The prospect of domination of the nation's scholars by federal employment, project allocations, and the power of money is ever present—and is gravely to be regarded.

Yet, in holding scientific research and discovery in respect, as we should, we must also be alert to the equal and opposite danger that public policy could itself become the captive of a scientific-technological elite.

It is the task of statesmanship to mold, to balance, and to integrate these and other forces, new and old, within the principles of our democratic system—ever aiming toward the supreme goals of our free society.

Another factor in maintaining balance involves the element of time. As we peer into society's future, we—you and I, and our government—must avoid the impulse to live only for today, plundering, for our own ease and convenience, the precious resources of tomorrow. We cannot mortgage the material assets of our grandchildren without risking the loss also of their political and spiritual heritage. We want democracy to survive for all generations to come, not to become the insolvent phantom of tomorrow.

Down the long lane of the history yet to be written America knows that this world of ours, ever growing smaller, must avoid becoming a community of dreadful fear and hate, and be, instead, a proud confederation of mutual trust and respect.

Such a confederation must be one of equals. The weakest must come to the conference table with the same confidence as do we, protected as we are by our moral, economic, and military strength. That table, though scarred by many past frustrations, cannot be abandoned for the certain agony of the battlefield.

Disarmament, with mutual honor and confidence, is a continuing imperative. Together we must learn how to compose differences, not with arms, but with intellect and decent purpose. Because this need is so sharp and apparent I confess that I lay down my official responsibilities in this field with a definite sense of disappointment. As one who has witnessed the horror and the lingering sadness of war—as one who knows that another war could utterly destroy this civilization which has been so slowly and painfully built over thousands of years—I wish I could say tonight that a lasting peace is in sight.

Happily, I can say that war has been avoided. Steady progress toward our ultimate goal has been made. But, so much remains to be done. As a private citizen, I shall never cease to do what little I can to help the world advance along that road. . . .

34

◆
_____

THE DEFENSE OF FREEDOM

Although the New Frontier of President John F. Kennedy had a significant domestic component centering on civil rights and social welfare programs, Kennedy's primary emphasis, as his inaugural address,
reprinted below, makes clear, was on the development of a vigorous
foreign policy. Kennedy perceived the Soviet threat in much the same
way that Richard M. Nixon, his Republican opponent, had perceived
it during the 1960 presidential campaign: as ubiquitous and unremitting and therefore to be countered at every turn. But Kennedy's views
held significant differences from the policy pursued by the Eisenhower
administration.

Kennedy was more willing than Eisenhower to increase defense
spending; he was also more skeptical about the value of responding
to revolutions in the Third World by threatening thermonuclear war.
Departing from the policies of his predecessor, Kennedy moved toward
a doctrine of "flexible response" that stressed conventional forces over
atomic weapons and emphasized international propaganda and public
relations over armaments. At once idealistic and demanding, like the
1961 inaugural address itself, Kennedy's views led to the signing of
treaties with the Soviet Union that banned atmospheric nuclear testing
and to the establishment of emergency communications between the
White House and the Kremlin. But these same views also led to the
sending of more and more military personnel to South Vietnam, to
prevent Ho Chi Minh, the Communist leader of North Vietnam, from
unifying Vietnam under his rule.

John F. Kennedy was born in 1917 to a wealthy Irish-American
family. After graduating with honors from Harvard in 1940, he served
for a time as secretary to his father, who was then U.S. ambassador
to Great Britain. _Why England Slept_—his best-selling book on British
military policies during the 1930s—was published in 1940. During
World War II he served in the U.S. Navy and won the Navy and
Marine Corps Medal for his heroism. After the war he entered politics
in Massachusetts, winning election to the House of Representatives in
1946 and to the Senate in 1952. His book _Profiles in Courage_, published in 1956, won the Pulitzer Prize, and in 1960 he narrowly bested
Richard Nixon in a contest for the presidency. The youngest man and

the only Roman Catholic ever elected president, Kennedy projected an image of intelligence, vitality, and sophistication. Worldwide mourning occurred after he was assassinated in Dallas, Texas, on November 22, 1963.

Questions to Consider. Some historians have argued that in this address Kennedy formally shifted the focus of the cold war from Europe to the nonaligned or economically underdeveloped part of the world. Do you agree or disagree? If you agree, do you also believe there was a connection between this shift and Kennedy's emphasis on feeding and clothing the world—on winning by doing good? Was there also a connection between this shift and Kennedy's preference for invoking human rights instead of democracy? Historians have also read the address as an unprecedented fusion of "adversarialism" with "universalism." Again, do you agree or disagree? Was this fusion connected with Kennedy's sense of facing an "hour of maximum danger" in which Americans might have to "pay any price" for liberty?

◆

Inaugural Address (1961)

JOHN F. KENNEDY

We observe today not a victory of party but a celebration of freedom—symbolizing an end as well as a beginning—signifying renewal as well as change. For I have sworn before you and Almighty God the same solemn oath our forbears prescribed nearly a century and three-quarters ago.

The world is very different now. For man holds in his mortal hands the power to abolish all forms of human poverty and all forms of human life. And yet the same revolutionary beliefs for which our forbears fought are still at issue around the globe—the belief that the rights of man come not from the generosity of the state but from the hand of God.

We dare not forget today that we are the heirs of that first revolution. Let the word go forth from this time and place, to friend and foe alike, that the torch has been passed to a new generation of Americans—born in this century, tempered by war, disciplined by a hard and bitter peace, proud of our ancient heritage—and unwilling to witness or permit the slow undoing of those human rights to which this nation has always been committed, and to which we are committed today at home and around the world.

From *The New York Times,* January 21, 1961.

John F. Kennedy. Kennedy, with his wife Jacqueline sitting at his side, during the presidential inauguration, 1961. (© 1960 Paul Schutzer/LIFE Magazine, Time-Warner, Inc.)

Let every nation know, whether it wishes us well or ill, that we shall pay any price, bear any burden, meet any hardship, support any friend, oppose any foe to assure the survival and the success of liberty.

This much we pledge—and more.

To those old allies whose cultural and spiritual origins we share, we pledge the loyalty of faithful friends. United, there is little we cannot do in a host of co-operative ventures. Divided, there is little we can do—for we dare not meet a powerful challenge at odds and split asunder.

To those new states whom we welcome to the ranks of the free, we pledge our word that one form of colonial control shall not have passed away merely to be replaced by a far more iron tyranny. We shall not always expect to find them supporting our view. But we shall always hope to find them strongly supporting their own freedom—and to remember that, in the past, those who foolishly sought power by riding the back of the tiger ended up inside.

To those people in the huts and villages of half the globe struggling to break the bonds of mass misery, we pledge our best efforts to help them help themselves, for whatever period is required—not because the Communists may be doing it, not because we seek their votes, but because it is right. If a free society cannot help the many who are poor, it cannot save the few who are rich.

To our sister republics south of our border, we offer a special pledge—to convert our good words into good deeds—in a new alliance for progress—to assist free men and free governments in casting off the chains of poverty. But this peaceful revolution of hope cannot become the prey of hostile powers. Let all our neighbors know that we shall join with them to oppose aggression or subversion anywhere in the Americas. And let every other power know that this hemisphere intends to remain the master of its own house.

To that world assembly of sovereign states, the United Nations, our last best hope in an age where the instruments of war have far outpaced the instruments of peace, we renew our pledge of support—to prevent it from becoming merely a forum for invective—to strengthen its shield of the new and the weak—and to enlarge the area in which its writ may run.

Finally, to those nations who would make themselves our adversary, we offer not a pledge but a request: that both sides begin anew the quest for peace, before the dark powers of destruction unleashed by science engulf all humanity in planned or accidental self-destruction.

We dare not tempt them with weakness. For only when our arms are sufficient beyond doubt can we be certain beyond doubt that they will never be employed.

But neither can two great and powerful groups of nations take comfort from our present course—both sides overburdened by the cost of modern weapons, both rigidly alarmed by the steady spread of the deadly atom, yet both racing to alter that uncertain balance of terror that stays the hand of mankind's final war.

So let us begin anew—remembering on both sides that civility is not a sign of weakness, and sincerity is always subject to proof. Let us never negotiate out of fear. But let us never fear to negotiate.

Let both sides explore what problems unite us instead of belaboring those problems which divide us.

Let both sides, for the first time, formulate serious and precise proposals for the inspection and control of arms—and bring the absolute power to destroy other nations under the absolute control of all nations.

Let both sides seek to invoke the wonders of science instead of its terror. Together let us explore the stars, conquer the deserts, eradicate disease, tap the ocean depths, and encourage the arts and commerce.

Let both sides unite to heed in all corners of the earth the command of Isaiah—to "undo the heavy burdens . . . [and] let the oppressed go free."

And if a beachhead of co-operation may push back the jungle of suspicion, let both sides join in creating a new endeavor, not a new balance of power, but a new world of law, where the strong are just and the weak secure and the peace preserved.

All this will not be finished in the first one hundred days. Nor will it be finished in the first one thousand days, nor in the life of this administration, nor even perhaps in our lifetime on this planet. But let us begin.

In your hands, my fellow citizens, more than mine, will rest the final success or failure of our course. Since this country was founded, each generation of Americans has been summoned to give testimony to its national loyalty. The graves of young Americans who answered the call to service surround the globe.

Now the trumpet summons us again—not as a call to bear arms, though arms we need—not as a call to battle, though embattled we are—but a call to bear the burden of a long twilight struggle, year in and year out, "rejoicing in hope, patient in tribulation"—a struggle against the common enemies of man: tyranny, poverty, disease, and war itself.

Can we forge against these enemies a grand and global alliance, North and South, East and West, that can assure a more fruitful life for all mankind? Will you join in that historic effort?

In the long history of the world, only a few generations have been granted the role of defending freedom in its hour of maximum danger. I do not shrink from this responsibility—I welcome it. I do not believe that any of us would exchange places with any other people or any other generation. The energy, the faith, the devotion which we bring to this endeavor will light our country and all who serve it—and the glow from that fire can truly light the world.

And so, my fellow Americans: ask not what your country can do for you—ask what you can do for your country.

My fellow citizens of the world: ask not what America will do for you, but what together we can do for the freedom of man.

Finally, whether you are citizens of America or citizens of the world, ask of us here the same high standards of strength and sacrifice which we ask of you. With a good conscience our only sure reward, with history the final judge of deeds, let us go forth to lead the land we love, asking His blessing and His help, but knowing that here on earth God's work must truly be our own.

35

◆

BLANK CHECK

American involvement in Vietnam began modestly enough with a promise in 1945 to help France restore colonial rule there. The United States backed France because Ho Chi Minh, the leader of the struggle for Vietnamese independence, was a Communist. American policy makers were more impressed by Ho's Communism than by his nationalism; they viewed him as a tool of the Kremlin, although he had the backing of many non-Communists in Indochina who wanted freedom from French control. In 1954, Ho's forces defeated the French, and the French decided to withdraw from Vietnam. At this point the United States stepped in, backed a partition of Vietnam, and gave aid to the South Vietnamese government in Saigon. American policy continued to be based on the belief that Communism in Vietnam was inspired by China or the Soviet Union, if not both. If Vietnam went Communist, Washington warned, other countries in Asia might topple like so many dominoes, and Communist influence in the world would grow at the expense of America's.

U.S. military personnel entered the Vietnamese conflict between North and South under presidents Eisenhower and Kennedy. American bombers began raiding North Vietnam in 1965, after the reelection of Kennedy's successor, Lyndon B. Johnson. By 1969, American troops in South Vietnam numbered around 550,000, and American planes had dropped more bombs in Vietnam than had been dropped on Germany and Japan during World War II. Yet the Vietcong (the South Vietnamese insurgents), aided by North Vietnamese military units, seemed stronger than ever. International opinion had now turned against the United States.

A key episode in Lyndon Johnson's escalation came with the so-called Tonkin Gulf incident. On August 2, 1964, the U.S.S. *Maddox,* an American destroyer supporting South Vietnamese commando raids against North Vietnam, came under attack by enemy patrol boats. The attackers suffered heavy damage; the *Maddox* was unharmed. Two days later the *Maddox* and another U.S. destroyer again moved into North Vietnamese waters. Although the weather was bad, sonar equipment indicated enemy torpedoes. When the captain of the *Maddox* later questioned members of his crew, no one could recall any enemy attacks, and subsequent investigations of the incident likewise turned up no evidence of hostile fire. The American destroyers nevertheless reportedly leveled heavy fire against North Vietnamese patrol boats. President Johnson, despite the questionable evidence and without admitting that U.S. ships were supporting raids against the North, ordered air strikes on North Vietnamese naval bases and announced on television that he was retaliating for "unprovoked" attacks. U.S. planes would now, he said, bomb North Vietnam.

On August 5, Johnson, in the address excerpted below, asked Congress to give him authority to repel "any armed attack against the forces of the United States and to prevent further aggression." The resolution passed the House by 466 to 0 and passed the Senate by 88 to 2. The resolution, as Johnson eventually argued, was tantamount to a declaration of war—which Congress has not voted against any country since December 1941. Under its auspices, the president authorized not only the carpet-bombing of North Vietnam but the American build-up to over a half-million combat troops. Its effect in 1964 was to preempt criticism from Republican presidential candidate Barry Goldwater, a hawk on foreign policy, help raise Johnson's approval rating in the polls from 42 percent to 72 percent, and contribute to a major victory in that fall's election.

Born in the poor hill country of central Texas in 1908, Lyndon Johnson worked his way through Southwest Texas State Teachers College in San Marcos and went to Washington as assistant to a local congressman in 1931. An intensely ambitious and ardent New Deal Democrat, Johnson began his political career with his election to fill a congressional vacancy in 1937. He was elected to the U.S. Senate in 1948. Unmatched at arranging the compromises and distributing the favors and money on which congressional politics rested, he became Senate minority leader in 1953 and majority leader in 1955, when the Democrats regained control of the Senate. As the vice-presidential nominee in 1960, he helped John F. Kennedy carry enough Southern states to become president; he became president himself upon Kennedy's assassination in 1963. As president, Johnson helped enact the most sweeping civil rights legislation of the century, but he also dramatically escalated a fundamentally unpopular war. Faced with widespread opposition to his policies, he declined to run for reelection in 1968. He died in San Antonio in 1973.

Questions to Consider. On what grounds did Johnson defend the American presence in Vietnam? How did he deal with the problematic nature of the evidence of North Vietnamese attacks on U.S. ships? Johnson wanted authorization not only for limited retaliation over this specific incident but to attack North Vietnam on a large scale over a long period of time. How did he move in this address from the par-

ticular incident to the general goal? What parts of the speech might
have been especially effective in undercutting Barry Goldwater's criticism of the Democrats as "soft on Communism"? Was Johnson demanding, in effect, a declaration of war? If so, why didn't he ask for
that?

◆

Message to Congress on the Gulf of Tonkin (1964)

LYNDON B. JOHNSON

Last night I announced to the American people that the North Vietnamese
regime had conducted further deliberate attacks against U.S. naval vessels
operating in international waters, and that I had therefore directed air action
against gun boats and supporting facilities used in these hostile operations.
This air action has now been carried out with substantial damage to the
boats and facilities. Two U.S. aircraft were lost in the action.

After consultation with the leaders of both parties in the Congress, I
further announced a decision to ask the Congress for a Resolution expressing the unity and determination of the United States in supporting
freedom and in protecting peace in Southeast Asia.

These latest actions of the North Vietnamese regime have given a new
and grave turn to the already serious situation in Southeast Asia. Our
commitments in that area are well known to the Congress. They were first
made in 1954 by President Eisenhower. They were further defined in the
Southeast Asia Collective Defense Treaty approved by the Senate in February 1955.

This Treaty with its accompanying protocol obligates the United States
and other members to act in accordance with their Constitutional processes
to meet Communist aggression against any of the parties or protocol states.

Our policy in Southeast Asia has been consistent and unchanged since
1954. I summarized it on June 2 in four simple propositions:

1. *America keeps her word.* Here as elsewhere, we must and shall honor
our commitments.

2. *The issue is the future of Southeast Asia as a whole.* A threat to any nation
in that region is a threat to all, and a threat to us.

3. *Our purpose is peace.* We have no military, political or territorial ambitions in the area.

4. *This is not just a jungle war, but a struggle for freedom on every front of
human activity.* Our military and economic assistance to South Vietnam and

From *The New York Times,* August 6, 1964.

Laos in particular has the purpose of helping these countries to repel aggression and strengthen their independence.

The threat to the free nations of Southeast Asia has long been clear. The North Vietnamese regime has constantly sought to take over South Vietnam and Laos. This Communist regime has violated the Geneva Accords for Vietnam. It has systematically conducted a campaign of subversion, which includes the direction, training, and supply of personnel and arms for the conduct of guerrilla warfare in South Vietnamese territory. In Laos, the North Vietnamese regime has maintained military forces, used Laotian territory for infiltration into South Vietnam, and most recently carried out combat operations—all in direct violation of the Geneva Agreements of 1962.

In recent months, the actions of the North Vietnamese regime have become steadily more threatening. In May, following new acts of Communist aggression in Laos, the United States undertook reconnaissance flights over Laotian territory, at the request of the Government of Laos. These flights had the essential mission of determining the situation in territory where Communist forces were preventing inspection by the International Control Commission. When the Communists attacked these aircraft, I responded by furnishing escort fighters with instructions to fire when fired upon. Thus, these latest North Vietnamese attacks on our naval vessels are not the first direct attack on armed forces of the United States.

As President of the United States I have concluded that I should now ask the Congress, on its part, to join in affirming the national determination that all such attacks will be met, and that the U.S. will continue in its basic policy of assisting the free nations of the area to defend their freedom.

As I have repeatedly made clear, the United States intends no rashness, and seeks no wider war. We must make it clear to all that the United States is united in its determination to bring about the end of Communist subversion and aggression in the area. We seek the full and effective restoration of the international agreements signed in Geneva in 1954, with respect to South Vietnam, and again in Geneva in 1962, with respect to Laos.

I recommend a Resolution expressing the support of the Congress for all necessary action to protect our armed forces and to assist nations covered by the SEATO Treaty. At the same time, I assure the Congress that we shall continue readily to explore any avenues of political solution that will effectively guarantee the removal of Communist subversion and the preservation of the independence of the nations of the area.

The Resolution could well be based upon similar resolutions enacted by the Congress in the past—to meet the threat to Formosa in 1955, to meet the threat to the Middle East in 1957, and to meet the threat in Cuba in 1962. It could state in the simplest terms the resolve and support of the Congress for action to deal appropriately with attacks against our armed forces and to defend freedom and preserve peace in southeast Asia in accordance with the obligations of the United States under the southeast Asia Treaty. I urge the Congress to enact such a Resolution promptly and thus to give convincing evidence to the aggressive Communist nations, and to the world as a whole, that our policy in southeast Asia will be carried forward—and that the peace and security of the area will be preserved.

The events of this week would in any event have made the passage of a Congressional Resolution essential. But there is an additional reason for doing so at a time when we are entering on three months of political campaigning. Hostile nations must understand that in such a period the United States will continue to protect its national interests, and that in these matters there is no division among us.

36

◆

AGONY IN ASIA

The escalation of American involvement in Vietnam provoked perhaps
the greatest wartime opposition in American history. By the end of
1965, the first draft card burnings had occurred. Students in major
universities throughout the country had organized "teach-ins" (named
after the civil rights "sit-ins") to discuss the nature of the war and had
held the first antiwar march on Washington. By 1967, protest rallies
were drawing hundreds of thousands, and evasion of the draft among
middle-class students was widespread. Some of the country's most
prominent leaders, including the Reverend Martin Luther King, Jr.,
were vehemently criticizing the Johnson administration for its Vietnam
policy. The speech reprinted below, which King delivered at Riverside
Church in New York City, stressed the links between international
violence and domestic violence, war spending and social poverty, and
the suppression of independence movements abroad and minority
aspirations at home.

Martin Luther King's stance had special force because of his stature
as an advocate of peace and human rights. Born in Atlanta, Georgia,
in 1929, the son of a Baptist clergyman, King entered college at the
age of fifteen. He eventually received a doctorate in theology from
Boston University. In 1954 he was called to the ministry of a church
in Montgomery, Alabama, and in 1955 he became a leader in the
successful effort to integrate the local bus system. Calling on this experience and on his philosophy of nonviolence, King was soon promoting demonstrations against segregation throughout the South. In
August 1963 he spoke to 250,000 people in the nation's capital on
behalf of black voting rights, the first so-called March on Washington
and a model for later antiwar protests. In 1964 he won the Nobel
Peace Prize. In April 1968, having broken with the Johnson administration over the Vietnam war and on the eve of a vast "Poor People's
Campaign" for economic justice, King was assassinated in Memphis,
Tennessee. The death of the apostle of nonviolence triggered massive
race riots in the nation's cities. His funeral attracted 150,000 mourners.
The inscription on his tombstone, taken from his 1963 Washington
speech, reads: "Free at Last, Free at Last, Thank God Almighty, I'm
Free at Last."

Questions to Consider. Of the seven reasons King gave for deciding to "break silence" over Vietnam, which—as measurable by the rank and emphasis he gave them and by his rhetorical style—seem to have mattered most to him? Note how King inveighed first against racial injustice, then against violence, and finally against both issues. Was he right to link the two so closely? Would any perceptive critic of injustice have done so, or did this reflect King's particular way of seeing things and his personal experience in the civil rights movement? Many historians believe this speech marked a sharp political shift by King away from the struggle for civil rights and toward a broader struggle for economic justice and social transformation. Is there evidence for this interpretation in the speech? Why do you suppose King waited until 1967 to launch a public attack on American policy in Vietnam? Why was he careful to call his silence, rather than his attack, a "betrayal"?

◆

A Time to Break Silence (1967)

MARTIN LUTHER KING, JR.

I come to this magnificent house of worship tonight because my conscience leaves me no other choice. I join with you in this meeting because I am in deepest agreement with the aims and work of the organization which has brought us together: Clergy and Laymen Concerned About Vietnam. The recent statement of your executive committee are the sentiments of my own heart and I found myself in full accord when I read its opening lines: "A time comes when silence is betrayal." That time has come for us in relation to Vietnam. . . .

Over the past two years, as I have moved to break the betrayal of my own silences and to speak from the burnings of my own heart, as I have called for radical departures from the destruction of Vietnam, many persons have questioned me about the wisdom of my path. At the heart of their concerns this query has often loomed large and loud: Why are you speaking about the war, Dr. King? Why are you joining the voices of dissent? Peace and civil rights don't mix, they say. Aren't you hurting the cause of your people, they ask? And when I hear them, though I often understand the source of their concern, I am nevertheless greatly saddened, for such questions mean that the inquirers have not really known me, my commitment or my calling. Indeed, their questions suggest that they do not know the world in which they live.

From *Freedomways* (Spring 1967), 103–117. Reprinted by permission of Joan Daves Agency.
Copyright © 1967 by Martin Luther King, Jr.

Wartime remembrance. Another soldier returns from Vietnam. (© 1969 Constantine Manos/Magnum Photos)

In the light of such tragic misunderstanding, I deem it of signal importance to try to state clearly, and I trust concisely, why I believe that the path from Dexter Avenue Baptist Church—the church in Montgomery, Alabama, where I began my pastorate—leads clearly to this sanctuary tonight. . . .

Since I am a preacher by trade, I suppose it is not surprising that I have seven major reasons for bringing Vietnam into the field of my moral vision. There is at the outset a very obvious and almost facile connection between the war in Vietnam and the struggle I, and others, have been waging in America. A few years ago there was a shining moment in that struggle. It seemed as if there was a real promise of hope for the poor—both black and white—through the Poverty Program. There were experiments, hopes, new beginnings. Then came the build-up in Vietnam and I watched the program broken and eviscerated as if it were some idle political plaything of a society gone mad on war, and I knew that America would never invest the necessary funds or energies in rehabilitation of its poor so long as adventures like Vietnam continued to draw men and skills and money like some demonic destructive suction tube. So I was increasingly compelled to see the war as an enemy of the poor and to attack it as such.

Perhaps the more tragic recognition of reality took place when it became clear to me that the war was doing far more than devastating the hopes of the poor at home. It was sending their sons and their brothers and their husbands to fight and to die in extraordinarily high proportions relative to the rest of the population. We were taking the black young men who had been crippled by our society and sending them 8,000 miles away to guarantee liberties in Southeast Asia which they had not found in Southwest Georgia and East Harlem. So we have been repeatedly faced with the cruel irony of watching negro and white boys on TV screens as they kill and die together for a nation that has been unable to seat them together in the same schools. So we watch them in brutal solidarity burning the huts of a poor village, but we realize that they would never live on the same block in Detroit. I could not be silent in the face of such cruel manipulation of the poor.

My third reason moves to an even deeper level of awareness, for it grows out of my experience in the ghettos of the north over the last three years—especially the last three summers. As I have walked among the desperate, rejected and angry young men I have told them that Molotov cocktails and rifles would not solve their problems. I have tried to offer them my deepest compassion while maintaining my conviction that social change comes most meaningfully through nonviolent action. But they asked—and rightly so—what about Vietnam? They asked if our own nation wasn't using massive doses of violence to solve its problems, to bring about the changes it wanted. Their questions hit home, and I knew that I could never again raise my voice against the violence of the oppressed in the ghettos without having first spoken clearly to the greatest purveyor of violence in the world today—my own government. For the sake of those boys, for the sake of this government, for the sake of the hundreds of thousands trembling under our violence, I cannot be silent.

For those who ask the question, "Aren't you a Civil Rights leader?" and thereby mean to exclude me from the movement for peace, I have this further answer. In 1957 when a group of us formed the Southern Christian Leadership Conference, we chose as our motto: "To save the soul of America." We were convinced that we could not limit our vision to certain rights for black people, but instead affirmed the conviction that America would never be free or saved from itself unless the descendants of its slaves were loosed completely from the shackles they still wear. In a way we were agreeing with Langston Hughes, that black bard of Harlem, who had written earlier:

> *O, yes*
> *I say it plain,*
> *America never was America to me,*
> *And yet I swear this oath—*
> *America will be!*[1]

Now, it should be incandescently clear that no one who has any concern for the integrity and life of America today can ignore the present war. If America's soul becomes totally poisoned, part of the autopsy must read Vietnam. It can never be saved so long as it destroys the deepest hopes of men the world over. So it is that those of us who are yet determined that America will be are led down the path of protest and dissent, working for the health of our land.

As if the weight of such a commitment to the life and health of America were not enough, another burden of responsibility was placed upon me in 1964; and I cannot forget that the Nobel Prize for Peace was also a commission—a commission to work harder than I had ever worked before for "the brotherhood of man." This is a calling that takes me beyond national allegiances, but even if it were not present I would yet have to live with the meaning of my commitment to the ministry of Jesus Christ. To me the relationship of this ministry to the making of peace is so obvious that I sometimes marvel at those who ask me why I am speaking against the war. Could it be that they do not know that the good news was meant for all men—for Communists and capitalists, for their children and ours, for black and for white, for revolutionary and conservative? Have they forgotten that my ministry is in obedience to the one who loved his enemies so fully that he died for them? What can I say to the "Viet Cong" or to Castro or to Mao as a faithful minister of this one? Can I threaten them with death or must I not share with them my life?

1. Reprinted by permission of Harold Ober Associates Incorporated. Copyright 1938 by Langston Hughes. Copyright renewed 1965 by Langston Hughes.

Finally, as I try to delineate for you and for myself the road that leads from Montgomery to this place I would have offered all that was most valid if I simply said that I must be true to my conviction that I share with all men the calling to be a son of the Living God. Beyond the calling of race or nation or creed is this vocation of sonship and brotherhood, and because I believe that the Father is deeply concerned especially for his suffering and helpless and outcast children, I come tonight to speak for them. . . .

And as I ponder the madness of Vietnam and search within myself for ways to understand and respond to compassion my mind goes constantly to the people of that peninsula. I speak now not of the soldiers of each side, not of the junta in Saigon, but simply of the people who have been living under the curse of war for almost three continuous decades now. I think of them too because it is clear to me that there will be no meaningful solution there until some attempt is made to know them and hear their broken cries. . . .

They languish under our bombs and consider us—not their fellow Vietnamese—the real enemy. They move sadly and apathetically as we herd them off the land of their fathers into concentration camps where minimal social needs are rarely met. They know they must move or be destroyed by our bombs. So they go—primarily women and children and the aged.

They watch as we poison their water, as we kill a million acres of their crops. They must weep as the bulldozers roar through their areas preparing to destroy the precious trees. They wander into the hospitals, with at least twenty casualties from American firepower for one "Viet Cong"-inflicted injury. So far we may have killed a million of them—mostly children. They wander into the towns and see thousands of the children, homeless, without clothes, running in packs on the streets like animals. They see the children degraded by our soldiers as they beg for food. They see the children selling their sisters to our soldiers, soliciting for their mothers.

What do the peasants think as we ally ourselves with the landlords and as we refuse to put any action into our many words concerning land reform? What do they think as we test out our latest weapons on them, just as the Germans tested out new medicine and new tortures in the concentration camps of Europe? Where are the roots of the independent Vietnam we claim to be building? Is it among these voiceless ones?

We have destroyed their two most cherished institutions: the family and the village. We have destroyed their land and their crops. We have co-operated in the crushing of the nation's only non-communist revolutionary political force—the unified Buddhist Church. We have supported the enemies of the peasants of Saigon. We have corrupted their women and children and killed their men. What liberators! . . .

At this point I should make it clear that while I have tried in these last few minutes to give a voice to the voiceless on Vietnam and to understand the arguments of those who are called enemy, I am as deeply concerned about our own troops there as anything else. For it occurs to me that what we are submitting them to in Vietnam is not simply the brutalizing process that goes on in any war where armies face each other and seek to destroy. We are adding cynicism to the process of death, for they must know after a short period there that none of the things we claim to be fighting for are really involved. Before long they must know that their government has sent them into a struggle among Vietnamese, and the more sophisticated surely realize that we are on the side of the wealthy and the secure while we create a hell for the poor.

Somehow this madness must cease. We must stop now. I speak as a child of God and brother to the suffering poor of Vietnam. I speak for those whose land is being laid waste, whose homes are being destroyed, whose culture is being subverted. I speak for the poor of America who are paying the double price of smashed hopes at home and death and corruption in Vietnam. I speak as a citizen of the world, for the world as it stands aghast at the path we have taken. I speak as an American to the leaders of my own nation. The great initiative in this war is ours. The initiative to stop it must be ours. . . .

In 1957 a sensitive American official overseas said that it seemed to him that our nation was on the wrong side of a world revolution. During the past ten years we have seen emerge a pattern of suppression which now has justified the presence of U.S. military "advisers" in Venezuela. This need to maintain social stability for our investments accounts for the counterrevolutionary action of American forces in Guatemala. It tells why American helicopters are being used against guerrillas in Colombia and why American napalm and green beret forces have already been active against rebels in Peru. It is with such activity in mind that the words of the late John F. Kennedy come back to haunt us. Five years ago he said, "Those who make peaceful revolution impossible will make violent revolution inevitable."

Increasingly, by choice or by accident, this is the role our nation has taken—the role of those who make peaceful revolution impossible by refusing to give up the privileges and the pleasures that come from the immense profits of overseas investment.

I am convinced that if we are to get on the right side of the world revolution, we as a nation must undergo a radical revolution of values. We must rapidly begin the shift from a "thing-oriented" society to a "person-oriented" society. When machines and computers, profit motives and property rights are considered more important than people, the giant triplets of racism, materialism, and militarism are incapable of being conquered.

A true revolution of values will soon cause us to question the fairness and justice of many of our past and present policies. On the one hand we are called to play the Good Samaritan on life's roadside; but that will be only an initial act. One day we must come to see that the whole Jericho Road must be transformed so that men and women will not be constantly beaten and robbed as they make their journey on Life's highway. True compassion is more than flinging a coin to a beggar; it is not haphazard and superficial. It comes to see that an edifice which produces beggars needs restructuring. A true revolution of values will soon look uneasily on the glaring contrast of poverty and wealth. With righteous indignation, it will look across the seas and see individual capitalists of the West investing huge sums of money in Asia, Africa and South America, only to take the profits out with no concern for the social betterment of the countries, and say: "This is not just." It will look at our alliance with the landed gentry of Latin America and say: "This is not just." The Western arrogance of feeling that it has everything to teach others and nothing to learn from them is not just. A true revolution of values will lay hands on the world order and say of war: "This way of settling differences is not just."

Now let us begin. Now let us rededicate ourselves to the long and bitter—but beautiful—struggle for a new world. This is the calling of the sons of God, and our brothers wait eagerly for our response. Shall we say the odds are too great? Shall we tell them the struggle is too hard? Will our message be that the forces of American life militate against their arrival as full men, and we send our deepest regrets? Or will there be another message, of longing, of hope, of solidarity with their yearnings, of commitment to their cause, whatever the cost? The choice is ours, and though we might prefer it otherwise we must choose in this crucial moment of human history.

Martin Luther King, Jr. Martin Luther King, Jr., delivers his soaring "I have a dream speech" at the Lincoln Memorial, August 1963. (© 1963 Bob Adelman/ Magnum Photos)

CHAPTER SEVEN

◆

Uncertain Trumpets

37

◆

DESEGREGATION BEGINS

Racial segregation was a fact of life everywhere in the South until the middle of this century. Organizations such as the National Association for the Advancement of Colored People (NAACP) and the Congress of Racial Equality (CORE) fought hard against segregation and its hand-maiden, disfranchisement of blacks. But in 1896 the Supreme Court had ruled in *Plessy* v. *Ferguson* that separate facilities for blacks and whites were legal, and there seemed little recourse from this decree, especially given the unsympathetic racial views of the national government in this period. Only in 1947 did some tentative preliminary change come with the integration of major-league baseball for commercial reasons, the integration of the armed forces by presidential order, and the integration of Southern law schools by a Supreme Court decision that year arguing that such schools were inherently unequal because they denied opportunities to those excluded.

Then, in 1954, in an NAACP lawsuit entitled *Brown* v. *The Board of Education of Topeka,* the Supreme Court extended its reasoning from law schools to the entire segregated school system, thereby reversing the "separate-but-equal" doctrine some sixty years after its adoption. Written by Chief Justice Earl Warren on behalf of a unanimous Court, at first this momentous decision, reprinted below, was met with bitter resentment and resistance from most Southern whites. Yet it marked the beginning of the end for legally segregated schools in the nation. Together with the massive civil rights movement led by Martin Luther King, Jr., and others, it outlawed all segregated public facilities, whether buses, beaches, lunch counters, voting booths, or schools.

Earl Warren was born in Los Angeles in 1891. After he was graduated from the University of California at Berkeley, he practiced law in the San Francisco area until joining the army during World War I. In the 1920s Warren embarked on a successful political career in California, serving as district attorney, state attorney general, and governor. His only electoral defeat came as Republican vice-presidential candidate in 1948. When President Eisenhower appointed him chief justice in 1953, Warren was considered a rather traditional Republican moderate. His leadership of the Court, however, brought an unexpected burst of judicial activism that strengthened not only minority rights but also the rights of voters, trial defendants, and witnesses before congressional committees. Warren resigned from the Court in 1969 and died in Washington in 1974.

Questions to Consider. Compare Earl Warren's assumptions and reasoning in this case with those of Henry Billings Brown in *Plessy* v. *Ferguson* (1896). Note, for example, that Warren virtually disregarded what Brown had believed to be so crucial—the actual differences between the races. Note, too, that Warren read very large public purposes into the bountiful commitment of local governments to public education: good citizenship, values, training, and social adjustment. Were these two factors—colorblindness and purposeful public education—enough to account for the Court's 1954 decision? If so, why did Warren introduce psychological studies into his argument? Was it merely a reflection of the findings of modern social science? Or was it because Brown had already reasoned from psychological effects in *Plessy*? In what other areas besides education might modern courts attempt to use the equal protection clause of the Fourteenth Amendment as construed by the Warren Court?

◆

Brown v. *The Board of Education of Topeka* (1954)

EARL WARREN

These cases come to us from the States of Kansas, South Carolina, Virginia, and Delaware. They are premised on different facts and different local conditions, but a common legal question justifies their consideration together in this consolidated opinion.

In approaching this problem, we cannot turn the clock back to 1868 when the Amendment was adopted, or even to 1896 when *Plessy* v. *Ferguson* was written. We must consider public education in the light of its full development and its present place in American life throughout the Nation. Only in this way can it be determined if segregation in public schools deprives these plaintiffs of the equal protection of the laws.

Today, education is perhaps the most important function of state and local governments. Compulsory school attendance laws and the great expenditures for education both demonstrate our recognition of the importance of education to our democratic society. It is required in the performance of our most basic public responsibilities, even service in the armed forces.

Brown v. *The Board of Education of Topeka,* 347 U.S. 483 (1954).

Resistance to desegregation. Federal troops escort black students into Central High School, Little Rock, Arkansas, in obedience to a court order to desegregate the public schools "with all deliberate speed," 1957. President Eisenhower sent U.S. troops to the scene after the Arkansas governor vowed to resist the desegregation order. (© 1957 Burt Glinn/Magnum Photos)

It is the very foundation of good citizenship. Today it is a principal instrument in awakening the child to cultural values, in preparing him for later professional training, and in helping him to adjust normally to his environment. In these days, it is doubtful that any child may reasonably be expected to succeed in life if he is denied the opportunity of an education. Such an opportunity, where the state has undertaken to provide it, is a right which must be made available to all on equal terms.

We come then to the question presented: Does segregation of children in public schools solely on the basis of race, even though the physical facilities and other "tangible" factors may be equal, deprive the children of the minority group of equal educational opportunities? We believe that it does.

In *Sweatt* v. *Painter*, . . . in finding that a segregated law school for Negroes could not provide them equal educational opportunities, this Court relied in large part on "those qualities which are incapable of objective measurement but which make for greatness in a law school." In *McLaurin*

v. *Oklahoma State Regents, . . .* the Court, in requiring that a Negro admitted to a white graduate school be treated like all other students, again resorted to intangible considerations: " . . . his ability to study, to engage in discussions and exchange views with other students, and, in general, to learn his profession." Such considerations apply with added force to children in grade and high schools. To separate them from others of similar age and qualifications solely because of their race generates a feeling of inferiority as to their status in the community that may affect their hearts and minds in a way unlikely ever to be undone. The effect of this separation on their educational opportunities was well stated by a finding in the Kansas case by a court which nevertheless felt compelled to rule against the Negro plaintiffs:

> Segregation of white and colored children in public schools has a detrimental effect upon the colored children. The impact is greater when it has the sanction of the law; for the policy of separating the races is usually interpreted as denoting the inferiority of the Negro group. A sense of inferiority affects the motivation of a child to learn. Segregation with the sanction of the law, therefore, has a tendency to retard the educational and mental development of Negro children and to deprive them of some of the benefits they would receive in a racially integrated school system.

Whatever may have been the extent of psychological knowledge at the time of *Plessy* v. *Ferguson,* this finding is amply supported by modern authority. Any language in *Plessy* v. *Ferguson* contrary to this finding is rejected.

We conclude that in the field of public education the doctrine of "separate but equal" has no place. Separate educational facilities are inherently unequal. Therefore, we hold that the plaintiffs and others similarly situated for whom the actions have been brought are, by reason of the segregation complained of, deprived of the equal protection of the laws guaranteed by the Fourteenth Amendment. . . .

38

◆

NONVIOLENCE AND PROTEST

When the Supreme Court ordered public schools desegregated in 1954, the country's leading civil rights organizations—the NAACP, CORE, and the National Urban League—were all situated in the North. They drew their strength mainly from teachers, journalists, lawyers, students, businesspeople, and other persons who made up the tiny black middle class, and challenged racial oppression mostly through lawsuits and political lobbying. The initiatives of these organizations might affect Southern blacks and change the lives of black rural and urban workers, who comprised most blacks, because most blacks still lived in the South and did manual labor. But the organizations themselves were not based on this Southern black majority and so were unable to involve these blacks in the civil rights struggle or to mount direct challenges to racial injustice in the section of the country where it mattered most.

By the late 1950s the situation was changing. In part this resulted from efforts to implement the Brown decision, particularly in New Orleans, Louisiana, and Little Rock, Arkansas. There militant whites met black students with violence, prompting not only federal intervention but black demonstrations in support of desegregation. Southern NAACP chapters now grew rapidly, giving that organization a regional strength it had not enjoyed before. Even more important were the direct actions against segregated public facilities led by the Reverend Martin Luther King, Jr., and the civil rights group he founded in 1957, the Southern Christian Leadership Conference (SCLC). The first of these actions was precipitated by an incident in Montgomery, Alabama, in December 1955, when a woman named Rosa Parks refused to move to a seat at the back of the bus, where bus regulations required blacks to sit. When Parks was arrested, Montgomery blacks, acting under King's general leadership, began a boycott of the bus system that involved unprecedented mass meetings in local black churches and lasted until the city finally desegregated its public transportation a year later. This success spurred similar actions elsewhere against the racial caste system and propelled King and the SCLC to the forefront of civil rights protest.

In the early 1960s CORE sent "freedom riders" on the bus trips into the South to find out whether interstate bus facilities were integrated. A new group, the Student Nonviolent Coordinating Committee (SNCC), organized sit-ins in segregated cafes, stand-ins at segregated theaters, and swim-ins at segregated beaches. Then in early 1963, King and the SCLC organized boycotts and marches in the industrial city of Birmingham, Alabama, during which thousands of black men, women, and children were beaten, shot at, attacked by dogs, sprayed with hoses, and imprisoned. Among the imprisoned was King; while in jail, in answer to an "open letter" by several white clergymen, he wrote a statement, reprinted below, on the goals and methods of the civil rights movement and SCLC's controversial philosophy of nonviolent protest. The Birmingham protests ended after important city business and civic leaders pledged to begin the process of local desegregation.

Questions to Consider. King organized his famous letter around points that local ministers had raised in an open letter critical of the demonstrations. Do you find his responses compelling? Is his explanation of the philosophy of nonviolence adequate? King himself acknowledged that many in the black community, especially in the North, found nonviolence too passive, deferential, and submissive. Were they likely to find his letter satisfactory? To defend lawbreaking, King divided laws into two categories and attempted to distinguish between why he advocated breaking unjust laws and opposed breaking just ones. Is his distinction valid? Finally, what evidence can you find in the style of the letter that it was written in jail by a minister?

◆

Letter from Birmingham Jail (1963)

MARTIN LUTHER KING, JR.

My Dear Fellow Clergymen:

While confined here in the Birmingham city jail, I came across your recent statement calling my present activities "unwise and untimely." . . .

I think I should indicate why I am here in Birmingham, since you have been influenced by the view which argues against "outsiders coming in."

I have the honor of serving as president of the Southern Christian Leadership Conference, an organization operating in every southern state, with headquarters in Atlanta, Georgia. We have some eighty-five affiliated organizations across the South, and one of them is the Alabama Christian Movement for Human Rights. Frequently we share staff, educational and financial resources with our affiliates. Several months ago the affiliate here in Birmingham asked us to be on call to engage in a nonviolent direct-action program if such were deemed necessary. We readily consented, and when the hour came we lived up to our promise. So I, along with several members of my staff, am here because I was invited here. I am here because I have organizational ties here.

But more basically, I am in Birmingham because injustice is here. Just as the prophets of the eighth century B.C. left their villages and carried their "thus saith the Lord" far beyond the boundaries of their home towns, and just as the Apostle Paul left his village of Tarsus and carried the gospel of Jesus Christ to the far corners of the Greco-Roman world, so am I compelled to carry the gospel of freedom beyond my own home town. Like Paul, I must constantly respond to the Macedonian call for aid.

Moreover, I am cognizant of the interrelatedness of all communities and states. I cannot sit idly by in Atlanta and not be concerned about what happens in Birmingham. Injustice anywhere is a threat to justice everywhere. We are caught in an inescapable network of mutuality, tied in a single garment of destiny. Whatever affects one directly, affects all indirectly. Never again can we afford to live with the narrow, provincial "outside agitator" idea. Anyone who lives inside the United States can never be considered an outsider anywhere within its bounds.

You deplore the demonstrations taking place in Birmingham. But your statement, I am sorry to say, fails to express a similar concern for the conditions that brought about the demonstrations. I am sure that none of you would want to rest content with the superficial kind of social analysis that deals merely with effects and does not grapple with underlying causes. It is unfortunate that demonstrations are taking place in Birmingham, but it is even more unfortunate that the city's white power structure left the Negro community with no alternative.

In any nonviolent campaign there are four basic steps: collection of the facts to determine whether injustices exist; negotiation; self-purification; and direct action. We have gone through all these steps in Birmingham. There can be no gainsaying the fact that racial injustice engulfs this community. Birmingham is probably the most thoroughly segregated city in the United States. Its ugly record of brutality is widely known. Negroes have experienced grossly unjust treatment in the courts. There have been more unsolved bombings of Negro homes and churches in Birmingham than in any other city in the nation. These are the hard, brutal facts of the case. On the basis of these conditions, Negro leaders sought to negotiate with the city fathers. But the latter consistently refused to engage in good-faith negotiation. . . .

As in so many past experiences, our hopes had been blasted, and the shadow of deep disappointment settled upon us. We had no alternative except to prepare for direct action, whereby we would present our very bodies as a means of laying our case before the conscience of the local and the national community. Mindful of the difficulties involved, we decided to undertake a process of self-purification. We began a series of workshops on nonviolence, and we repeatedly asked ourselves: "Are you able to accept blows without retaliating?" "Are you able to endure the ordeal of jail?" We decided to schedule our direct-action program for the Easter season, realizing that except for Christmas, this is the main shopping period of the year. . . .

You may well ask: "Why direct action? Why sit-ins, marches and so forth? Isn't negotiation a better path?" You are quite right in calling for negotiation. Indeed, this is the very purpose of direct action. Nonviolent direct action seeks to create such a crisis and foster such a tension that a community which has constantly refused to negotiate is forced to confront the issue. It seeks so to dramatize the issue that it can no longer be ignored. My citing the creation of tension as part of the work of the nonviolent resister may sound rather shocking. But I must confess that I am not afraid of the word "tension." I have earnestly opposed violent tension, but there is a type of constructive, nonviolent tension which is necessary for growth.

The purpose of our direct-action program is to create a situation so crisis-packed that it will inevitably open the door to negotiation. I therefore concur with you in your call for negotiation. Too long has our beloved Southland been bogged down in a tragic effort to live in monologue rather than dialogue. . . .

We know through painful experience that freedom is never voluntarily given by the oppressor; it must be demanded by the oppressed. Frankly, I have yet to engage in a direct-action campaign that was "well timed" in the view of those who have not suffered unduly from the disease of seg-regation. For years now I have heard the word "Wait!" It rings in the ear of every Negro with piercing familiarity. This "Wait" has almost always meant "Never." We must come to see, with one of our distinguished jurists, that "justice too long delayed is justice denied."

We have waited for more than 340 years for our constitutional and God-given rights. The nations of Asia and Africa are moving with jetlike speed toward gaining political independence, but we still creep at horse-and-buggy pace toward gaining a cup of coffee at a lunch counter. Perhaps it is easy for those who have never felt the stinging darts of segregation to say "Wait." But when you have seen vicious mobs lynch your mothers and fathers at will and drown your sisters and brothers at whim; when you have seen hate-filled policemen curse, kick and even kill your black softening of the labor market generally in the 1970s, poor education, continuing discrimination, and a reciprocal sense of defeatism among some inner-city and rural men. There is no question but that the number of Americans who wanted to work and could not find jobs was larger in 1980 brothers and sisters; when you see the vast majority of your twenty million Negro brothers smothering in an airtight cage of poverty in the midst of an affluent society; when you suddenly find your tongue twisted and your speech stammering as you seek to explain to your six-year-old daughter why she can't go to the public amusement park that has just been advertised on television, and see tears welling up in her eyes when she is told that Funtown is closed to colored children, and see ominous clouds of inferiority beginning to form in her little mental sky, and see her beginning to distort her personality by developing an unconscious bitterness toward white people; when you have to concoct an answer for a five-year-old son who is asking, "Daddy, why do white people treat colored people so mean?"; when you take a cross-country drive and find it necessary to sleep night after night in the uncomfortable corners of your automobile because no motel will accept you; when you are humiliated day in and day out by nagging signs reading "white" and "colored"; when your first name becomes "nigger," your middle name becomes "boy" (however old you are) and your last name becomes "John," and your wife and mother are never given the respected title "Mrs."; when you are harried by day and haunted by night by the fact that you are a Negro, living constantly at tiptoe stance, never quite knowing what to expect next, and are plagued with inner fears and outer resentments; when you are forever fighting a degenerating sense of "nobodiness"—then you will understand why we find it difficult to wait. There comes a time when the cup of endurance runs over, and men are no longer willing to be plunged into the abyss of despair. I hope, sirs, you can understand our legitimate and unavoidable impatience.

You express a great deal of anxiety over our willingness to break laws. This is certainly a legitimate concern. Since we so diligently urge people to obey the Supreme Court's decision of 1954 [*Brown* v. *The Board of Education of Topeka*] outlawing segregation in the public schools, at first glance it may seem rather paradoxical for us consciously to break laws. One may well ask: "How can you advocate breaking some laws and obeying others?" The answer lies in the fact that there are two types of laws: just and unjust. . . .

Now, what is the difference between the two? How does one determine whether a law is just or unjust? A just law is a man-made code that squares with the moral law or the law of God. An unjust law is a code that is out of harmony with the moral law. To put it in the terms of St. Thomas Aquinas [Catholic theologian]: An unjust law is a human law that is not rooted in eternal law and natural law. Any law that uplifts human personality is just. Any law that degrades human personality is unjust. All segregation statutes are unjust because segregation distorts the soul and damages the personality. It gives the segregator a false sense of superiority and the segregated a false sense of inferiority. Segregation, to use the terminology of the Jewish philosopher Martin Buber, substitutes an "I-it" relationship for an "I-thou" relationship and ends up relegating persons to the status of things. Hence segregation is not only politically, economically and sociologically unsound, it is morally wrong and sinful. Paul Tillich [Protestant theologian] has said that sin is separation. Is not segregation an existential expression of man's tragic separation, his awful estrangement, his terrible sinfulness? Thus it is that I can urge men to obey the 1954 decision of the Supreme Court, for it is morally right; and I can urge them to disobey segregation ordinances, for they are morally wrong. . . .

I hope you are able to see the distinction I am trying to point out. In no sense do I advocate evading or defying the law, as would the rabid segregationist. That would lead to anarchy. One who breaks an unjust law must do so openly, lovingly, and with a willingness to accept the penalty. I submit that an individual who breaks a law that conscience tells him is unjust, and who willingly accepts the penalty of imprisonment in order to arouse the conscience of the community over its injustice, is in reality expressing the highest respect for the law. . . .

You speak of our activity in Birmingham as extreme. At first I was rather disappointed that fellow clergymen would see my nonviolent efforts as those of an extremist. I began thinking about the fact that I stand in the middle of two opposing forces in the Negro community. One is a force of complacency, made up in part of Negroes who, as a result of long years of oppression, are so drained of self-respect and a sense of "somebodiness" that they have adjusted to segregation; and in part of a few middle-class Negroes who, because of a degree of academic and economic security and because in some ways they profit by segregation, have become insensitive to the problems of the masses. The other force is one of bitterness and hatred, and it comes perilously close to advocating violence. It is expressed in the various black nationalist groups that are springing up across the nation, the largest and best-known being Elijah Muhammad's Muslim movement. Nourished by the Negro's frustration over the continued existence of racial discrimination, this movement is made up of people who have lost faith in America, who have absolutely repudiated Christianity, and who have concluded that the white man is an incorrigible "devil."

I have tried to stand between these two forces, saying that we need emulate neither the "do-nothingism" of the complacent nor the hatred and despair of the black nationalist. For there is the more excellent way of love and non-violent protest. I am grateful to God that, through the influence of the Negro church, the way of nonviolence became an integral part of our struggle. . . .

[T]hough I was initially disappointed at being categorized as an extremist, as I continued to think about the matter I gradually gained a measure of satisfaction from the label. Was not Jesus an extremist for love: "Love your enemies, bless them that curse you, do good to them that hate you, and pray for them which despitefully use you, and persecute you." Was not Amos an extremist for justice: "Let justice roll down like waters and righteousness like an ever-flowing stream." Was not Paul an extremist for the Christian gospel: "I bear in my body the marks of the Lord Jesus." Was not Martin Luther an extremist: "Here I stand: I cannot do otherwise, so help me God." And John Bunyan: "I will stay in jail to the end of my days before I make a butchery of my conscience." And Abraham Lincoln: "This nation cannot survive half slave and half free." And Thomas Jefferson: "We hold these truths to be self-evident, that all men are created equal . . ." So the question is not whether we will be extremists, but what kind of extremists we will be. Will we be extremists for hate or for love? Will we be extremists for the preservation of injustice or for the extension of justice? . . .

Before closing I feel impelled to mention one other point in your statement that has troubled me profoundly. You warmly commended the Birmingham police force for keeping "order" and "preventing violence." I doubt that you would have so warmly commended the police force if you had seen its dogs sinking their teeth into unarmed, nonviolent Negroes. I doubt that you would so quickly commend the policemen if you were to observe their ugly and inhumane treatment of Negroes here in the city jail; if you were to watch them push and curse old Negro women and young Negro girls; if you were to see them slap and kick old Negro men and young boys; if you were to observe them, as they did on two occasions, refuse to give us food because we wanted to sing our grace together. I cannot join you in your praise of the Birmingham police department. . . .

I wish you had commended the Negro sit-inners and demonstrators of Birmingham for their sublime courage, their willingness to suffer and their amazing discipline in the midst of great provocation. One day the South will recognize its real heroes. They will be the James Merediths,[1] with the noble sense of purpose that enables them to face jeering and hostile mobs, and with the agonizing loneliness that characterizes the life of the pioneer. They will be old, oppressed, battered Negro women, symbolized in a seventy-two-year-old woman in Montgomery, Alabama, who rose up with a sense of dignity and with her people decided not to ride segregated buses, and who responded with ungrammatical profundity to one who inquired about her weariness: "My feets is tired, but my soul is at rest." They will be the young high school and college students, the young ministers of the gospel and a host of their elders, courageously and nonviolently sitting in at lunch counters and willingly going to jail for conscience' sake. One day the South will know that when these disinherited children of God

---

1. **James Meredith:** The first black student at the University of Mississippi. His efforts to enter the university in 1962 were met by white demonstrations and violence.—Eds.

sat down at lunch counters, they were in reality standing up for what is best in the American dream and for the most sacred values in our Judaeo-Christian heritage, thereby bringing our nation back to those great wells of democracy which were dug deep by the founding fathers in their formulation of the Constitution and the Declaration of Independence.

Never before have I written so long a letter. I'm afraid it is much too long to take your precious time. I can assure you that it would have been much shorter if I had been writing from a comfortable desk, but what else can one do when he is alone in a narrow jail cell, other than write long letters, think long thoughts and pray long prayers?

39

◆

Women's Liberation

After its bright triumph of the early 1920s, interest in the movement for women's rights lagged, then gathered new steam in the 1950s. This resurgence resulted partly from a trend in the workforce: 27 percent of adult women worked outside the home in 1940, 33 percent in 1960, and 50 percent in 1980. With so many women in the workforce, they gradually made their concerns heard: equal pay for equal work; managerial positions in heretofore all-male administrations; elimination of sexual and physical harassment. Working wives, it turned out, often strained traditional male-dominant marriages, and both the divorce rate and the need for new child-care arrangements increased. Also, married or not, working women saw their lives focusing less exclusively on children and domesticity. They therefore looked increasingly to modern birth control devices and to abortion. (The Supreme Court declared abortion legal in 1973.) From 1960 to 1980, the birth rate decreased 50 percent.

But if these trends provided the underpinnings for the modern women's movement, true feminism—the struggle for women's liberation—came only with the addition of "consciousness raising" to these socioeconomic tendencies. Here, too, there was a crucial underlying trend: many more women were college-educated than ever before. In 1940 approximately 15 percent of American women had completed at least one year of college, and women earned about one-fourth of all bachelor's degrees given by U.S. colleges. By 1960, about 20 percent of all women had gone to college, and women earned one-third of all bachelor's degrees. By 1980, the percentage of women attending college had increased to 40 percent and women earned nearly half of all U.S. bachelor's degrees.

In part, Betty Friedan was addressing these millions of educated but underemployed women in her pathbreaking *The Feminine Mystique,* published in 1963 and excerpted below. Friedan attacked the mass media for brainwashing women into models of domesticity. The National Organization for Women (NOW), created in 1966 with Friedan's support, pressed for eliminating all discriminatory legal sexual distinctions. A half-century after the suffrage amendment, politics witnessed major gains for women. They became governors in numerous states, including Texas, one of the three largest. Women senators were elected from several states, including Florida, another of the three largest. Mayors in many of the nation's largest cities, including Chicago and Houston, were women. They held three cabinet positions under Jimmy Carter and one each under Reagan and Bush. A woman was appointed Supreme Court justice, and one ran as a Democratic party vice-presidential candidate. Women were commonplace in the American military force sent to the Persian Gulf in 1991, although not initially in official combat roles.

Some feminists, meanwhile, worked to erase cultural stereotypes, producing, for example, school texts in which men sometimes did housework and women flew airplanes. The word *chair* replaced *chairman* at meetings or on organizational charts. In some denominations, feminists brought about the modification of hymns or carols—"God rest ye merry gentle*folk*" instead of "gentle*men*." Others formed women's support groups to deal with women's concerns, particularly health care, sexuality, and domestic violence, and to promote the establishment of family planning clinics, women's health collectives, and battered women's shelters.

The issue of sexuality was a tricky one for feminists. "Our Bodies, Ourselves," was a slogan of one part of the movement. It signaled a concern not only for more female-oriented medicine but also for loosening the bonds on female sexuality, so that women could become sex subjects and partners instead of mere sex objects. A powerful early statement of this point of view was contained in Germaine Greer's *The Female Eunuch,* published in 1970, which advocated more uninhibited female sexuality. The publication of a widely read interview with Greer in the January 1972 issue of *Playboy* magazine (excerpted below) illustrated the difficulties involved in pursuing this goal. *Playboy* had become the foremost "men's" magazine of the day largely by pioneering in the publication of pictures of nude women interspersed with "high-brow" writing and glossy advertisements for expensive consumer goods. The effect of *Playboy* was to make so-called soft pornography both fashionable and respectable. It was therefore a significant force in stripping inhibitions from, or sexualizing, the culture as a whole. After *Playboy's* success, other publications—including women's publications—could more easily acknowledge and discuss the central role of sexuality and sexual pleasure in the lives of both men and women, thus facilitating the liberation of "our bodies, ourselves."

The downside, as feminists (including Greer) readily saw, was twofold. First, *Playboy* and its many imitators prospered largely by exploiting images of women's bodies for commercial purposes. Second, the images of the female body in *Playboy* reinforced the assumption that women were mere subordinate sex objects rather than presenting women as equal sex partners, as feminists desired. Feminists were not the only critics of the cultural influence of the *Playboy* phenomenon; Christian fundamentalists profoundly regretted it as well, especially for its potentially pernicious effect on traditional family values. One of the striking political developments of the 1980s was the occasional alliance of feminism and fundamentalism against pornography.

Betty Friedan was born in 1921 in Illinois and attended Smith College and the University of California at Berkeley. In the early 1960s Friedan was a wife and mother who, having lost her job as a newspaper reporter, was contributing to popular magazines. Noticing that editors frequently cut her references to women's careers in favor of more material on homemaking, she began to analyze the housewife fantasy and to interview housewives themselves. The result was *The Feminine Mystique* (1963), an instant best seller that catapulted its author to the forefront of the women's movement and earned her countless offers to lecture and teach. Friedan was the founding president of the National Organization for Women from 1966 to 1970 and also helped found the National Women's Political Caucus and the National Association to Repeal Abortion Laws. None of it was easy. "A lot of people," she recalled, "treated me like a leper."

Germaine Greer was born in Australia in 1939, attended the Universities of Melbourne and Sydney, and received a doctorate from Cambridge University in 1967. Described in *Newsweek* as "a dazzling combination of erudition, eccentricity, and eroticism," Greer's basic argument is that "women's sexuality is both denied and misrepresented by being identified as passivity." Her popularity in the United States signifies not only the rage for reading and arguing about sexuality that swept the country in the 1960s and 1970s, but an almost equally powerful admiration for British cultural figures, among them the Beatles and Rolling Stones.

Questions to Consider. Betty Friedan argued in *The Feminine Mystique* that American women suffered from a "problem that has no name." What was that problem? Was she the first to discover it? What were her methods of investigating and reporting it? Why did it have no name? Did Friedan name it? Would all American women have responded to Friedan's arguments? What kinds of women would have been most likely to respond? How revolutionary was her message? What social or political measures would be required to deal effectively with this problem?

In her *Playboy* interview, Germaine Greer was severely critical of a "*Playboy*-type orgy." Why did Greer describe the "orgy" she attended in this way? What effect was she trying to achieve? How persuasive do you find her argument against censorship? How effective is her argument against conventional sex manuals? Why did she call them "counterrevolutionary"? Did Greer think there might be inherent differences between men and women? Did she think that was an important question? Did she argue ultimately for uniformity or diversity?

◆

The Feminine Mystique (1963)

BETTY FRIEDAN

The suburban housewife—she was the dream image of the young American women and the envy, it was said, of women all over the world. The American housewife—freed by science and labor-saving appliances from the drudgery, the dangers of childbirth and the illnesses of her grandmother. She was healthy, beautiful, educated, concerned only about her husband, her children, her home. She had found true feminine fulfillment. As a housewife and mother, she was respected as a full and equal partner to man in his world. She was free to choose automobiles, clothes, appliances, supermarkets; she had everything that women ever dreamed of.

In the fifteen years after World War II, this mystique of feminine fulfillment became the cherished and self-perpetuating core of contemporary American culture. Millions of women lived their lives in the image of those pretty pictures of the American suburban housewife, kissing their husbands goodbye in front of the picture window, depositing their stationwagonsful of children at school, and smiling as they ran the new electric waxer over the spotless kitchen floor. They baked their own bread, sewed their own and their children's clothes, kept their new washing machines and dryers running all day. They changed the sheets on the beds twice a week instead of once, took the rug-hooking class in adult education, and pitied their poor frustrated mothers, who had dreamed of having a career. Their only dream was to be perfect wives and mothers; their highest ambition to have five children and a beautiful house, their only fight to get and keep their husbands. They had no thought for the unfeminine problems of the world outside the home; they wanted the men to make the major decisions. They gloried in their role as women, and wrote proudly on the census blank: "Occupation: housewife."

For over fifteen years, the words written for women, and the words women used when they talked to each other, while their husbands sat on the other side of the room and talked shop or politics or septic tanks, were about problems with their children, or how to keep their husbands happy,

From Betty Friedan, *The Feminine Mystique* (W.W. Norton, New York, 1963), 3–18. Reprinted from *The Feminine Mystique* by Betty Friedan, by permission of W.W. Norton & Company, Inc. Copyright © 1963 by Betty Friedan. Copyright renewed 1991.

A NOW rally. A demonstration at the Statue of Liberty on behalf of equal rights for women, August 1970. The raised clenched fist was by now a standard symbol of angry radical protest. (© 1970 Jack Manning/New York Times Picture Service)

or improve their children's school, or cook chicken or make slipcovers. Nobody argued whether women were inferior or superior to men; they were simply different. Words like *emancipation* and *career* sounded strange and embarrassing; no one had used them for years. . . .

But on an April morning in 1959, I heard a mother of four, having coffee with four other mothers in a suburban development fifteen miles from New York, say in a tone of quiet desperation, "the problem." And the others knew, without words, that she was not talking about a problem with her husband, or her children, or her home. Suddenly they realized they all shared the same problem, the problem that has no name. They began, hesitantly, to talk about it. Later, after they had picked up their children at nursery school and taken them home to nap, two of the women cried, in sheer relief, just to know they were not alone. . . .

Just what was this problem that has no name? What were the words women used when they tried to express it? Sometimes a woman would say "I feel empty somehow . . . incomplete." Or she would say, "I feel as if I don't exist." Sometimes she blotted out the feeling with a tranquilizer. Sometimes she thought the problem was with her husband, or her children, or that what she really needed was to redecorate her house, or move to a better neighborhood, or have an affair, or another baby. Sometimes, she went to a doctor with symptoms she could hardly describe: "A tired feeling . . . I get so angry with the children it scares me . . . I feel like crying without any reason." (A Cleveland doctor called it "the housewife's syndrome.") A number of women told me about great bleeding blisters that break out on their hands and arms. "I call it the housewife's blight," said a family doctor in Pennsylvania. "I see it so often lately in these young women with four, five and six children who bury themselves in their dishpans. But it isn't caused by detergent and it isn't cured by cortisone." . . .

In 1960, the problem that has no name burst like a boil through the image of the happy American housewife. In the television commercials the pretty housewives still beamed over their foaming dishpans and *Time's* cover story on "The Suburban Wife, an American Phenomenon" protested: "Having too good a time . . . to believe that they should be unhappy." But the actual unhappiness of the American housewife was suddenly being reported—from the *New York Times* and *Newsweek* to *Good Housekeeping* and CBS Television ("The Trapped Housewife"), although almost everybody who talked about it found some superficial reason to dismiss it. . . .

Of the growing thousands of women currently getting private psychiatric help in the United States, the married ones were reported dissatisfied with their marriages, the unmarried ones suffering from anxiety and, finally, depression. Strangely, a number of psychiatrists stated that, in their experience, unmarried women patients were happier than married ones. So the door of all those pretty suburban houses opened a crack to permit a glimpse of uncounted thousands of American housewives who suffered alone from a problem that suddenly everyone was talking about, and beginning to take for granted, as one of those unreal problems in American life that can never be solved—like the hydrogen bomb. . . .

I do not accept the answer that there is no problem because American women have luxuries that women in other times and lands never dreamed of; part of the strange newness of the problem is that it cannot be understood in terms of the age-old material problems of man: poverty, sickness, hunger, cold. The women who suffer this problem have a hunger that food cannot fill. . . .

Are the women who finished college, the women who once had dreams beyond housewifery, the ones who suffer the most? According to the experts they are, but. . . . housewives of all educational levels suffer the same feeling of desperation.

The fact is that no one today is muttering angrily about "women's rights," even though more and more women have gone to college. In a recent study of all the classes that have graduated from Barnard College, a significant minority of earlier graduates blamed their education for making them want "rights," later classes blamed their education for giving them career dreams, but recent graduates blamed the college for making them feel it was not enough simply to be a housewife and mother; they did not want to feel guilty if they did not read books or take part in community activities. But if education is not the cause of the problem, the fact that education somehow festers in these women may be a clue.

If the secret of feminine fulfillment is having children, never have so many women, with the freedom to choose, had so many children, in so few years, so willingly. If the answer is love, never have women searched for love with such determination. And yet there is a growing suspicion that the problem may not be sexual, though it must somehow be related to sex. I have heard from many doctors evidence of new sexual problems between man and wife—sexual hunger in wives so great their husbands cannot satisfy it. . . .

Can the problem that has no name be somehow related to the domestic routine of the housewife? When a woman tries to put the problem into words, she often merely describes the daily life she leads. What is there in this recital of comfortable domestic detail that could possibly cause such a feeling of desperation? Is she trapped simply by the enormous demands of her role as modern housewife: wife, mistress, mother, nurse, consumer, cook, chauffeur; expert on interior decoration, child care, appliance repair, furniture refinishing, nutrition, and education? . . .

If I am right, the problem that has no name stirring in the minds of so many American women today is not a matter of loss of femininity or too much education, or the demands of domesticity. It is far more important than anyone recognizes. It is the key to these other new and old problems which have been torturing women and their husbands and children, and puzzling their doctors and educators for years. It may well be the key to our future as a nation and a culture. We can no longer ignore that voice within women that says: "I want something more than my husband and my children and my home."

◆

Playboy Interviews Germaine Greer (1972)

Playboy: Why did you call your book *The Female Eunuch?*

Greer: The term *eunuch* was used by Eldrige Cleaver to describe blacks. It occurred to me that women were in a somewhat similar position. Blacks had been emancipated from slavery but never given any kind of meaningful freedom, while women were given the vote but denied sexual freedom.

G. Barry Golson, ed., *The Playboy Interview* (Wideview Books, n.p., 1981), 330–334, 340, 348. Excerpted from "*Playboy* Interview:Germaine Greer," *Playboy* Magazine (January 1972);

In the final analysis, women aren't really free until their libidos are recognized as separate entities. Some of the suffragettes understood this. They could see the connection among the vote, political power, independence and being able to express their sexuality according to their own experience, instead of in reference to a demand by somebody else. But they were regarded as crazy and were virtually crucified. Thinking about them, I suddenly realized, Christ, we've been castrated and that's what it's all about. . . .

Playboy: You're physically imposing, bright, well educated and enormously successful. Nobody would describe *you* as an emasculated woman. Yet you've called yourself a female eunuch. Why?

Greer: Because it's useless to think of liberating oneself in a vacuum. You can't liberate yourself *by* yourself. Women can become free only insofar as circumstances allow them to. It's a slow business and involves constant compromise. Indeed, neither of the sexes is truly liberated at this time.

Playboy: What will make them free?

Greer: Only true equality, which is best understood in terms of Plato's concept of love. You see, it's impossible for superiors and inferiors to love, since the superior can only condescend and the inferior can only admire. Whereas what you really want is recognition between two equals, which means that they don't need to exploit each other. They simply rejoice in each other's presence, because what they see is a reflection of themselves in the other. The brotherhood of man would work only if this were the case—if we became more impressed by our similarities than by our differences. . . . As a judge at the Wet Dream Film Festival, I was invited to an orgy. It turned out to be a *Playboy*-type orgy.

Playboy: It must have been some other company's orgy. We don't merchandise them.

Greer: Says you. It was in this really beautiful apartment. Oh, my God, I can see it now, just like the *Playboy* gatefolds, with all that stained wood and rose-pink lighting and heavy drapes and full cocktail cabinets and bearskin rugs and—sure enough—the door was opened by the host, naked, with a drink in his hand. He said, with wit characteristic of your "Party Jokes" page, "Come in and take your clothes off!" There were two other men and two girls. The girls were blonde and long-legged and lovely. They had taken their clothes off already and you could see that they'd never had any children, which is one of the essential characteristics of your Playmate: No signs of actual *use* of the body have ever interposed themselves, not so much as a callus. I was with a really nice boy and we sort of obediently climbed out of our clothes, because we were supposed to be in favor of that kind of liberated behavior. It was so awful I can't tell you. . . .

Playboy: Where did you pick up these weird fantasies about *Playboy*?

Greer: I know what a *Playboy* pad looks like and I know what a Playmate looks like, too, so they're hardly fantasies. For one thing, your girls are so excessively young. What does this do to the man who looks at them? His wife's legs have been ruined by childbearing or her bum sags. . . . I don't like the breast fetishism that I see in *Playboy*. There's no connection between the breasts you show and satisfactory sexual activity. And you display your girls as if they were a commodity. Sex ought not to be that. It ought to be a means of communication between people. It's not something you can buy for whatever an issue of *Playboy* costs.

Playboy: At first you condemned the fact that our Playmates are young. Then you seemed to be arguing that their figures are too good. Now, when you bring up the commodity argument, you appear to be joining those critics who think we shouldn't publish nude pictures of *any* girls, young or old, beautiful or ugly.

Greer: I'm simply against showing girls as if they were pork chops. Why should women's bodies be this sort of physical fetish? Why can't their bodies just be an extension of their personalities, the way a man supposes *his* body is? No, I'm not against nudity, and I will pay dues to *Playboy* when it runs a man in the gatefold. You can even keep the Playmate.

Playboy: As a matter of fact, we do on occasion run pictures of nude men. As for putting them in featured spots such as the centerfold, ours is a men's magazine and we assume that our readers aren't terribly interested in looking at nude males. Even if *Playboy* were a general magazine with a large female circulation, we doubt that pictures of naked men would be a major attraction, since women don't generally turn on to graphic images of sex.

Greer: I know that as well as you do—that women are not voyeurs; but women are not the clients for prostitutes, either—male or female. And this disparity has to be understood. Women do not regard men as a commodity they may have if they pay for it—even to look at. . . .

Playboy: From what direction are you casting stones? As a contributing editor of an underground sex paper called *Suck,* you must have noticed that, among other things, it contains pictures of young children locked in sexual embrace, women copulating with machines, homosexuals penetrating each other while wearing Nazi uniforms and references to people being forced to eat and drink human waste. Do you find these images less offensive than the Playmate?

Greer: I don't approve of the sadomasochistic stuff that appears in *Suck,* and an editorial statement by me was run in a recent issue about that very thing. I said, essentially, that the editors don't approve of censorship, that it's our principal enemy. But that's why we carry things that make us sick. Because contemporary sexuality is sick, because people are twisted and impotent and incapable of straightforward sexual expression. Insofar as we're dedicated to writing a paper about sex actualities, this sort of thing is going to have to appear in it. But we don't endorse it, and we reserve the right to vomit. That's where it's at. The minute we start to apply censorship, we're just in the same bag as everybody else. . . .

Playboy: Why *did* you grant the interview? Other feminists won't come this close even to insult us.

Greer: I'm not sure why I did, but basically I guess it's because you seem to be trying to go in a decent direction. Although I disapprove of the entire subliminal message in *Playboy*, I suppose your editorial matter is more liberal than that of other large-circulation magazines. And I probably feel that some people will read this interview and drop some of their more ridiculous notions about the women's movement. I really think that the basis of every political movement is people. And you have to have some faith in people, even people like your readers who pay money to drool over pink Playmates. If you don't have confidence that these people will understand you when you say something clearly enough and will begin to see how your statements reflect on their own lives, then you've got no reason to be a revolutionary. I suppose I'm really being arrogant, thinking that what I'm about will come across, even if there should be a pinup interleaved thickly between every 500 words of discourse.

Playboy: What *are* you about? Do you carry the banner for any particular feminist organization?

Greer: No, I don't belong to anything. My role is simply to preach to the unconverted. I'm the one who talks to *Playboy*. . . .

Playboy: The male's ability to turn on at a moment's notice—and at the slightest provocation—is one of those sexual differences that really seems to bother women. Do you think the slower female response is something women are born with, or is it simply retarded by social repression?

Greer: I think it's obvious that female response has been retarded. But if you want to talk about being bothered, there's nothing more bothersome than being a woman in a situation where a man believes he has to work to make you come. He's trying to make a good impression and he wants you to like him, so he tills your vineyard for hours on end. You might just as well be doing something else, because the real sexual excitement comes from a sense of urgency, not from the efforts of a guy who's trying to remember what some sex manual told him about turning women on. . . . That's not my idea of ecstasy.

Playboy: What is?

Greer: It's the combination of what we call the erotic with what Freud called the oceanic impulse—a sort of identification with a huge, cosmic order of things. It doesn't happen when people go around twiddling knobs and trying to give you titillating sensations in the extremities of your body. All the sex in the manuals is localized genitality, and you just isolate it more and more when you play the push-button game. I think the sex manuals that teach marriage partners how to develop a kind of characteristic play, in order to satisfy each other with no sweat and strain, are absolutely counterrevolutionary and deeply arid. . . .

Playboy: Do you think that most of the different qualities men and women have are conditioned rather than inborn?

Greer: I think they're substantially conditioned, but I can't really say. We just don't know what the genuine innate sexual differences are, because we've obscured them by cultural sexual differences. There may, indeed, be some biological disparities, but I don't know that they're very pronounced. I mean, do you think you'd be better off being attacked by a lion than a lioness? Or vice versa? In any case, what small differences may exist don't justify the great degree of sexual discrimination we see in our ordinary lives.

Playboy: Would you like to see men and women play pretty much the same roles in society?

Greer: One of the troubles with the world as it exists now is that the number of differences has been decreased. Uniformity is the desideratum. What one would hope for is a world in which there were myriad differences. But these would be *individual* differences rather than deep differences between groups that are pacing out the same kinds of steps according to their sex or class. People would be genuinely developing different psychic possibilities and living in endlessly variable ways. The whole point about abolishing the sexual polarity is not to make the world less interesting but to make it *more* interesting.

40

◆

A Turn to Militancy

The modern civil rights movement began with *Brown* v. *The Board of Education* in 1954 and the Montgomery bus boycott in 1955. For the next few years two groups provided the movement with leadership: the NAACP, which worked mainly through the courts and enjoyed a national membership; and the SCLC, which was based in the Southern churches and used the tactics of nonviolent demonstrations and boycotts. Though differing in methods, the two organizations shared important characteristics. Their chief objective was the integration of public facilities, including schools. And although they both had predominantly black membership, they accepted white support and participation.

In the early 1960s, however, the civil rights movement began to change. Its primary focus moved from efforts to integrate public facilities to efforts to secure black voting rights. This brought fierce white resistance and much violence, particularly during the "freedom summers" of 1964 and 1965, when black and white college students ran voter registration campaigns in various parts of the South. The violence and the racially selective nature of the registration drives in turn sparked a reaction among young black activists against white participation in the movement. The new militant black position—articulated by the Student Nonviolent Coordinating Committee in the following 1966 position paper—gained plausibility from the outbreak of rioting in the black slums of Northern cities and from the example of liberation struggles in the Third World. After 1966, then, the civil rights movement became increasingly ethnocentric, militant, and fragmented. By 1970 it hardly existed in its original form.

SNCC had been founded in 1960 at a conference called by Martin Luther King., Jr., who imbued its early members with his philosophy of nonviolence. The decisive shift in position occurred early in 1966 when Stokely Carmichael, the principal author of the position paper reprinted below, became chairman. Carmichael was born in 1941 on the West Indian island of Trinidad. After moving with his family to New York City, he lived first in mostly black Harlem and then in the mostly white Bronx. He attended the High School of Science in the Bronx and Howard University in Washington, D.C., and went to jail twenty-seven times during the Southern civil rights campaigns. Under Carmichael, SNCC dropped "Nonviolent" from its name, and its leaders urged angry blacks to undertake a militant black-power position. Carmichael himself later married singer Miriam Makeba and moved to West Africa, where he took the name Kwame Ture and announced, "Africa is my home. I'm staying."

Questions to Consider. The SNCC paper on black power prompted vigorous debate. Those distressed by the statement characterized it as belligerent, damaging, and despairing. Sympathizers called it necessary, determined, and reasonable. Does one set of adjectives seem more accurate than the other in assessing this statement? (Recently, scholars have used both sets of adjectives simultaneously in judging it!) Consider, too, the following points. Was it accurate to say in 1966 that no black could ever "represent" Americans and no white could ever "relate" to blacks? Did the paper propose to change this or accept it as a fact of life? Why were there so many references to popular culture in so political a paper? Why did the paper conclude by stressing the task of "identification"? Where did SNCC expect to find new sources of identity?

◆

Position Paper of the Student Nonviolent Coordinating Committee (1966)

The myth that the Negro is somehow incapable of liberating himself, is lazy, etc., came out of the American experience. In the books that children read, whites are always "good" (good symbols are white), blacks are "evil" or seen as savages in movies, their language is referred to as a "dialect," and black people in this country are supposedly descended from savages.

Any white person who comes into the movement has these concepts in his mind about black people if only subconsciously. He cannot escape them because the whole society has geared his subconscious in that direction.

Miss America coming from Mississippi has a chance to represent all of America, but a black person from either Mississippi or New York will never represent America. So that white people coming into the movement cannot relate to the black experience, cannot relate to the word "black," cannot relate to the "nitty gritty," cannot relate to the experience that brought such a word into being, cannot relate to chitterlings, hog's head cheese, pig feet, hamhocks, and cannot relate to slavery, because these things are

Published by the Student Nonviolent Coordinating Committee. Reprinted by permission.

not a part of their experience. They also cannot relate to the black religious experience, nor to the black church unless, of course, this church has taken on white manifestations.

Negroes in this country have never been allowed to organize themselves because of white interference. As a result of this, the stereotype has been reinforced that blacks cannot organize themselves. The white psychology that blacks have to be watched, also reinforces this stereotype. Blacks, in fact, feel intimidated by the presence of whites, because of their knowledge of the power that whites have over their lives. One white person can come into a meeting of black people and change the complexion of that meeting, whereas one black person would not change the complexion of that meeting unless he was an obvious Uncle Tom. People would immediately start talking about "brotherhood," "love," etc.; race would not be discussed.

If people must express themselves freely, there has to be a climate in which they can do this. If blacks feel intimidated by whites, then they are not liable to vent the rage that they feel about whites in the presence of whites—especially not the black people whom we are trying to organize, i.e. broad masses of black people. A climate has to be created whereby blacks can express themselves. The reason that whites must be excluded is not that one is anti-white, but because the efforts that one is trying to achieve cannot succeed because whites have an intimidating effect. Oftentimes the intimidating effect is in direct proportion to the amount of degradation that black people have suffered at the hands of white people. How do blacks relate to other blacks as such? How do we react to Willie Mays as against Mickey Mantle? What is our response to Mays hitting a home run against Mantle performing the same deed? One has to come to the conclusion that it is because of black participation in baseball. Negroes still identify with the Dodgers because of Jackie Robinson's efforts with the Dodgers. Negroes would instinctively champion all-black teams if they opposed all-white or predominantly white teams. The same principle operates for the movement as it does for baseball: a mystique must be created whereby Negroes can identify with the movement.

Thus an all-black project is needed in order for the people to free themselves. This has to exist from the beginning. This relates to what can be called "coalition politics." There is no doubt in our minds that some whites are just as disgusted with this system as we are. But it is meaningless to talk about coalition if there is no one to align ourselves with, because of the lack of organization in the white communities. There can be no talk of "hooking up" unless black people organize blacks and white people organize whites. If these conditions are met then perhaps at some later date— and if we are going in the same direction—talks about exchange of personnel, coalition, and other meaningful alliances can be discussed.

These facts do not mean that whites cannot help. They can participate on a voluntary basis. We can contract work out to them, but in no way can they participate on a policy-making level.

The charge may be made that we are "racists," but whites who are sensitive to our problems will realize we must determine our own destiny.

In an attempt to find a solution to our dilemma, we propose that our organization (SNCC) should be black-staffed, black-controlled and black-financed. We do not want to fall into a similar dilemma that other civil rights organizations have fallen into. If we continue to rely upon white financial support we will find ourselves entwined in the tentacles of the white power complex that controls this country. It is also important that a black organization (devoid of cultism) be projected to our people so that it can be demonstrated that such organizations are viable.

More and more we see black people in this country being used as a tool of the white liberal establishment. Liberal whites have not begun to address themselves to the real problem of black people in this country; witness their bewilderment, fear and anxiety when nationalism is mentioned concerning black people. An analysis of their (white liberal) reaction to the word alone (nationalism) reveals a very meaningful attitude of whites of any ideological persuasion toward blacks in this country. It means previous solutions to black problems in this country have been made in the interests of those whites dealing with these problems and not in the best interests of black people in this country. Whites can only subvert our true search and struggle for self-determination, self-identification, and liberation in this country. Re-evaluation of the white and black roles must NOW take place not so that black people play but rather black people define white people's roles.

Too long have we allowed white people to interpret the importance and meaning of the cultural aspects of our society. We have allowed them to tell us what was good about our Afro-American music, art and literature. How many black critics do we have on the "jazz" scene? How can a white person who is not a part of the black psyche (except in the oppressor's role) interpret the meaning of the blues to us who are manifestations of the songs themselves? It must also be pointed out that on whatever level of contact that blacks and whites come together, that meeting or confrontation is not on the level of the whites. This only means that our everyday contact with whites is a reinforcement of the myth of white supremacy. Whites are the ones who must try to raise themselves to our humanistic level. We are not, after all, the ones who are responsible for a genocidal war in Vietnam; we are not the ones who are responsible for neocolonialism in Africa and Latin America; we are not the ones who held a people in animalistic bondage over 400 years. We reject the American dream as defined by white people and must work to construct an American reality defined by Afro-Americans.

One of the criticisms of white militants and radicals is that when we view the masses of white people we view the over-all reality of America, we view the racism, the bigotry, and the distortion of personality, we view man's inhumanity to man; we view in reality 180 million racists. The sensitive white intellectual and radical who is fighting to bring about change is conscious of this fact, but does not have the courage to admit this. When he admits this reality, then he must also admit his involvement because he is a part of the collective white America. It is only to the extent that he recognizes this that he will be able to change his reality.

Another concern is how does the white radical view the black community and how does he view the poor white community in terms of organizing. So far we have found that most white radicals have sought to escape the horrible reality of America by going into the black community and attempting to organize black people while neglecting the organization of their own people's racist communities. How can one clean up someone else's yard when one's own yard is untidy?

A thorough reexamination must be made by black people concerning the contributions that we have made in shaping this country. If this reexamination and reevaluation is not made and black people are not given their proper due and respect, then the antagonisms and contradictions are going to become more and more glaring, more and more intense until a national explosion may result.

When people attempt to move from these conclusions it would be faulty reasoning to say they are ordered by racism, because, in this country and in the West, racism has functioned as a type of white nationalism when dealing with black people. We all know the habit that this has created throughout the world and particularly among nonwhite people in this country.

Therefore any reevaluation that we must make will, for the most part, deal with identification. Who are black people, what are black people; what is their relationship to America and the world?

It must be repeated that the whole myth of "Negro citizenship," perpetuated by the white elite, has confused the thinking of radical and progressive blacks and whites in this country. The broad masses of black people react to American society in the same manner as colonial peoples react to the West in Africa and Latin America, and have the same relationship—that of the colonized toward the colonizer.

41

◆

WATERGATE

On June 17, 1972, five men were arrested for rifling the files and tapping the telephones of the Democratic National Committee in the Watergate office building in Washington, D.C. Thus was born the Watergate affair that transfixed the nation for the next two years. All five burglars, it turned out, were former agents of the Central Intelligence Agency (CIA). Two of the men, James McCord and G. Gordon Liddy, were currently working for the Committee to Re-elect the President (CRP, or, popularly, CREEP), an independent organization supporting President Richard Nixon's bid for re-election. McCord and Liddy had connections with another former CIA agent, E. Howard Hunt, who, like Liddy, now served as a White House aide. The other burglars were Cubans who had been associated with the Bay of Pigs operation in Cuba.

After the trial and conviction of the five burglars, McCord broke silence by indicating, first, that the head of CRP himself, none other than former Attorney General John N. Mitchell, had approved the break-in and, second, that White House agents had paid "hush money" to the burglars. Newspaper reporters, the Federal Bureau of Investigation, and a special Senate committee on campaign practices opened investigations and soon learned that CRP had used extortionist tactics to raise an illegal slush fund from corporations for the 1972 presidential campaign, and that CRP had used this fund to pay for burglaries, wiretaps, forgeries, phony demonstrations, and other "dirty tricks" to discredit and punish Nixon critics.

By the summer of 1973 it was clear that President Nixon's closest aides, including advisers H.R. Haldeman and John D. Ehrlichman and counsel John W. Dean, had tried to interfere with the Watergate investigations and were withholding valuable evidence, notably tapes of White House conversations during the period under question. When the Senate committee, wondering who (including President Nixon) knew what, requested access to the tapes, Nixon pleaded executive privilege and refused to release them; and when Archibald Cox, a special Watergate prosecutor whom Nixon had appointed, asked for the tapes, the president ordered Cox's dismissal, even though several Justice Department officials resigned in protest.

During the next few months more than thirty former Nixon advisers were indicted for federal crimes, including Dean, Ehrlichman, Haldeman, Mitchell, and former Secretary of Commerce and CRP finance chairman Maurice Stans. The House Judiciary Committee began preparing articles of impeachment against the president. On August 4, 1974, the Supreme Court ordered Nixon to release the tapes. Investigators, hoping to unearth the "smoking pistol" (direct evidence, if it existed, that the president himself had authorized the cover-up), were eager to examine them.

As suggested in the brief excerpts reprinted below, the tapes did indeed provide such evidence. According to the June 1972 conversations, Nixon knew of the Watergate break-in forty-eight hours after it happened; he also withheld evidence, authorized bribes, and used the FBI and the CIA to thwart Congressional investigators. The September 1972 excerpt suggests Nixon's intent, in the aftermath of Watergate, to use the FBI and the Justice Department against the administration's enemies. In March 1973, the president elaborated on the nature of his enemies. A week later, in response to Dean's concern about washing money—"the sort of thing Mafia people can do"—for paying blackmail, Nixon replied that the money could be obtained. With such conversations made public and facing almost certain impeachment, Richard Nixon announced his resignation of the presidency on August 8, 1974. In the end, Nixon's bold diplomacy in foreign affairs seemed swallowed up by domestic sordidness.

Questions to Consider. The Watergate episode, as revealed in these tape transcriptions, illustrated the remarkable size and complexity of the White House staff and executive bureaucracy in the last third of this century; the constant, almost casual resort to the new technology of wiretapping and secret surveillance; and the phenomenal importance of money in high-level politics and the apparent ease of raising it. Might these features of the modern presidency have tended in themselves to promote the kind of domineering mentality that characterized the Nixon White House? Did the fact that Nixon felt assailed (not unlike Senator Joseph McCarthy) by "upper intellectual types" and a "dying" establishment affect his actions? How prominently did activist, Kennedy-style cold war attitudes and habits—the use of CIA operatives, references to the Bay of Pigs and national security—figure in the episode? Do future Watergate threats lie mainly in the nature of the modern presidency, or mainly in a special combination of anticommunism and status anxiety?

◆

White House Conversations (1972–1973)

June 23, 1972

HALDEMAN: Now, on the investigation, you know the Democratic breakin thing, we're back in the problem area because the FBI is not under control, because [Director Patrick] Gray doesn't exactly know how to control it and they have—their investigation is now leading into some productive areas. . . . They've been able to trace the money—not through the money itself—but through the bank sources—the banker. And it goes in some directions we don't want it to go. Ah, also there have been some [other] things—like an informant came in off the street to the FBI in Miami who was a photographer or has a friend who is a photographer who developed some films through this guy [Bernard] Barker and the films had pictures of Democratic National Committee letterhead documents and things. So it's things like that that are filtering in. . . . [John] Mitchell came up with yesterday, and John Dean analyzed very carefully last night and concludes, concurs now with Mitchell's recommendation that the only way to solve this . . . is for us to have [CIA Assistant Director Vernon] Walters call Pat Gray and just say, "Stay to hell out of this—this is ah, [our] business here. We don't want you to go any further on it." That's not an unusual development, and ah, that would take care of it.

PRESIDENT: What about Pat Gray—you mean Pat Gray doesn't want to?

HALDEMAN: Pat does want to. He doesn't know how to, and he doesn't have any basis for doing it. Given this, he will then have the basis. He'll call [FBI Assistant Director] Mark Felt in, and the two of them—and Mark Felt wants to cooperate because he's ambitious—

PRESIDENT: Yeah.

HALDEMAN: He'll call him in and say, "We've got the signal from across the river to put the hold on this." And that will fit rather well because the FBI agents who are working the case, at this point, feel that's what it is.

PRESIDENT: This is CIA? They've traced the money? Who'd they trace it to?

HALDEMAN: Well, they've traced it to a name, but they haven't gotten to the guy yet.

PRESIDENT: Would it be somebody here?

HALDEMAN: Ken Dahlberg.

PRESIDENT: Who the hell is Ken Dahlberg?

From Hearings Before the Committee on the Judiciary, House of Representatives, 93rd Congress, 2nd Session (Government Printing Office, Washington, D.C., 1974).

HALDEMAN: He gave $25,000 in Minnesota and, ah, the check went directly to this guy Barker.

PRESIDENT: It isn't from the Committee though, from [Maurice] Stans?

HALDEMAN: Yeah. It is. It's directly traceable and there's some more through some Texas people that went to the Mexican bank which can also be traced to the Mexican bank—they'll get their names today.

PRESIDENT: Well, I mean, there's no way—I'm just thinking if they don't cooperate, what do they say? That they were approached by the Cubans? That's what Dahlberg has to say, the Texans too.

HALDEMAN: Well, if they will. But then we're relying on more and more people all the time. That's the problem and they'll [the FBI] . . . stop if we could take this other route.

PRESIDENT: All right.

HALDEMAN: [Mitchell and Dean] say the only way to do that is from White House instructions. And it's got to be to [CIA Director Richard] Helms and to—ah, what's his name? . . . Walters.

PRESIDENT: Walters.

HALDEMAN: And the proposal would be that . . . [John] Ehrlichman and I call them in, and say, ah—

PRESIDENT: All right, fine. How do you call him in—I mean you just—well, we protected Helms from one hell of a lot of things.

HALDEMAN: That's what Ehrlichman says.

PRESIDENT: Of course; this [Howard] Hunt [business.] That will uncover a lot of things. You open that scab there's a hell of a lot of things and we just feel that it would be very detrimental to have this thing go any further. This involves these Cubans, Hunt, and a lot of hanky-panky that we have nothing to do with ourselves. Well, what the hell, did Mitchell know about this?

HALDEMAN: I think so. I don't think he knew the details, but I think he knew.

PRESIDENT: He didn't know how it was going to be handled though—with Dahlberg and the Texans and so forth? Well who was the asshole that did? Is it [G. Gordon] Liddy? Is that the fellow? He must be a little nuts!

HALDEMAN: He is.

PRESIDENT: I mean he just isn't well screwed on, is he? Is that the problem?

HALDEMAN: No, but he was under pressure, apparently, to get more information, and as he got more pressure, he pushed the people harder.

PRESIDENT: Pressure from Mitchell?

HALDEMAN: Apparently. . . .

PRESIDENT: All right, fine, I understand it all. We won't second-guess Mitchell and the rest. Thank God it wasn't [special White House counsel Charles] Colson.

HALDEMAN: The FBI interviewed Colson yesterday. They determined that would be a good thing to do. To have him take an interrogation, which he did, and the FBI guys working the case concluded that there were one or two possibilities—one, that this was a White House (they don't think that there is anything at the Election Committee) they think it was either a White House operation and they had some obscure reasons for it—non-political, or it was a—Cuban [operation] and [involved] the CIA. And after their interrogation of Colson yesterday, they concluded it was not the White House, but are now convinced it is a CIA thing, so the CIA turnoff would—

PRESIDENT: Well, not sure of their analysis, I'm not going to get that involved. I'm (unintelligible).

HALDEMAN: No, sir, we don't want you to.

PRESIDENT: You call them in.

HALDEMAN: Good deal.

PRESIDENT: Play it tough. That's the way they play it and that's the way we are going to play it. . . .

*   *   *   *   *

PRESIDENT: O.K. . . . Just say (unintelligible) very bad to have this fellow Hunt, ah, he knows too damned much. . . . If it gets out that this is all involved, the Cuba thing, it would be a fiasco. It would make the CIA look bad, it's going to make Hunt look bad, and it is likely to blow the whole Bay of Pigs thing which we think would be very unfortunate—both for CIA, and for the country, at this time, and for American foreign policy. Just tell him to lay off. Don't you [think] so?

HALDEMAN: Yep. That's the basis to do it on. Just leave it at that. . . .

September 15, 1972

PRESIDENT: We are all in it together. This is a war. We take a few shots and it will be over. We will give them a few shots and it will be over. Don't worry. I wouldn't want to be on the other side right now. Would you?

DEAN: Along that line, one of the things I've tried to do, I have begun to keep notes on a lot of people who are emerging as less than our friends because this will be over some day and we shouldn't forget the way some of them have treated us.

PRESIDENT: I want the most comprehensive notes on all those who tried to do us in. They didn't have to do it. If we had had a very close election and they were playing the other side I would understand this. No—they were doing this quite deliberately and they are asking for it and they are going to get it. We have not used the power in this first four years, as you know. We have never used it. We have not used the Bureau, and we have not used the Justice Department, but things are going to change now. And they are either going to do it right or go.

DEAN: What an exciting prospect.

PRESIDENT: Thanks. It has to be done. We have been (adjective deleted) fools for us to come into this election campaign and not do anything with regard to the Democratic Senators who are running, et cetera. And who the hell are they after? They are after us. It is absolutely ridiculous. It is not going to be that way any more.

March 13, 1973

PRESIDENT: How much of a crisis? It will be—I am thinking in terms of— the point is, everything is a crisis. (expletive deleted) it is a terrible lousy thing—it will remain a crisis among the upper intellectual types, the soft heads, our own, too—Republicans—and the Democrats and the rest. Average people won't think it is much of a crisis unless it affects them. (unintelligible)

DEAN: I think it will pass. I think after the [Senator Sam] Ervin hearings, they are going to find so much—there will be some new revelations. I don't think that the thing will get out of hand. I have no reason to believe it will.

PRESIDENT: As a matter of fact, it is just a bunch of (characterization deleted). We don't object to such damn things anyway. On, and on and on. No. I tell you this it is the last gasp of our hardest opponents. They've just got to have something to squeal about it.

DEAN: It is the only thing they have to squeal—

PRESIDENT: (Unintelligible) They are going to lie around and squeal. They are having a hard time now. They got the hell kicked out of them in the election. There is not a Watergate around in this town, not so much our opponents, even the media, but the basic thing is the establishment. The establishment is dying, and so they've got to show that despite the successes we have had in foreign policy and in the election, they've got to show that it is just wrong, just because of this. They are trying to use this as the whole thing.

March 21, 1973

DEAN: So that is it. That is the extent of the knowledge. So where are the soft spots on this? Well, first of all, there is the problem of the continued blackmail which will not only go on now, but it will go on while these people are in prison, and it will compound the obstruction of justice situation. It will cost money. It is dangerous. People around here are not pros at this sort of thing. This is the sort of thing Mafia people can do: washing money, getting clean money, and things like that. We just don't know about those things, because we are not criminals and not used to dealing in that business.

PRESIDENT: That's right.

DEAN: It is a tough thing to know how to do.

PRESIDENT: Maybe it takes a gang to do that.

DEAN: That's right. There is a real problem as to whether we could even do it. Plus there is a real problem in raising money. Mitchell has been working on raising some money. He is one of the ones with the most to lose. But there is no denying the fact that the White House, in Ehrlichman, Haldeman and Dean, are involved in some of the early money decisions.

PRESIDENT: How much money do you need?

DEAN: I would say these people are going to cost over a million dollars over the next two years.

PRESIDENT: We could get that. On the money, if you need the money you could get that. You could get a million dollars. You could get it in cash. I know where it could be gotten. It is not easy, but it could be done. But the question is who the hell would handle it? Any ideas on that?

DEAN: That's right. Well, I think that is something that Mitchell ought to be charged with.

PRESIDENT: I would think so too.

42

◆

CHOICE AND LIFE

Except for a brief "baby boom" period after 1945, the number of children born to the average American woman has steadily decreased since the early nineteenth century. She had seven children on average in the early 1800s, four in the late 1800s, three in the early 1900s, two in the late 1900s. In the nineteenth century, the chief methods for limiting births were primitive contraception, abstinence, and, especially, abortion. In the early twentieth century, however, abortion became illegal in most states, and abstinence in marriage was less acceptable to husbands and wives. Improved contraception and delays in first marriages therefore became increasingly important birth-limiting measures. The falling birthrate since 1960 has come chiefly from a dramatic improvement in contraceptive techniques, especially contraceptive sterilization, the pill, the intrauterine device, and the vaginal sponge. Less important but still significant has been a rise in abortion rates, most notably in the five years that followed the historic 1973 Supreme Court decision in *Roe* v. *Wade,* which ruled restrictive state abortion laws unconstitutional.

Roe v. *Wade* reflected major changes in American society. These included advances in birth control technology, a desire to limit family size, and, especially, increased attention to the rights of women. One of these rights, according to modern feminists, is "reproductive freedom," of which abortion on demand was a crucial part. *Roe* v. *Wade* also typified a notable long-term shift in how the Supreme Court has viewed Constitutional "rights"—or at least the question of which rights are the truly vital ones. In theory, all rights in the Constitution are of equal value, but over the years the Court, reflecting changes in social values, has always cherished some rights as more important than others. In the nation's early days, private property was given special consideration; later this came to include the rights of businesses and liberty of contract. Then, in the 1930s and 1940s, economic rights lost pride of place to the rights enumerated in the First Amendment. In recent years the right to vote and to attend racially integrated schools has been judged to be of fundamental importance. With the *Roe* v. *Wade* decision, so has the right to privacy.[1]

Justice Harry Blackmun's decision, which invalidated the statutes of thirty states that forbade abortions except to save the mother's life, sparked bitter controversy. "Pro-life" forces, most affiliated with religious denominations and uncompromisingly opposed to abortion, denounced the ruling. They called for a Constitutional amendment defining human life as beginning at conception, picketed abortion clinics, and successfully urged Congress to curtail most Medicaid funds for abortions. Meanwhile, "pro-choice" advocates organized in support of the right of a woman (rather than the state) to choose whether or not to have an abortion. They also supported doctors' rights to perform abortions and poor women's rights to obtain them. By the 1980s, a political candidate's position on abortion could make or break a campaign, just as a Supreme Court nominee's position on *Roe* v. *Wade* could make or break a Court nomination.

Harry Blackmun, author of the *Roe* v. *Wade* decision, was born in Illinois in 1908. He grew up in the Minneapolis-St. Paul area and then headed east to attend Harvard College and Harvard Law School. Blackmun returned to Minneapolis to open a private practice before moving to Rochester, Minnesota, as legal counsel for the world-famous Mayo Clinic. A hard-working, serious-minded, moderate Republican, he was first appointed to the federal judiciary by President Dwight Eisenhower in 1959. Blackmun, a boyhood friend of Chief Justice Warren Burger, was promoted to the Supreme Court in 1970 after the Senate had rejected Richard Nixon's first two nominations to fill a recent vacancy. Although Blackmun was initially perceived as Burger's "Minnesota twin," the *Roe* v. *Wade* ruling (from which Justices Byron White and William Rehnquist dissented) marked the beginning of his drift away from the conservative Burger wing of the Court toward the more liberal wing associated with Justice William Brennan.

Questions to Consider. On what two Constitutional grounds did the appellant seek to overturn restrictive Texas abortion laws? Of the three reasons commonly given to justify restricting abortions since the nineteenth century, which did Blackmun consider most important? Where in the Constitution did he find grounds for the right to privacy claimed by the appellant? Did Blackmun consider a woman's right to privacy a guarantee of an absolute right to abortion? The State of Texas (the appellee) argued that states could restrict abortion because the state

---

[1]In *Rust* v. *Sullivan* (May 23, 1991) the Supreme Court decided that medical personnel in family planning clinics receiving federal funds may not mention abortion or abortion facilities to clients.

has a "compelling interest" in protecting the right of an unborn fetus under the provisions of the Fourteenth Amendment. How did Blackmun deal with this argument? Why did he call Texas's position "one theory of life"? Why did Blackmun discuss "trimesters" and "viability" at such length? If medical technology were to shift the point of viability from the third to the second trimester, would that undercut the force of *Roe v. Wade?*

◆

Roe v. *Wade* (1973)

HARRY BLACKMUN

The principal thrust of appellant's attack on the Texas statutes is that they improperly invade a right, said to be possessed by the pregnant woman, to choose to terminate her pregnancy. Appellant would discover this right in the concept of personal "liberty" embodied in the Fourteenth Amendment's Due Process Clause; or in personal, marital, familial, and sexual privacy said to be protected by the Bill of Rights.

It perhaps is not generally appreciated that the restrictive criminal abortion laws in effect in a majority of States today are of relatively recent vintage. Those laws, generally proscribing abortion or its attempt at any time during pregnancy except when necessary to preserve the pregnant woman's life, are not of ancient or even of common law origin. Instead, they derive from statutory changes effected, for the most part, in the latter half of the nineteenth century. . . .

Three reasons have been advanced to explain historically the enactment of criminal abortion laws in the nineteenth century and to justify their continued existence.

It has been argued occasionally that these laws were the product of a Victorian social concern to discourage illicit sexual conduct. Texas, however, does not advance this justification in the present case, and it appears that no court or commentator has taken the argument seriously. . . .

A second reason is concerned with abortion as a medical procedure. When most criminal abortion laws were first enacted, the procedure was a hazardous one for the woman. . . . Modern medical techniques have altered this situation. Appellants refer to medical data indicating that abortion in early pregnancy, that is, prior to the end of first trimester, although not without its risk, is now relatively safe. . . . The State retains a definite interest in protecting the woman's own health and safety when an abortion is proposed at a late stage of pregnancy.

From *Roe v. Wade*, 410 U.S. 113 (1973).

The third reason is the State's interest—some phrase it in terms of duty—in protecting prenatal life. Some of the argument for this justification rests on the theory that a new human life is present from the moment of conception. The State's interest and general obligation to protect life then extends, it is argued, to prenatal life. Only when the life of the pregnant mother herself is at stake, balanced against the life she carries within her, should the interest of the embryo or fetus not prevail. Logically, of course, a legitimate State interest in this area need not stand or fall on acceptance of the belief that life begins at conception or at some other point prior to live birth. In assessing the State's interest, recognition may be given to the less rigid claim that as long as at least *potential* life is involved, the State may assert interests beyond the protection of the pregnant woman alone. . . .

The Constitution does not explicitly mention any right of privacy. In a line of decisions, however, going back perhaps as far as *Union Pacific R. Co.* v. *Botsford* (1891), the Court has recognized that a right of personal privacy, or a guarantee of certain areas or zones of privacy, does exist under the Constitution. . . . These decisions make it clear that only personal rights that can be deemed "fundamental" or "implicit in the concept of ordered liberty," are included in this guarantee of personal privacy. They also make it clear that the right has some extension to activities relating to marriage, procreation, contraception. . . . [1]

This right of privacy, whether it be founded in the Fourteenth Amendment's concept of personal liberty and restrictions upon state action, as we feel it is, or, as the District Court determined, in the Ninth Amendment's reservation of rights to the people, is broad enough to encompass a woman's decision whether or not to terminate her pregnancy. The detriment that the State would impose upon the pregnant woman by denying this choice altogether is apparent. Specific and direct harm medically diagnosable even in early pregnancy may be involved. Maternity, or additional offspring, may force upon the woman a distressful life and future. Psychological harm may be imminent. Mental and physical health may be taxed by child care. There is also the distress, for all concerned, associated with the unwanted child, and there is the problem of bringing a child into a family already unable, psychologically and otherwise, to care for it. In other cases, as in this one, the additional difficulties and continuing stigma of unwed motherhood may be involved. All these are factors the woman and her responsible physician necessarily will consider in consultation. . . .

On the basis of elements such as these, appellants argue that the woman's right is absolute and that she is entitled to terminate her pregnancy at whatever time, in whatever way, and for whatever reason she alone

---

1. References to prior court decisions have been omitted.

chooses. With this we do not agree. Appellant's arguments that Texas either has no valid interest at all in regulating the abortion decision, or no interest strong enough to support any limitation upon the woman's sole determination, is unpersuasive. The Court's decisions recognizing a right of privacy also acknowledge that some state regulation in areas protected by that right is appropriate. As noted above, a State may properly assert important interests in safeguarding health, in maintaining medical standards, and in protecting potential life. At some point in pregnancy, these respective interests become sufficiently compelling to sustain regulation of the factors that govern the abortion decision. The privacy right involved, therefore, cannot be said to be absolute. In fact, it is not clear to us that the claim . . . that one has an unlimited right to do with one's body as one pleases bears a close relationship to the right of privacy previously articulated in the Court's decisions. The Court has refused to recognize an unlimited right of this kind in the past.

We therefore conclude that the right of personal privacy includes the abortion decision, but that this right is not unqualified and must be considered against state interests in regulation. . . .

Appellee [the state of Texas] argues that the State's determination to recognize and protect prenatal life from and after conception constitutes a compelling state interest. We do not agree fully. . . .

The Constitution does not define "person" in so many words. Section 1 of the Fourteenth Amendment contains three references to "person." The first, in defining "citizens," speaks of "persons born or naturalized in the United States." The word also appears both in the Due Process Clause and in the Equal Protection Clause. "Person" is used in other places in the Constitution. . . . But in nearly all these instances, the use of the word is such that it has application only postnatally. None indicates, with any assurance, that it has any possible prenatal application. All this, together with our observation, that throughout the major portion of the nineteenth century prevailing legal abortion practices were far freer than they are today, persuades us that the word "person," as used in the Fourteenth Amendment, does not include the unborn. . . .

Texas urges that, apart from the Fourteenth Amendment, life begins at conception and is present throughout pregnancy, and that, therefore, the State has a compelling interest in protecting that life from and after conception. We need not resolve the difficult question of when life begins. When those trained in the respective disciplines of medicine, philosophy, and theology are unable to arrive at any consensus, the judiciary, at this point in the development of man's knowledge, is not in a position to speculate as to the answer.

In view of all this, we do not agree that, by adopting one theory of life, Texas may override the rights of the pregnant woman that are at stake. We repeat, however, that the State does have an important and legitimate interest in preserving and protecting the health of the pregnant woman, whether she be a resident of the State or a nonresident who seeks medical consultation and treatment there, and that it has still *another* important and legitimate interest in protecting the potentiality of human life. These interests are separate and distinct. Each grows in substantiality as the woman approaches term and, at a point during pregnancy, each becomes "compelling."

With respect to the State's important and legitimate interest in the health of the mother, the "compelling" point, in the light of present medical knowledge, is at approximately the end of the first trimester. This is so because of the now established medical fact, referred to above . . . that until the end of the first trimester mortality in abortion is less than mortality in normal childbirth. It follows that, from and after this point, a State may regulate the abortion procedure to the extent that the regulation reasonably relates to the preservation and protection of maternal health. Examples of permissible state regulation in this area are requirements as to the qualifications of the person who is to perform the abortion; as to the licensure of that person; as to the facility in which the procedure is to be performed, that is, whether it must be a hospital or may be a clinic or some other place of less-than-hospital status; as to the licensing of the facility; and the like.

This means, on the other hand, that, for the period of pregnancy prior to this "compelling" point, the attending physician, in consultation with his patient, is free to determine, without regulation by the State, that in his medical judgment the patient's pregnancy should be terminated. If that decision is reached, the judgment may be effectuated by an abortion free of interference by the State.

With respect to the State's important and legitimate interest in potential life, the "compelling" point is at viability. This is so because the fetus then presumably has the capability of meaningful life outside the mother's womb. State regulation protective of fetal life after viability thus has both logical and biological justifications. If the State is interested in protecting fetal life after viability, it may go so far as to proscribe abortion during that period except when it is necessary to preserve the life or health of the mother.

Measured against these standards, the Texas Penal Code, in restricting legal abortions to those "procured or attempted by medical advice for the purpose of saving the life of the mother," sweeps too broadly.

To summarize and to repeat:

A state criminal abortion statute of the current Texas type, that excepts from criminality only a *life saving* procedure on behalf of the mother, without regard to pregnancy stage and without recognition of the other interests involved, is violative of the Due Process Clause of the Fourteenth Amendment.

(a) For the stage prior to approximately the end of the first trimester, the abortion decision and its effectuation must be left to the medical judgment of the pregnant woman's attending physician.

(b) For the stage subsequent to approximately the end of the first trimester, the State, in promoting its interest in the health of the mother, may, if it chooses, regulate the abortion procedure in ways that are reasonably related to maternal health.

(c) For the stage subsequent to viability the State, in promoting its interest in the potentiality of human life, may, if it chooses, regulate, and even proscribe, abortion except where it is necessary, in appropriate medical judgment, for the preservation of the life or health of the mother.

43

◆

TECHNOLOGY UNBOUND

After population growth, cheap land, and bountiful resources, it was technological innovation—the work of creative individuals, such as Eli Whitney, Isaac M. Singer, Andrew Carnegie, and Henry Ford—that was the driving force of American industrialization. After World War II, modern industries like petrochemicals, aerospace, and electronics helped power an unprecedented twenty-five years of almost uninterrupted growth in real national income. At every hand, it seemed, technology yielded products of prosperity: plastics and pharmaceuticals, satellites and jetliners, televisions and computers.

By the 1970s, however, doubts had appeared concerning the benefits of technology. These doubts stemmed in part from the "oil shocks" of 1973 and 1979, when exploding petroleum prices produced not only stagflation—a combination of high unemployment and rising prices—but concern about whether science could discover usable substitutes for hydrocarbon fuels. Another source of doubt came from fear that technology was destructive as well as creative. Evidenced by a spreading ecology movement, this fear centered chiefly on nuclear-powered electric plants with their radiation dangers and on the petrochemical industry, whose "unnatural" nonbiodegradable products and byproducts polluted the nation's air, water, and soil.

Despite the passage of Clean Air and Water Acts and the establishment of the Environmental Protection Agency (1970) and the Nuclear Regulatory Commission (1975), concern did not reach a peak until early 1979 when the discovery of a toxic chemical dump (called, ironically, Love Canal) led to the partial evacuation of a town in upstate New York and when the near meltdown of the Three Mile Island nuclear plant near Harrisburg, Pennsylvania, sent tremors of anxiety through that region. The first selection below, reprinted from the "Notes and Comment" section of the *New Yorker* magazine, illustrates the public reaction to the Three Mile Island ordeal, which resulted in killing plans to build more nuclear plants and intensified technological fears, at least toward nuclear power.

A final source of technological doubt concerned not whether we could find new energy supplies or could avoid poisoning ourselves but whether, given continuing stagflation and the success of foreign competitors such as Germany and Japan, the United States was technologically competitive—that is, was technological enough. The second selection reprinted below (by physicist Robert Jastrow) summarizes these concerns and provides an answer that was characteristic of the early 1980s, when many of the novel technologies Jastrow mentions were first becoming known to the general public.

"Notes and Comment," where the "Three Mile Island" remarks appeared, is a regular anonymous feature of the *New Yorker,* one of America's most literate, stylish, and genteel publications. Robert Jastrow was founder of the Goddard Institute for Space Studies of the National Aeronautics and Space Administration and chairman of the committee that set priorities for the early investigations of the moon. Once called "one of the rare scientists with the gift of making the unimaginable imaginable," Jastrow is currently professor of earth science at Dartmouth College. His books include *Red Giants and White Dwarfs* and *God and the Astronomers.*

Questions to Consider. In reading "Three Mile Island," consider why words such as "forever" and "human error" had so great an impact. Consider, too, the relevance to the Three Mile Island affair of John Hersey on Hiroshima. Remember also that Upton Sinclair had described the ravages of technology as early as 1906. How do the tone and intent of *The Jungle* differ from the tone and intent of "Three Mile Island"?

In reading "Science and the American Dream," consider four questions in particular. First, with whom does it appear that Jastrow was arguing in this essay? Second, can Jastrow be accurately placed within the tradition of probusiness writers such as Andrew Carnegie? Third, can Jastrow be accurately fitted into the conventional liberal or conservative categories of modern American politics? Finally, if Jastrow's argument is correct, would his argument reassure some people more than others?

◆

Three Mile Island (1979)

THE NEW YORKER

A recent headline in the *Washington Post* concerning the afflicted nuclear power plant on Three Mile Island, in Pennsylvania, read, "Aides Wonder If Contamination May Close Plant Forever." The plant may have been rendered permanently inoperable, the story that followed explained, be-

From "Notes and Comment," *The New Yorker* (April 9, 1979), 25. Reprinted by permission; © 1979 The New Yorker Magazine Inc.

Three Mile Island. The towers of Three Mile Island nuclear plant near Harrisburg, Pennsylvania, became sinister symbols after they sprang radioactive leaks in the spring of 1979. The Three Mile Island episode probably struck special terror into American hearts because it coincided with the appearance of The China Syndrome, a movie about a nuclear power near-disaster. Hollywood, in fact, had conditioned people to fear radiation as early as the 1950s with movies about mutant monsters—giant ants, flies, bees, and locusts, to name a few. (Wide World Photos)

cause of the release into the reactor-containment chamber of large quantities of radioactive isotopes, some of which will remain dangerous for as much as a thousand years. And within the reactor there are damaged fuel rods containing radioactive elements with half-lives of some twenty-four thousand years. That "Forever" stood out on the page; we could not remember having seen the word used in a newspaper headline before. (In human terms, twenty-four thousand years—roughly five times the span of recorded history, or the equivalent of almost a thousand generations of men—is forever.) Journalism has always dealt with what is historical and is therefore transient—even empires rise and decline—but now the papers were discussing a future of incomprehensible remoteness, as though they had given up on human affairs and instead interested themselves in the doings of immortal beings. The appearance in news stories of words like *forever* is one more clear signal, if we still need it, that with the discovery of nuclear energy events of a new order of magnitude, belonging to a new dimension of time, have broken into the stream of history. In unleashing nuclear chain reactions, we have brought a cosmic force, virtually never found in terrestrial nature, onto the earth—a force that, both in its visible, violent form of nuclear explosions and in its invisible, impalpable form of radiation, is alien and dangerous to earthly life, and can, through damage to life's genetic foundation, break the very frame on which the generations of mankind are molded. In the midst of the ups and downs of human fortunes, decisions of everlasting consequence have presented themselves. Last week, these decisions were being made in Pennsylvania. "We all live in Pennsylvania!" West German antinuclear demonstrators shouted in an inversion of President Kennedy's famous declaration *"Ich bin ein Berliner."* The danger of extinction is posed above all by nuclear war, but it was nevertheless symbolized during last week's disaster by the evacuation of children and pregnant women—who represent the future generations—from the vicinity of the plant. The lesson was plain: when atomic fission is brought in, the human future is driven out.

Another headline that caught our attention was one in the *News* which read, "Human Error Probed In Leak." The concept of "human error" has cropped up often during the Pennsylvania crisis. The alleged error referred to in the *News* story was an operator's decision to turn off a certain cooling system at an untimely moment, and this was contrasted with possible "technical" errors that could supposedly be made by machinery alone. But, even assuming that operators made mistakes, the question remains of who designed the plant in such a way that one or two untimely decisions could lead to a complete breakdown. Gods did not design the plant; human beings, each one as capable of error as any operator, did. That being so, it appears that the larger human error must lie in the decision to build plants of that design in the first place. But even this conclusion is too narrow—fails to get to the bottom of this matter of human error. The most striking aspect of the Pennsylvania disaster was not that a very unlikely (or "astronomically improbable," as the advocates of nuclear energy used to like to say) series of events occurred but that so many *entirely unpredicted* problems developed, the most important one to date being, of course, the sudden appearance inside the reactor of the explosive hydrogen bubble, which Harold Denton, the chief of reactor regulation for the Nuclear Regulatory Commission, called "a new twist." Events at the plant have turned out to be not at all like the well-ordered scenarios of the nuclear experts but, instead, to be like almost everything else in life—full of new twists. And the surprises within the plant were compounded by rumor and misinformation outside it, so that even when the scientists at the plant were in possession of reliable technical information Governor Richard Thornburgh, who had final responsibility for the lives of the people in the area, often was not. "There are a number of conflicting versions of every event that seems to occur," he observed to reporters at one point. In short, the conditions—reminiscent of New York's blackout two summers ago—that prevailed during this crisis were no different from the ones that prevail in almost every large crisis: erroneous prediction, more or less inadequate preparation, mass confusion and misunderstanding of the facts (accompanied by large amounts of cynicism and black humor), and official sleeplessness and improvisation. The main thing that planners concerned with nuclear power left out of their scenarios was not the correct workings of some valve or control panel. It was the thing that no scenario can take into account: simple human fallibility per se—an ineradicable ingredient in the actions not only of power-plant operators but also of power-plant designers, of government officials, and of the general public as well. What the experts know and most of the rest of us will never know is how to build a nuclear power plant. What we know and they seem to have forgotten is that human imperfection is ingrained in everything that human beings undertake. In almost every enterprise—for example, in air travel—mistakes are somehow tolerated, but in this one case they cannot be, because the losses, which include not only the lives of tens of thousands of people but the habitability of our country and of the earth, are so high, and are "forever." At the deepest level, then, the human error in our nuclear program may be the old Socratic flaw of thinking that we know what we don't know and can't know. The Faustian[1] proposal that the experts make to us is to let them lay their fallible human hands on eternity, and it is unacceptable.

◆

Science and the American Dream (1983)

ROBERT JASTROW

Industrial productivity depends on technical innovations, engineering and general knowhow—areas in which American prowess has been unchallenged. How is it possible that American productivity leveled off in the last ten years, while the productivity of Japan and Germany increased rapidly? What happened? The experts have given many answers. They all sound convincing, but when I began to look into the situation I found that none passes the test of a comparison with the facts. Here are some frequently heard opinions on the causes of our decline, and the data that test their validity.

American labor has priced itself out of the market. The Japanese have captured our market with cheap labor.

---

1. *Faust*: A literary figure modeled after a sixteenth-century alchemist who supposedly promised his immortal soul to Satan in exchange for power in the physical world—*Eds.*

From Robert Jastrow, "Science and the American Dream," *Science Digest* (March 1983), 46–48. First appeared in *Science Digest*, © 1983 by The Hearst Corporation. Reprinted by permission of the author.

True once but no longer. Japanese wages were pennies an hour in 1950, but factory wages in Japan are now about $10 an hour, nearly the same as in America. Steel and automobile workers in America make more than their counterparts in Japan but that is not true for industry across the board for the two countries.

We spend too much on social welfare, on defense, on government as a whole; the tax burden is oppressive.

The United States spends a smaller fraction of its GNP on social welfare than do its leading industrial competitors, Japan and West Germany. This item is surely not the main brake on American productivity.

And although we spend considerably more on defense than Japan and somewhat more than Germany, during the 1970s defense costs averaged only 5.5 percent of the American GNP—significant, but not large enough to slow down the whole economy.

In general, the United States spends approximately the same fraction of its GNP on government as Japan does—about 30 percent—and a considerably smaller fraction of GNP than West Germany spends.

Federal deficits are excessive; the federal debt has zoomed to astronomical levels.

Deficits in the federal budgets of our main competitors, Japan and Germany, are far greater than ours—three to four times larger as a fraction of GNP in recent years.

The federal debt in the United States has increased only 20 percent since 1954, when corrected for inflation. The astronomical zoom reflects inflated dollars.

Antipollution laws have increased the cost of doing business in America.

True, but no more so than in Japan, and less in some cases. In the steel industry, for example, although Japanese steel manufacturers spent nearly twice as much as we did on pollution control in the 1970s—$3.6 billion versus $1.9 billion between 1971 and 1977—they still had lower prices, and took away much of our market. In the automobile industry, Japanese restrictions on the emission of pollutants in automobile exhausts are far more stringent than the limits set by our own government, yet Japanese auto manufacturing costs are far lower.

American industry is not spending enough on R&D.

U.S. expenditures on industrial R&D are considerably higher than in Japan, as a fraction of GNP. The fraction of scientists and engineers engaged in R&D in industry is also higher. Furthermore, U.S. spending on industrial R&D increased throughout most of the '70s, during the period in which our economic growth was slowing down. This factor cannot explain the poor performance of the U.S. economy in the past decade.

The United States is not training enough engineers.

True; in recent years the Japanese have been turning out twice as many engineers as America in proportion to population. That growing pool of bright young engineers is a time bomb for America. Still, at the moment we lead the world in the number of scientists and engineers engaged in

R&D in proportion to the size of the labor force, and we have done so throughout the recent period of slow economic growth in the United States.

Investment in plant and equipment is inadequate.

Total capital investment as a fraction of GNP is low in the United States compared with other countries. However, in the manufacturing industries—such as steel, autos, machine tools—investment in machinery and equipment increased nearly 40 percent as a fraction of total production between 1960 and 1978, just when industrial productivity growth was declining. Many economists favor this explanation, but it cannot be a major factor.

Business gets more help from the government in Japan than in the United States.

Differences between Japan and America in this respect are not as great as generally believed. U.S. government purchases of semiconductors, computers and aircraft for the defense and space agencies in the 1950s and 1960s nurtured the great growth industries in computing, semiconductors and aircraft, when they were weak and struggling, by paying a large part of their R&D costs and buying up most of their products. Between 1955 and 1967 the government bought 57 percent of all computers made in the United States, 40 percent of all semiconductors, and more than half of all aircraft. In America, as in Japan, these hi-tech industries prospered because of government support. . . .

There is no villain. The trauma we are passing through now is not a depression, but a natural interlude between two great waves of economic growth. American industry is shedding its skin, casting off old technologies and developing new ones. But the new skin has not yet hardened. Industries based on the new technologies—mainly computers and microelectronics but also robots, fiberoptics, long-distance communications, biotechnology, and exotic new materials—are still young. They have not yet developed to the point where they can take up the slack in employment and industrial output created by the decline of the aging enterprises—the smokestack industries of steel, chemicals, autos, and so on.

The potential for growth in the new hi-tech industries is mind-boggling in terms of new jobs and new wealth. The computing industry alone is expected to grow from its current $50 billion to at least $100 billion and growing at the rate of 18 percent a year. Robots, another major new industry, pack a double wallop. Not only do they increase industrial productivity, but the construction of robots itself is showing phenomenal growth, from $200 million in 1980 to a projected $2 billion by 1985.

Fiberoptics is another rapidly growing technology. These light-pipes, made from glass fibers the thickness of a horsehair, can carry voices and data in a stream of tiny laser pulses at the rate of millions of pulses a second. AT&T plans to use a message-carrying light-pipe in a telephone cable between Boston and Richmond. The new cable would have taken 2 million pounds of copper with the old-fashioned wire technology.

There is little question that growth in the hi-tech industries will more than make up for the decline in the smokestack industries. Projected growth of $50 billion in the computing industry alone in the next four years is enough to offset the combined losses in the shrinking steel and auto industries. And new jobs go with the growth—easily sufficient to replace the jobs lost in the smokestack industries. Hewlett-Packard, one of the medium-size hi-tech companies, employs 57,000 people, Xerox more than 100,000. Two more Hewlett-Packards and a Xerox in the 1980s will make up for all the jobs lost in the auto industry.

Other countries will vie with us for a share in the wealth generated by the new technologies. Japan is the most formidable competitor. That nation graduated 87,000 engineers in 1980, compared with 63,000 in the United States, and is rapidly closing the gap in total numbers of scientists and engineers engaged in R&D in industry. The Japanese built their initial successes on technology borrowed from the United States, as we once borrowed our technology from Europe. Now, still following in our tracks, they are working very hard to acquire their own base of innovative research in semiconductors, computing, robotics, fiber optics, superplastics and biotechnology.

I would bet my money on America in this competition. The Japanese have the advantages of long-range planning and very productive management of people. But their industrial organization tends to stifle initiative, especially youthful initiative. "The nail that stands up gets hammered down," says a Japanese proverb. Conformity and respect for elders are highly valued traits in Japan.

We Americans have the advantages of an open society and an upward mobility that gives free rein to the innovativeness and entrepreneurial energy of human beings. This is what counts most of all—human capital, and a society in which it is utilized to its maximum potential.

Homeless in the 90s. A homeless man begs for change in the nation's capital. (© 1988 Brad Markel/Gamma-Liaison, Inc.)

CHAPTER EIGHT

◆

Modern Times

44

◆

ENTERPRISE UNLEASHED

Ronald Reagan first made his mark in politics with a televised appeal in 1964 on behalf of conservative Senator Barry Goldwater, the Republican presidential candidate. Reagan argued a position popular with the Sunbelt and the suburbs where Republicans were beginning to show strength—that federal government high taxes, social programs, and regulations were strangling individual freedom and threatening to drag the country "down to the ant heap of totalitarianism." He also showed himself to be a brilliant speaker—relaxed, confident, earnest, and poised, with a warm voice, a gift for turning a phrase, and a knack for seeming simultaneously friendly and determined. The speech failed to rescue Goldwater's foundering campaign, but it did launch Reagan's own political career, which led first to the California governor's mansion and then to the White House.

Reagan's major victory in the presidential election of 1980 can be traced to several sources. The Democratic candidate, incumbent Jimmy Carter, was widely perceived as a weak president, unable to lift the country from a lingering economic slump or to rescue American diplomatic hostages from the clutches of Moslem fundamentalists in Iran. But Reagan was himself a strong candidate, promising repeatedly (as he had on Goldwater's behalf sixteen years before) to cut taxes, deregulate business, balance the federal budget, and increase military spending—in brief, to restore unregulated capitalism and global supremacy, the twin pillars of the American system. That some of these promises appeared contradictory, mutually exclusive, or impossible was no problem, Reagan argued. According to "supply-side economics," which Reagan popularized, the country could accomplish these ends simply by cutting taxes enough to trigger massive investment and rapid growth, thus generating higher tax revenues despite lower tax rates. Reagan's Republican rival, George Bush, dismissed this notion as "voodoo economics." Nevertheless, Reagan's form of voodoo proved enormously popular with the American business community, which aggressively supported and financed his candidacy. President Reagan's inaugural address, excerpted below, signaled his determination to follow through on his campaign promises.

Born in 1914, Ronald Reagan won initial fame in Hollywood, where he worked in films and was president of the Screen Actors' Guild. During the 1950s he appeared on television and did publicity for General Electric Company. A two-term governor of California, he was by 1980 both a seasoned politician and a seasoned actor—photogenic, comfortable before the cameras, and possessing a mellifluous, compelling voice. No president since Franklin D. Roosevelt, with whom Reagan has often compared himself, used the electronic media so effectively or to such political advantage. His critics labeled him "the Teflon president" because he managed for years to escape unscathed from scandal or policy gaffes. But his friends called him "the Great Communicator," perhaps the finest of the century.

Questions to Consider. What was the nature of the "crisis" that Reagan saw in the United States in 1981? How did this crisis manifest itself at the government level? Why did Reagan say "government is the problem"? Did the president propose specific steps to deal with this? What steps did he propose for forcing government to live "within its means"? How, given these principles, was it possible for Reagan to oversee the biggest increase in the federal deficit in American history?

◆

First Inaugural Address (1981)

RONALD REAGAN

These United States are confronted with an economic affliction of great proportions. We suffer from the longest and one of the worst sustained inflations in our national history. It distorts our economic decisions, penalizes thrift, and crushes the struggling young and the fixed-income elderly alike. It threatens to shatter the lives of millions of our people.

Idle industries have cast workers into unemployment, causing human misery and personal indignity. Those who do work are denied a fair return for their labor by a tax system which penalizes successful achievement and keeps us from maintaining full productivity.

But great as our tax burden is, it has not kept pace with public spending. For decades, we have piled deficit upon deficit, mortgaging our future and our children's future for the temporary convenience of the present. To continue this long trend is to guarantee tremendous social, cultural, political, and economic upheavals.

From *The New York Times,* January 21, 1981.

The winning team. President-elect Ronald Reagan and Vice-President-elect George Bush at their first post-election news conference, November 7, 1980, after demolishing the Democratic ticket in the wake of the Iran hostage crisis. (© 1980 AP/Wide World Photos)

You and I as individuals can, by borrowing, live beyond our means, but only for a limited period of time. Why, then, should we think that collectively, as a nation, we are not bound by that same limitation? . . .

In this present crisis, government is not the solution to our problem. Government is the problem.

From time to time, we have been tempted to believe that society has become too complex to be managed by self-rule, that government by an elite group is superior to government for, by, and of the people. But if no one among us is capable of governing himself, then who among us has the capacity to govern someone else?

All of us together, in and out of government, must bear the burden. The solutions we seek must be equitable, with no one group singled out to pay a higher price.

We hear much of special interest groups. Our concern must be for a special interest group that has been too long neglected. It knows no sectional boundaries or ethnic and racial divisions, and it crosses political party lines. It is made up of men and women who raise our food, patrol our streets, man our mines and our factories, teach our children, keep our homes, and heal us when we are sick—professionals, industrialists, shopkeepers, clerks, cabbies, and truckdrivers. They are, in short, "We the people," this breed called Americans. . . .

So, as we begin, let us take inventory. We are a nation that has a government—not the other way around. And this makes us special among the nations of the earth. Our government has no power except that granted it by the people. It is time to check and reverse the growth of government, which shows signs of having grown beyond the consent of the governed.

It is my intention to curb the size and influence of the federal establishment and to demand recognition of the distinction between the powers granted to the federal government and those reserved to the states or to the people.

All of us need to be reminded that the federal government did not create the states; the states created the federal government.

So there will be no misunderstanding, it is not my intention to do away with government. It is, rather, to make it work—work with us, not over us; to stand by our sides, not ride on our backs. Government can and must provide opportunity, not smother it—foster productivity, not stifle it.

If we look to the answer as to why, for so many years, we achieved so much, prospered as no other people on earth, it was because here, in this land, we unleashed the energy and individual genius of man to a greater extent than has ever been done before. Freedom and the dignity of the individual have been more available and assured here than in any other place on earth. The price for this freedom has been high at times. But we have never been unwilling to pay that price.

It is no coincidence that our present troubles parallel and are proportionate to the intervention and intrusion in our lives that result from unnecessary and excessive growth of government. . . .

So with all the creative energy at our command, let us begin an era of national renewal. Let us renew our determination, our courage, and our strength. And let us renew our faith and our hope. We have every right to dream heroic dreams. . . .

In the days ahead, I will propose removing the roadblocks that have slowed our economy and reduced productivity. Steps will be taken aimed at restoring the balance between the various levels of government. Progress may be slow—measured in inches and feet, not miles—but we will progress. It is time to reawaken this industrial giant, to get government back within its means, and to lighten our punitive tax burden. And these will be our first priorities; on these principles there will be no compromise.

45

◆

THE EVIL EMPIRE

The main theme of Ronald Reagan's first inaugural address was the need to stimulate the American economy by cutting taxes and getting the government "off our backs." This position was dear to the hearts of the "Old Right"—traditional business conservatives concerned chiefly with economic policies. But Reagan's triumphant campaign of 1980 had also energized the so-called "New RIght"—groups concerned chiefly with restoring traditional morality both by combating abortion, pornography, homosexuality, and women's liberation and by returning prayer to the public schools.

The heartland of the New Right was the Old South, where the liberalism of the Democratic party had alienated white voters and where Protestant fundamentalism, strengthened by television evangelists, was growing rapidly. Long a target of Republican strategists, the South became a natural base for Ronald Reagan, who skillfully tailored his appeals to the region by couching them in terms of morality rather than race. Such appeals would in turn attract all voters wanting to restore traditional authority and morals. One of Reagan's great political achievements was to bring these New Right voters decisively into the Republican camp.

Increasingly, moreover, the president linked the new morality to the old struggle against Communism. In part, he did this to forge a connection between his domestic agenda and the immense military build-up undertaken during his administration. He also knew that both old and new conservatives could unite behind an aggressive foreign policy. Perhaps the most famous instance of his linking diplomacy with moral conservatism came in a speech, excerpted below, to the National Association of Evangelicals. In this speech Reagan called Soviet Communism "the focus of evil in the modern world." Ironically, during his second administration Ronald Reagan met with Soviet Premier Mikhail Gorbachev on several occasions and signed a path-breaking treaty with the USSR banning intermediate-range nuclear forces in Europe.

Questions to Consider. What were the "tried and time-tested values" Reagan referred to early in his speech? Were they only the "concern for others and respect for the rule of law under God" that he had mentioned earlier, or did he mean something more? How did he think government support for birth-control services for girls would undermine the values of concern for others and the rule of law under God? What did Reagan's efforts to cut funds for teenage birth control share with the struggle against abortion? What did he mean when he called the Soviets the "focus of evil in the modern world"? Do you think Reagan really meant to imply that proponents of a freeze on building and deploying nuclear weapons were under the influence of Satan (old Screwtape)?

◆

Speech to the National Association of Evangelicals (1983)

RONALD REAGAN

This administration is motivated by a political philosophy that sees the greatness of America in you, her people, and in your families, churches, neighborhoods, communities—the institutions that foster and nourish values like concern for others and respect for the rule of law under God.

Now, I don't have to tell you that this puts us in opposition to, or at least out of step with, a prevailing attitude of many who have turned to a modern-day secularism, discarding the tried and time-tested values upon which our very civilization is based. No matter how well intentioned, their value system is radically different from that of most Americans. And while they proclaim that they're freeing us from superstitions of the past, they've taken upon themselves the job of superintending us by government rule and regulation. Sometimes their voices are louder than ours, but they are not yet a majority.

An example of that vocal superiority is evident in a controversy now going on in Washington. And since I'm involved, I've been waiting to hear from the parents of young America. How far are they willing to go in giving to government their prerogatives as parents?

Let me state the case as briefly and simply as I can. An organization of citizens, sincerely motivated and deeply concerned about the increase in illegitimate births and abortions involving girls well below the age of consent, sometime ago established a nationwide network of clinics to offer help to these girls and, hopefully, alleviate this situation. Now, again, let me say, I do not fault their intent. However, in their well-intentioned effort,

From *The New York Times*, March 9, 1983.

these clinics have decided to provide advice and birth control drugs and devices to underage girls without the knowledge of their parents.

For some years now, the Federal Government has helped with funds to subsidize these clinics. In providing for this, the Congress decreed that every effort would be made to maximize parental participation. Nevertheless, the drugs and devices are prescribed without getting parental consent or giving notification after they've done so. Girls termed "sexually active"— and that has replaced the word "promiscuous"—are given this help in order to prevent illegitimate birth or abortion.

Well, we have ordered clinics receiving Federal funds to notify the parents such help has been given. One of the Nation's leading newspapers has created the term "squeal rule" in editorializing against us for doing this, and we're being criticized for violating the privacy of young people. A judge has recently granted an injunction against an enforcement of our rule. I've watched TV panel shows discuss this issue, seen columnists pontificating on our error, but no one seems to mention morality as playing a part in the subject of sex.

Is all of Judeo-Christian tradition wrong? Are we to believe that something so sacred can be looked upon as a purely physical thing with no potential for emotional and psychological harm? And isn't it the parents' right to give counsel and advice to keep their children from making mistakes that may affect their entire lives? . . .

More than a decade ago, a Supreme Court decision literally wiped off the books of fifty States statutes protecting the rights of unborn children. Abortion on demand now takes the lives of up to 1.5 million unborn children a year. Human life legislation ending this tragedy will some day pass the Congress, and you and I must never rest until it does. Unless and until it can be proven that the unborn child is not a living entity, then its right to life, liberty, and the pursuit of happiness must be protected.

You may remember that when abortion on demand began, many, and, indeed, I'm sure many of you, warned that the practice would lead to a decline in respect for human life, that the philosophical premises used to justify abortion on demand would ultimately be used to justify other attacks on the sacredness of human life—infanticide or mercy killing. Tragically enough, those warnings proved all too true. Only last year a court permitted the death by starvation of a handicapped infant. . . .

Now, I'm sure that you must get discouraged at times, but you've done better than you know, perhaps. There's a great spiritual awakening in America, a renewal of the traditional values that have been the bedrock of America's goodness and greatness.

One recent survey by a Washington-based research council concluded that Americans were far more religious than the people of other nations; 95 percent of those surveyed expressed a belief in God and a huge majority believed the Ten Commandments had real meaning in their lives. And another study has found that an overwhelming majority of Americans disapprove of adultery, teenage sex, pornography, abortion, and hard drugs. And this same study showed a deep reverence for the importance of family ties and religious belief. . . .

And this brings me to my final point today. During my first press conference as President, in answer to a direct question, I pointed out that, as good Marxist-Leninists, the Soviet leaders have openly and publicly declared that the only morality they recognize is that which will further their cause, which is world revolution. I think I should point out I was only quoting Lenin, their guiding spirit, who said in 1920 that they repudiate all morality that proceeds from supernatural ideas—that's their name for religion—or ideas that are outside class conceptions. Morality is entirely subordinate to the interests of class war. . . .

They must be made to understand we will never compromise our principles and standards. We will never give away our freedom. We will never abandon our belief in God. And we will never stop searching for a genuine peace. But we can assure none of these things America stands for through the so-called nuclear freeze solutions proposed by some.

The truth is that a freeze now would be a very dangerous fraud, for that is merely the illusion of peace. The reality is that we must find peace through strength. . . .

Yes, let us pray for the salvation of all of those who live in that totalitarian darkness—pray they will discover the joy of knowing God. But until they do, let us be aware that while they preach the supremacy of the state, declare its omnipotence over individual man, and predict its eventual domination of all peoples on the Earth, they are the focus of evil in the modern world. . . .

So, I urge you to speak out against those who would place the United States in a position of military and moral inferiority. You know, I've always believed that old Screwtape reserved his best efforts for those of you in the church. So, in your discussions of the nuclear freeze proposals, I urge you to beware the temptation of pride—the temptation of blithely declaring yourselves above it all and label both sides equally at fault, to ignore the facts of history and the aggressive impulses of an evil empire, to simply call the arms race a giant misunderstanding and thereby remove yourself from the struggle between right and wrong and good and evil.

46

◆

URBAN ANGUISH

The rise of Reagan conservatism moved serious discussion of the problems of poverty and urban blight to the edges of party politics. That there *were* such problems was apparent. It was difficult to travel in any American city without encountering unprecedented numbers of homeless people, so many that census takers barely counted them, lawyers barely represented them, doctors barely treated them, and public health officers barely coped with their existence. It was also difficult to follow the daily news without being assailed by instances of criminal violence. Large sections of cities became off-limits for many people; at night most sections became off-limits for nearly everyone. Drug dealers carried deadlier weapons than most police officers. School administrators frisked pupils for firearms.

The statistics told their own story: life expectancy among black urban males was falling; real income for urban workers was also falling. Rates of illegitimate birth were rising, as were rates of urban drug addiction and rates of domestic violence, rape, and murder. For a time, Detroit became the murder capital of the world, only to be displaced soon after by Houston—which in turn was overtaken by Washington, D.C. And there were the comparisons. Calcutta, the sprawling Indian city, has long been a byword for nightmarish squalor. In 1990 a group of foreign businessmen maintained that life in Calcutta, though desperate, might be preferable to the misery and viciousness of New York City. An American journalist agreed.

But serious as these problems were, they were largely problems of the poor at a time when the national mood and the national leadership were unsympathetic to reforms. Nevertheless, those who have a will to reform often find a way, usually by changing the terms of debate and organizing from outside. Faced with an unwillingness to debate poverty, reformers in the 1980s talked instead about the needs of children. Faced with an unwillingness to debate violence, they talked instead about the ravages of firearms. Thus arose two of the most visible and influential initiatives of the 1980s—the Children's Defense Fund and Handgun Control, Inc.—and the careers of Marian Wright Edelman and Sarah Brady, the women who led them.

Marian Wright Edelman was born in 1939 in South Carolina. She attended Spelman College and Yale Law School and, in 1963, became a staff attorney for the National Association for the Advancement of Colored People. She was congressional liaison for Martin Luther King's Poor People's Campaign in 1968 and director of the Harvard Center for Law and Education before founding the Children's Defense Fund in Washington, D.C. The purpose of the Fund was to monitor and propose improvements in government policies and programs in child-related areas: child and maternal health, education, child care, child welfare, adolescent pregnancy prevention, youth employment, and family support systems. Called "the 101st senator on children's issues" and "the nation's most effective lobbyist on behalf of children," Edelman, with the Children's Defense Fund, initiated a major long-term campaign in 1983 to prevent teenage pregnancy and provide positive life options for youth. The following excerpt is from her 1987 book, *Families in Peril,* which encapsulated many of the arguments and data that earned the Fund its high reputation for effective advocacy.

Sarah Brady, the daughter of an agent of the Federal Bureau of Investigation, was born in Virginia in 1943. In January 1981 her husband, James Brady, became Ronald Reagan's first presidential press secretary. On March 30, 1981, John Hinckley, a would-be assassin, fired several shots at Reagan. One of them pierced Jim Brady's forehead, penetrated his brain, and left him partially paralyzed. Within a few years Sarah Brady was the driving force behind Handgun Control, Inc., the nation's foremost advocate of controlling the availability of lethal firearms—including handguns of the kind Hinckley used. Brady had a formidable adversary, she quickly discovered: the National Rifle Association (NRA). Possibly the most powerful lobby in America, the NRA had successfully deflected numerous attempts to register firearms, to prohibit the sale of particularly deadly firearms and ammunition, and to require a waiting period for firearm purchases. Sarah Brady's growing involvement—plus the national epidemic of firearm killings—made Handgun Control, Inc., a significant force also. By the late 1980s, when Brady became chair, the organization had a million members and was a widely imitated direct-mail raiser of funds. It was a major force behind the passage of gun control legislation in numerous states as well as in Washington, D.C., and was the creator of the Center to Prevent Handgun Violence. Brady became so well known that her endorsement was instrumental in restricting assault rifles, and a proposal to require background checks for handgun purchases quickly became known as "the Brady Bill." Her 1987 testimony on behalf of the measure appears below. *Ms.* magazine named Sarah Brady one of its "Women of the Year" for 1988.

Questions to Consider. What single factor, in Marian Wright Edelman's view, best accounted for black family deterioration? Why did she stress the point that both white and black children were suffering from poverty? Do any of her statistics surprise you? Of the six reasons she gave for child poverty generally, which do you find most, and least, persuasive? What is the "highest ideal" that Edelman referred to in her final paragraph?

What part of Sarah Brady's 1987 testimony might U.S. senators have found compelling? Were her methods of persuasion the same as those of Marian Wright Edelman? Brady's advocacy had, by this time, made her a somewhat controversial figure. Did the controversy stem from her demands or from her as a person and from her chief adversary? Was the NRA right to argue that the Brady Bill was only the beginning— that the goal of gun control supporters was actually to prohibit the private ownership of firearms? Would Marian Wright Edelman have endorsed Brady's remarks?

◆

Defending Children (1987)

MARIAN WRIGHT EDELMAN

A 1985 Children's Defense Fund (CDF) study, *Black and White Children in America: Key Facts*, found that black children have been sliding backward. Black children today are more likely to be born into poverty, lack early prenatal care, have a single mother or unemployed parent, be unemployed as teenagers, and not go to college after high school graduation than they were in 1980. . . .

We also found that:

- Only four out of every ten black children, compared to eight out of every ten white children live in two-parent families.
- Births to unmarried teenagers occur five times more often among blacks than whites, although birth rates for black teens, married and unmarried, have been *declining*, while the birth rate among white unmarried teens has been *increasing* in recent years.
- In 1983, 58 percent of all births to black women were out of wedlock. Among black women under the age of twenty, the proportion was over 86 percent. For thirty years these out-of-wedlock ratios have increased inexorably. They have now reached levels that essentially

From Marian Wright Edelman, *Families in Peril*, 1–3, 10, 13–15, 23–26, 29, 35–44, 113. Reprinted by permission of the publishers from *Families In Peril* by Marian Wright Edelman, Cambridge, Mass.: Harvard University Press. Copyright © 1987 by the President and Fellows of Harvard College.

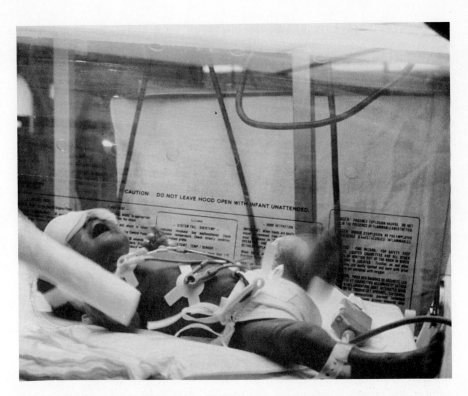

An innocent victim. A "crack baby," addicted to cocaine because the mother was an addict. Addictive illegal drugs were a plague throughout urban America. "Crack" cocaine, easily affordable and quickly addictive, was particularly deadly. (© 1990 John Chiasson/Gamma-Liaison, Inc.)

guarantee the poverty of many black children for the unforeseeable future.

Since the main reason that black children live with only a mother is that most unmarried pregnant black women do not marry before giving birth, what has become of the fathers? They remain single. The pattern is quite clear. . . .

One crucial question is: When did the rate of marriage formation drop among young black males? In the 1970s it paralleled the decline of employment prospects of young black males, which resulted in only 29.8 percent of black teens and 61 percent of black twenty- to twenty-four-year-old men being employed by 1978. From 1978 to 1985 things got a bit worse for both black teens and males in their twenties.

Why did this economic disaster for black men occur? It is difficult to say precisely, but I think that the other factors which contributed included the softening of the labor market generally in the 1970s, poor education, continuing discrimination, and a reciprocal sense of defeatism among some inner-city and rural men. There is no question but that the number of Americans who wanted to work and could not find jobs was larger in 1980 than it had been in 1970. The economy absorbed unprecedented numbers of baby-boomers, women, and immigrants; in the process it left behind the same people who have always been at the end of the American line. . . .

The American family crisis is not just a black family crisis. Both public and private sector neglect and anti-family policy have contributed to a downward spiral for families and children, black and white. Those who suffer the most are of course the poor. Although the data on poverty, family dissolution, and teenage pregnancy are grimmer for blacks than for whites, the data for whites and for our society as a whole are themselves quite grim. In some respects (education, income of two-parent families, women's earnings, child nutrition, infant mortality) black rates have been improving and narrowing the gap between whites—or were doing so until the budget cuts and near-depression of the early 1980s. In certain other respects the gap has been narrowing because blacks have been standing still while whites are slipping backward. . . .

We must recognize that, if only by dint of their overwhelmingly majority status, whites make up most of the children and young adults about whom we should be concerned.

Nearly half of all black children in the United States are poor, an ap- palling figure. But a sixth of white children are poor, and that is also appalling. There are 8.1 million poor *white* children in the U.S., and 4.3 million poor black children—a two to one ratio. Together, more than one out of five American children are poor, including nearly one out of four children under the age of six.

Overall, children in America have become far poorer than other age groups. During the past fifteen years their poverty rates have soared, even as poverty among adults generally has stayed stable. . . .

Poverty is the greatest child killer in the affluent United States of the mid-1980s. More American children die each year from poverty than from traffic fatalities and suicide combined. Over a five-year period, more Amer- ican children die from poverty than the total number of American battle deaths during the Vietnam War. . . .

Children are poor because our nation has lost its moral bearings. We must work to change the national climate and focus attention on families and children. Recent federal government policy has spawned a new set of beatitudes which measure success not by how many needy pregnant women can be provided cost-effective prenatal care to prevent infant deaths and birth defects, but by how many families can be denied Medicaid and turned away from public health clinics. . . .

Children are poor because their parents cannot find work. Today unemploy- ment is at historically high levels, given the context of well over three years of economic recovery. . . .

Millions of children remain locked in poverty because hard-working parents cannot make enough income to provide for their basic needs. Recent governmental and private sector policies have resulted not only in high unemployment but in low wages for those who are working, increasing poverty and making the struggle of poor families harder. . . .

Poor families struggling to survive on meager wages have faced another burden: skyrocketing federal taxes. In 1979 a family of four with earnings at the poverty line paid less than 2 percent of its income in federal Social Security and income taxes. In 1986 that same family, if still earning (inflation-adjusted) poverty-line wages, has nearly 11 percent of its income taken by the federal government. Tax rates for single-parent families are even higher. . . .

Children are poor because of decreasing government support at a time of increasing need, which has resulted from economic recession, unemployment, low wages, and increased taxes on the poor. The America of the 1980s presents a cruel paradox: while the rich are getting richer and often getting more government help, the poor are getting poorer and receiving less help. The decline in federal assistance for children has made living in poverty a harsher existence for 13 million children, and it has crippled the efforts of their families to struggle back up out of poverty. . . .

Children are poor because of demographic changes and the growth of female-headed families. In 1970 one baby in nine was born to a single mother. In 1983 one baby in five was. If the trends continue, by 1990 one out of five white babies and three out of four black babies will be born into female-headed households. . . .

The United States today has the challenge and opportunity of showing the world a living justice by eradicating child poverty and putting a floor of decency under every American family. To do less is to betray our highest ideal. This task cannot be relegated just to government or to somebody else. Every individual has a responsibility to try to make a difference, to give imaginative flesh to the ideal of justice. We should aim high.

♦

Testimony on Handgun Legislation (1987)

SARAH BRADY

I am here today in support of S. 466, legislation to establish a seven-day waiting period and allow for a background check for handgun purchases.

I live in Northern Virginia with my husband, Jim, and our eight-year-old son, Scott. Jim and I met through politics and our lives—very much like yours—have been on a campaign-to-campaign basis—hectic and filled

From *Judiciary Committee Hearings, U.S. Senate, 100th Congress, 1st Session* (Government Printing Office, Washington, D.C., 1987), 14–16. Reprinted with permission of Sarah Kemp Brady and Handgun Control, Inc.

with many ups and downs. We, in fact, both worked here on Capitol Hill for a while, Jim here in the Senate and me in the House.

Let me ask you to think back to the day when you won your first election—the exhilaration—the culmination of your many days of hard work and handshaking. January 2, 1981, was a day like that for Jim Brady. After many years of toiling in the vineyards, he was called by President-elect Reagan, asking him to serve as Press Secretary. This was a dream come true for Jim, the top job in his profession. Jim was on a high like you have never seen.

On the morning of March 30, 1981, as Jim was leaving for the White House at about 5:30 in the morning, he decided to go upstairs and get Scott, then 2, from his crib for a romp. It was almost a portent. He saw so little of Scott in those days. It was to be the last time Jim would climb those stairs or see Scott's bedroom, for at 2:30 p.m. on that day our lives would change forever. On that day, my husband was shot through the head by a deranged young man. He nearly died. The President nearly died, and two of his security men were seriously wounded.

It has now been more than six years, and Jim gets better every day, but it has been a long, and slow painful recovery for him. Jim's strong character, his determination and the support of a great many loving, caring people are pulling him through.

Still, there have been many times over these years that I have found myself thinking, "Why is it possible for the John Hinckleys of this world to walk into a store, buy a handgun and go out and shoot people because they hear voices or have strange visions?"

Politically, I am a Republican and a conservative. Many people who share my political outlook say that the way to keep handguns out of the wrong hands is to add mandatory long sentences for those who are convicted of crimes involving handguns. I agree, that helps and I am for mandatory sentencing, but it addresses only part of the problem. And in any case, locking up John Hinckley did not take back the bullet that nearly killed Jim Brady, nor has it spared him years of pain.

Now, I know in a few minutes you are going to hear from the NRA about how John Hinckley bought his gun, but I want you to know the facts. John Hinckley walked into a Dallas pawn shop and in minutes purchased the handgun he later used to shoot Jim. He committed a felony when he used a false address on the Federal form he was required to complete, but this went unnoticed because there was no requirement under Texas law that Hinckley's statements be verified. A simple check may have stopped him—if the local police had been given an opportunity to discover his lies, John Hinckley might well have been in jail instead of on his way to Washington.

I firmly believe that if a reasonable waiting period and a provision for background checks had been in effect when John Hinckley walked into that Dallas pawn shop, my husband Jim would be spending his days pursuing a successful career and, in his spare time, climbing trees with our eight-year-old, rather than in hours of painful and rigorous physical therapy.

Public support for a waiting period and background check is strong. A 1981 Gallup Poll found that 91 percent of Americans want such a law. The 1981 Reagan Administration Task Force on Violent Crime recommended such a law. A 1985 Justice Department report stated that "at minimum, the acquisition of a firearm by a felon should be somewhat more complicated than just walking into a gun shop and buying one."

Last year . . . we achieved some major victories. We held the line on the 1968 Gun Control Act. We succeeded in stopping the importation of deadly Saturday night special parts, the kind of handgun John Hinckley used. And Congress banned the sale of new machine guns, the automatic weapons of war which had been legal in thirty-seven states.

Last year, Congress also voted to outlaw armor-piercing bullets, legislation opposed by the National Rifle Association. This year, the NRA has stated that its highest priority is to repeal the machine gun ban. The NRA is also opposing legislation which would ban plastic firearms which cannot be detected by x-ray and metal detection equipment. And now the NRA is opposing a seven-day waiting period on handgun purchases.

After looking at the NRA positions on machine guns, cop-killer bullets, and plastic guns, I find it difficult to believe that any Member of Congress could trust the judgment of the NRA on a national waiting period or any other legislation affecting American lives and public safety.

While the NRA opposes S. 466, it is interesting to note that several years ago in its own publication, the NRA stated that a waiting period would be effective as a means of "reducing crimes of passion and in preventing people with criminal records or dangerous mental illness from acquiring guns."

The NRA claims that waiting periods do not stop crime because criminals do not submit to waiting periods. However, in areas where waiting periods and background checks are required, prohibited persons have been stopped from obtaining handguns.

In California, in one year alone, 1,200 prohibited handgun buyers were screened out through the State's waiting period. The Chief of Police in Columbus, GA, says that the city's three-day waiting period catches two felons a week trying to buy handguns. And in Memphis, TN, a police sergeant reports that the State's fifteen-day waiting period screens out about fifty applicants a month, most of whom have criminal records.

The NRA argues that waiting periods do not prevent criminals from obtaining handguns because criminals get handguns from other sources. But a study by the Bureau of Alcohol, Tobacco and Firearms, "Project Identification," found that "the percentage of out-of-State handgun purchases is directly proportional to the strength of the local firearms regulations." For example, the study found that of handguns used in crime in

New York, only 4 percent were purchased in the State. With only a few exceptions, the rest were purchased in States without waiting periods or background checks.

The study also showed that in States without waiting periods or background checks, an overwhelming majority of the handguns used in crime were purchased in the same State. For example, of the handguns used in crime in Dallas, 87 percent were purchased in Texas.

While eighteen States and many localities have already passed waiting period laws, a national waiting period law is desperately needed.

I am one wife and mother who hopes the day will come when no American family has to go through what we have been through and who asks that you provide the leadership that will finally begin to make it possible for us to keep these terrible weapons out of the wrong hands.

47

◆

THRIFT

In the Old Testament of the Bible, the prophet Jeremiah laments the moral and religious degradation of the children of Israel and denounces his people for worshipping false gods. Seventeenth-century Puritan ministers thundered so frequently against the weaknesses of their flock that their sermons came to be called "jeremiads," and Protestant preachers resorted to the form in the eighteenth century and period-ically thereafter when the country's spiritual fiber seemed lacking. In modern times, particularly in such periods of unbridled acquisitiveness as the 1880s and 1920s, social reformers rather than ministers have done the preaching. The evils, however, have been mostly those the jeremiads have always assaulted: materialism, greed, selfishness, and a turning away from the civic virtues. Perhaps unsurprisingly, the jeremiad has recently reappeared—and once again it is directed against familiar targets.

The remarkable economic boom of the 1980s had one notable feature besides its length. Although total employment, the gross na-tional product, and the stock market all rose, so did the country's total indebtedness—to the staggering total, by 1990, of nearly $13 trillion, much of it created during the 1980s. A part of this debt arose from the budget deficits of the federal government, which averaged $175 billion per year after 1981. But much more of this total indebtedness was private corporate and consumer debt. The economic boom of the 1980s occurred, in fact, largely because businesses and individuals as well as government borrowed so heavily against the future.

But the fact that the boom sailed along on a vast tide of credit contributed to another of its distinctive features: the startling increase in business bankruptcies. Swollen with debt, industrial firms failed at the fastest pace since the 1920s, and in the financial sector the carnage was even worse. Insurance companies, for example, which had been extremely stable over the previous half-century, began to fail at the rate of twenty-five a year in 1985 and one hundred a year in 1989. In commercial banking, reliable since the early 1930s because of federal deposit insurance and federal regulation, there were twenty failures in 1980—and more than two hundred in 1988.

Our first jeremiad, by Michael Waldman of Public Citizen, a public interest organization associated with consumer advocate Ralph Nader, deals with the incredible debacle in the nation's savings and loan (S&L) industry. By the end of the decade the Federal Savings and Loan Insurance Corporation (FSLIC) had rescued several hundred institutions with assets totaling nearly $150 billion. FSLIC rescued the S&Ls by (1) guaranteeing their deposits, thus preventing runs on the institutions, and (2) finding someone, usually another S&L, to take them over. Many observers believed the price tag to the government would eventually reach $500 billion. That would make the S&L bailout, by all odds, the costliest financial scandal in U.S. history—and many critics fear the price could be even higher.

The second jeremiad is a commentary, by Lewis H. Lapham, editor of *Harper's* magazine, on the state of American financial and political morality in the late twentieth century. Lapham was born in 1935 to a San Francisco banking family. He attended Hotchkiss School and Yale University and did graduate work at Cambridge University in England. A reporter with California and New York newspapers from 1957 to 1962 and a magazine writer during the 1960s, he became managing editor of *Harper's* in 1971 and editor in 1975. The author of three books on class, status, and power in contemporary America, Lapham is a member of the Council of Foreign Relations. The following excerpt is from one of his monthly *Harper's* editorials.

Questions to Consider. According to Michael Waldman, who was most responsible for the S&L crisis of the 1980s? In which states were the biggest culprits apparently located? What role did the Reagan administration play in the scandal? Why did the S&L crisis turn out to be a nonpartisan issue? What was the role of Wall Street? What aspect of the scandal seems to have upset Waldman the most?

According to Lewis Lapham, were the vast financial scandals of the 1980s exceptional or typical? What bothered Lapham most, corruption or hypocrisy? Do you think the people Lapham castigated were in fact hypocrites? Or did they simply not see or comprehend the swindles?

◆

Who Robbed America? (1990)

MICHAEL WALDMAN

It was 1986, the height of the S&L boom, and Charles Keating, the owner of Lincoln Savings and Loan, was showing a camera crew the headquarters of his real estate and financial empire.

"How old are you now?" he asked one employee.

"Thirty-one."

"Thirty-one? Okay, you're going to be the first girl that started off as a secretary to make $100,000," Keating said boastfully in front of the cameras.

In 1989, Keating's S&L failed, following what a federal judge ruled was a systematic "looting."

The total estimated cost to the taxpayers: $2.5 billion.

*   *   *   *   *

In 1983, Vernon Savings and Loan of Dallas, Texas, sent its president, Don Dixon, on a "gastronomique fantastique" tour of Europe. He and his wife ate their way through six French cities, and hired a European nobleman as an "adviser."

"You think it's easy eating in three-star restaurants twice a day six days a week?" Dixon protested to a reporter. "By the end of the week, you want to spit it [the food] out."

By the time Vernon S&L was seized by regulators in 1987, some 90 percent of its loans were in default.

Estimated cost to the taxpayers: $1.3 billion.

*   *   *   *   *

Once, S&Ls invested their money in home mortgages. Miami Florida's CenTrust had a different idea. The spendthrift thrift bought a classic painting, Reuben's *Portrait of a Man as Mars*, for $12 million. CenTrust stored the painting "temporarily" at the mansion of its owner, David Paul, supposedly until its executive offices were finished. When regulators forced the S&L to sell the painting at an auction in 1989, it sold for $4 million less than the S&L had paid for it. CenTrust failed in 1990.

The estimated cost to the taxpayers: up to $2 billion.

*   *   *   *   *

From Michael Waldman, *Who Robbed America?: A Citizen's Guide to the Savings & Loan Scandal* (Random House New York, 1990). 2–10. Copyright © 1990 by *Public Citizen*. Reprinted by permission of Random House, Inc.

Anxious depositors. Depositors wait to withdraw their money from a failed thrift institution during the gargantuan savings-and-loan crisis of the late 1980s. (© 1990 Marty Katz/Time Pictures Syndication)

It was, young Neil Bush had to admit later, "an incredibly sweet deal."

Bush was referring to a $100,000 "loan" given to him in 1984 by Kenneth Good, a prominent Colorado developer. The loan had a special term: If Bush lost the money, he didn't have to pay it back; if he made a profit with the money, he could keep the extra funds. Bush still hasn't paid back the funds; nor has he declared the $100,000 as income, though now he says he will.

A year after receiving the loan, Bush joined the board of Silverado Banking S&L, which voted to lend huge sums to his benefactor Kenneth Good— only to have him default on $30 million worth of loans.

Total estimated cost to taxpayers of Silverado's failure: up to $1 billion.

*   *   *   *   *

Who robbed America?

Charles Keating, Don Dixon, David Paul, and, yes, Neil Bush: we might be tempted just to laugh and shake our heads at their flagrant excess and self-enrichment. But it wasn't their money they were gambling with; it was *ours*, because we, as taxpayers, insured the deposits in their banks. The result is an unprecedented government bailout, with an estimated cost of up to $15,000 per taxpayer.

The S&L scandal is the biggest and most expensive financial debacle in American history. The numbers are incomprehensible. After insisting for years that the cost would be much lower, the federal government now admits that the crisis will cost between $300 and $500 billion over the next decade alone. That sum is greater than the Marshall Plan (which rebuilt Europe after World War II), the New York City bailout, the Lockheed bailout, the Chrysler bailout and the Continental-Illinois bailouts *combined*, even when adjusted for inflation. The S&L bailout is beginning to approach the cost of the Korean War. . . .

*   *   *   *   *

The first thing to understand is that this crisis was not merely the product of adverse economic conditions, or an act of nature. Instead, it was the result of greed on an epic scale—what Al Capone called "the legitimate rackets." Bank robbers use guns and physical force. The thrift robbers saw a new method—persuading the government to enact laws that actually *allowed* them to empty the till.

The thrift robbers aren't shadowy figures, operating at the margins of society. Instead, they are some of the powerful and the wealthy, who were so celebrated in the money culture of the 1980s:

- *S&L owners and executives.* A platoon of riverboat gamblers took over many of America's savings and loans and threw the money away— or worse. There was the Beverly Hills thrift that hired nineteen Uzi-toting bodyguards to protect its chief executive officer. And then there was Texas—land of wild parties and wilder land deals. Prosecutors believe that these S&L high-flyers weren't just frivolous, they were fraudulent. At as many as six out of every ten failed S&Ls, insiders engaged in serious misconduct. And now some investigators believe that many failed S&Ls were linked through an elaborate network of fraud, involving ties to organized crime.
- *Ronald Reagan's deregulators.* The probusiness ideologues in the Reagan administration believed that letting the S&Ls gamble with taxpayer money was "the free market at work." When one official begged the White House for more enforcement personnel to combat the pervasive fraud, he was told, "The policy of the administration is to have fewer, not more, [bank] examiners."

- *A "kept" Congress.* Politicians of both parties took millions of dollars in campaign contributions and speech fees from the financial industry, and then voted to deregulate the S&Ls. Shills for the S&Ls included some of the most powerful men in Washington—from former Speaker of the House Jim Wright, who held vital legislation hostage for the benefit of a few cronies in the Texas S&L industry, to the notorious five senators who intervened for Lincoln Savings and Loan and took $1.4 million from Charles Keating. . . .
- *George Bush.* He wasn't president when the thrifts were looted, but he *is* responsible for much of the bailout cost—by insisting that it be paid for over four decades with bailout bonds instead of financing it now with taxes.
- *"Hired-gun" accountants and lawyers.* These professionals are supposed to abide by professional standards, but instead watched out for their fat fees. At one point, nearly every major accounting firm in the country was being sued by the government for negligence—or worse—in the S&L debacle.
- *Wall Street's "Masters of the Universe."* In the 1980s, Wall Street was where the action was. And aggressive investment bankers enmeshed the S&Ls into elaborate investment schemes more appropriate to Ivan Boesky than to Jimmy Stewart. Wealthy investors put billions of dollars in S&Ls, reaping extra-high interest rates and giving S&L owners taxpayer-insured money to invest. And these thrifts, in turn, poured billions of dollars into junk bonds, corporate mergers, and other financial shenanigans.
- *The press.* Our media watchdogs didn't bark while the rich plundered the S&Ls. They didn't cover it while it was happening, gave minimal coverage as the full extent of the blowout became clear, and still won't listen to anyone other than the official bureaucrats and pundits in Washington. . . .

Millions of dollars in PAC gifts . . . Floating Potomac River fund-raisers, on a yacht owned by a crooked S&L . . . Top White House aides trying to stymie strong enforcement . . . Chief regulators chosen by the industry they are supposed to oversee: The story of the S&Ls is also a story of the corruption now taken for granted in Washington.

Sadly, the politicians and officials, who are supposed to guard the public treasury, instead handed the keys to the plunderers. The scandal is bipartisan, soiling Republicans and Democrats, executive branch and legislative branch alike. The S&Ls are nothing less than a Watergate scandal for the entire government. There's no need to subpoena secret tapes; just read the *Congressional Record* and the campaign finance disclosure forms.

The reasons varied. Ronald Reagan's belief in deregulation was the core of his economic philosophy. Give the forces of unleashed business free rein, he promised, and the result would be an eruption of productive investment. But deregulation in practice meant looking the other way while private sector forces ran wild. Only two years after Ronald and Nancy Reagan returned to their ranch, the costs of deregulation are coming due. And they are larger than even his harshest critics imagined.

Congress, for its part, responded less to ideology than to the imperatives of campaign financing. The United States is the only western democracy in which legislative elections are entirely funded by private parties, mostly with an interest in legislation. The legalized bribery of PACs, large individual campaign contributions, and speech fees have created a perpetual reelection machine more responsive to contributors than to constituents. The S&L scandal is proof of just how badly Congress has lost touch with the people it is supposed to represent. . . .

In short, the savings and loan crisis has exposed deep fissures in the fabric of American democracy.

◆

The Visible Hand (1990)

LEWIS LAPHAM

The mechanics of the savings and loan swindle become somewhat easier to understand if the reader remembers to bear in mind the comparison to the financial workings of a Soviet collective farm or a Bulgarian steel mill. The operative economic principle was socialist, not capitalist; the money came and went for reasons that were political and ideological, not because it obeyed the rules of supply and demand.

The story of the swindle . . . makes a mockery of the national prayer to the idols of free enterprise. Instead of Adam Smith's benign and mysterious "invisible hand," what appears behind the curtain of fraud is the all-too-visible and familiar hand of venal and incompetent bureaucracy. As follows:

The American government conferred an urgent subsidy on an industry that certainly would have gone bankrupt if it had been left to the decision of anything as treacherous as a free market. In return for the subsidy, the grateful recipients (in Texas and California, as in Belorussia or the Ukraine) professed their fervent loyalty to the socioeconomic cant that enjoyed the blessing of the party in power. Whenever called upon to do so (in after-dinner speeches, while making campaign contributions, in letters to the editor of the *Wall Street Journal*), they expressed their belief in the joys of "risk taking" and the wonders of "entrepreneurship."

Because everybody tacitly acknowledged the political text of the subsidy, the government neglected to insist on a strict accounting, and the newly minted bankers obligingly clothed the nakedness of their stupidity and greed in the false reports of unalloyed success.

Understood as the rule rather than the exception, and measured by any standard other than its handsome cost (currently estimated at $500 billion over the next thirty or forty years), the swindle was in no way abnormal or un-American. By and large, and certainly in its primary and steadier movements, the national economy depends not only on systematic price-fixing and noncompetitive bidding but also on the guarantee of government intervention. The theory of the free market works at the margins of the economy—among cabdrivers and the owners of pizza parlors, for small businessmen who make the mistake of borrowing $20,000 instead of $20 million—but the central pillars of the American enterprise rest firmly on the foundation stones of state subsidy.

The federal treasury at the moment supplies 45 percent of the nation's income. Nearly three in every ten Americans live in a household receiving direct payments from the government; four of the remaining seven probably work for an enterprise dependent on the federal dole. The government subsidizes the growing of the nation's crops ($15 billion a year to the farmers) as well as the building of the nation's houses and the maintenance of the nation's roads. The television networks receive from the FCC the license that grants them (free of charge and without any risk) the use of the broadcasting frequencies. The commercial banks borrow money from the federal government at an interest rate two or three points below the rate they charge their best customers.

The politicians dress up the deals in the language of law or policy, but they're in the business of brokering the tax revenue. What keeps them in office is not their talent for oratory but their skill at redistributing the national income in a way that rewards their constituents, clients, patrons, and friends. They trade in every known commodity—school lunches, tax exemptions, water and mineral rights, aluminum siding, dairy subsidies, pension benefits, highway contracts, prison uniforms—and they work the levers of government like gamblers pulling at slot machines. . . .

As with the subsidizing of the farms and the defense industry, so also with paying off the bad debt acquired by savings and loan associations. Except for the taxpayers (who, as always, didn't know what was being promised in their name), nobody took the slightest risk. Always and whenever possible, the participants in the swindle zealously adhered to the fundamental American principles of "no money down" and "something for nothing."

The same economic maxims guided the settling of the old American frontier and the amassing of the gaudier fortunes synonymous with the decade of the Reagan prosperity. Sometimes it was the leveraged buy-out deal; sometimes it was the Wall Street practice of "insider trading"; sometimes it was a revision of the tax law or a contract bestowed by the Department of Housing and Urban Development. At HUD, the resident shills didn't even bother to pretend that they were playing with anything other than a marked deck. If the real-estate developer knew the right people in the administration, then he received the contract. If not, not. Explaining the procedure to a congressional committee investigating the extent of the fraud, DuBois L. Gilliam, formerly a deputy assistant secretary at HUD and now one of the few government officials serving a term in prison, described his public offices as ". . . the best political machine I've ever seen. We dealt strictly in politics.". . .

During the course of the summer, at the same time that I was reading daily bulletins from the frontiers of the savings and loan swindle, I also had occasion to read the Spring issue of *Policy Review*, a quarterly journal published by The Heritage Foundation that embodies the orthodox wisdom of the Republican Party, the larger corporations, and the Wall Street banks. Under the title "The Vision Thing: Conservativism for the Nineties," the editors presented brief essays by no fewer than thirty-nine well-known voices of the conservative conscience. . . .

They recited the national economic creed in the sweet soprano voices of a choir of castrati, and on reading their improving lessons, I was struck by the collective tone of inane complacence. It was as if I had been invited to an ideological variant of the Mad Hatter's tea party staged at an expensive conference center in Aspen or Palm Springs. I could imagine the guests dressed for croquet or golf, seated in white wicker chairs, admiring the postcard views of the sea or the mountains, busily arranging and rearranging their briefing papers, exchanging idiot solemnities with the aplomb of a club steward handing around the potted shrimp. Many of them had furnished the claptrap economic theory that justified the raids on the federal treasury during the heyday of the Reagan administration, but none of them seemed to have noticed the corollary damage done to the society's hope for the future. Nobody said a word about the debt, about the HUD or savings and loan swindles, about the numerous public officials indicted for theft or fraud, about the racial divisions in what's left of the American democracy, about the mismanagement of the military budget, about the squalor of the nation's cities and the wreckage of the nation's schools.

Everybody talked instead about the triumph of new money, which proved what one of their number described as the "moral superiority of the free economy over statism.". . .

I read the anthology of self-congratulation with the mounting suspicion that it might have been intended as a parody. So many of the remarks were so far removed from the realms of experience that I began to wonder if any of the ladies and gentlemen in the lawn chairs had ever met a defense contractor, watched network television, traveled to New York or Miami, seen a slum, or read an insurance claim. Every now and then one of their company admitted to having read something nasty in the newspapers or having heard—at a less refined conference—a really awful rumor (about illiteracy or crime or deviant sexual practice), but if the rumors were true (which probably they were not), then undoubtedly it was the fault of the "imperial Congress" or the "spiritual decay" said to be rotting the moral tissue of the nation's popular songs.

Nor did many of the guests of the symposium seem to have the least idea of what it might mean to sell their labor in a competitive market. Of the thirty-nine seers in residence, only a very few could be expected to pay their own bills. The majority owed their livings to some sort of subsidy or dole, either as politicians drawing an allowance of public money or as ministers of tax-exempt foundations relying on the largess of their corporate patrons.

The absurd humor of the performance in *Policy Review* was elaborated by George Bush in late June when he staged a show of fiscal conscience in the great hall of the Justice Department building in Washington. Wishing to express his alarm about the savings and loan swindle, Mr. Bush appeared against the backdrop of American flags, seconded by the marine band playing "God Bless America" and "Hail to the Chief." To an audience of United States attorneys Mr. Bush said, "These cheats have cost us billions, and they will pay us back with their dollars, and they will pay us back with years of their lives."

But the cheats always cost us billions. That is one of the great objects of the great American dream, and the reader who continues to cherish doubts on the point has only to consult the life and works of Donald Trump or reflect on the aerodynamic pretensions of the Stealth bomber. If Mr. Bush were to pursue his vengeance across the whole table of organization of American business enterprise, he would find that an embarrassing number of his golfing companions had declared bankruptcy or had gone suddenly to jail. Like the friends of the March Hare and the Mad Hatter placidly trading economic theories over cups of tax-deductible tea, Mr. Bush chooses to know as little as possible about the workings of the American economy. He prefers the mystical vision of "the free market" to the secular, workaday chores of the payoff, the kickback, the political favor, and the cost overrun. If the distinction interested him, he could apply for an explanation to his son, Neil, a director of a bankrupt savings and loan association in Denver who granted himself opulent lines of credit (as much as $900,000) at virtually no cost.

The boy is obviously a born entrepreneur, and if the father took the time to study the son's arithmetic, I am sure that as a politician quick to follow a popular trend he would discover that his fellow countrymen have a profound aversion for anything that remotely resembles a free market or an honest risk. What they know and like is the rigged price, the safe monopoly, and the sure percentage.

48

◆

BLOOD AND SAND

Since World War II, the Middle East, with its vast oil reserves, has been of strategic importance to both the United States and the Soviet Union. The presence there of Israel, a state with strong political and military ties to the United States virtually since Israel's founding in 1948, has made the area doubly important to American policy makers. As a consequence, every modern U.S. president has expended enormous financial and political resources to maintain American influence in the Middle East. There have been some successes from the standpoint of the American government. In 1953 President Dwight Eisenhower used the Central Intelligence Agency to replace an unfriendly government with a friendly one in oil-rich Iran; in 1958 he deployed the Sixth Fleet to maintain a friendly government in Lebanon. In 1978 Jimmy Carter helped bring about the so-called Camp David Accords between Israel and Egypt, the Arab world's most populous state.

But the United States has also experienced many failures in the region, not least in the very places where initial policies succeeded. In the late 1970s, for example, Islamic partisans seized control of Iran and its oil fields, taking fifty-two American hostages in the process. President Carter, unable to respond effectively, plummeted in public opinion polls and lost the 1980 election to Ronald Reagan partly because of his handling of the Iran crisis. President Reagan himself then came to grief when Israeli and Syrian invasions of Lebanon shattered that country's unity in 1982. Concerned about Syrian and Soviet influence, Reagan sent U.S. Marines to Beirut, the Lebanese capital, as part of a peacekeeping force, only to see more than two hundred of them killed in a terrorist attack. Just three months later, even though the president had called the American presence "essential," he ordered the force's withdrawal.

On August 2, 1990, Iraq, which had concluded a long and inconclusive war with Iran, invaded Kuwait, an oil-rich sheikdom abutting Iraq in the Persian Gulf not far from Kuwait's border with the desert kingdom of Saudi Arabia, the largest oil producer in the world. President George Bush immediately branded the Iraqi president, Saddam Hussein, a "bloody tyrant" and vowed that this brutal aggression "will not stand." During the following weeks the United States sent 250,000 troops to Saudi Arabia to protect it from Iraqi invasion and persuaded several European and Arab countries (including the dictator of Syria, a long-time U.S. foe) to send forces to join the Americans. The United States also obtained the backing of the United Nations Security Council for economic sanctions against Iraq, with a deadline of January 15, 1991, for Iraqi withdrawal from Kuwait. In November (after the congressional elections) another 200,000 American troops put still bigger teeth in the multinational force facing Iraqi soldiers across the borders of Kuwait.

In early January—after a historic debate that lasted several days and was broadcast live from gavel to gavel—the Senate and the House of Representatives voted to support President Bush's request for what everyone agreed was tantamount to a declaration of war: an endorsement of the U.N. resolution threatening military action if Iraq did not leave Kuwait by January 15. Saddam Hussein, however, made no move. On January 16, Bush ordered a full-scale air assault, including a dazzling array of electronic weaponry, against military targets in Kuwait and Iraq. That evening he delivered the following television address to explain and defend his decision.

Born in Connecticut in 1924, George Bush was the son of Prescott Bush, a Wall Street banker and U.S. senator. He attended private schools and, after service with the navy in World War II, took a degree in economics at Yale, where he also played baseball. Bush then moved to Texas, where he made money in the oil business. He lost a race on the Republican ticket for the U.S. Senate before, in 1966, winning election to Congress from Houston. During the Nixon years, Bush served as U.N. ambassador and chairman of the Republican National Committee; under Gerald R. Ford he was chief of the Liaison Office in China and director of the Central Intelligence Agency. Defeated by Ronald Reagan for the 1980 Republican presidential nomination, Bush agreed to run as Reagan's vice-presidential nominee. This was the ticket that trounced Jimmy Carter in 1980 and mauled Walter Mondale in 1984. With a record of party loyalty and Reagan's popularity behind him, Bush easily won the nomination for president in 1988 and, with Dan Quayle on the bottom of the ticket, thrashed Democrat Michael Dukakis to keep the White House in Republican hands.

Questions to Consider. President Bush gave several reasons for taking action against Iraq. Which of them seems to have been most important? What reasons did he give for taking military action rather than waiting for the economic sanctions possibly to produce results? Which reasons seem to have mattered most to him? What kind of war did the President seem to anticipate? What did he mean when he said this war would not be "another Vietnam"? What did he mean by "the new world order"?

◆

Address on the War with Iraq (1991)

GEORGE BUSH

Just two hours ago, allied air forces began an attack on military targets in Iraq and Kuwait. These attacks continue as I speak. Ground forces are not engaged.

This conflict started Aug. 2, when the dictator of Iraq invaded a small and helpless neighbor. Kuwait, a member of the Arab League and a member of the United Nations, was crushed, its people brutalized. Five months ago, Saddam Hussein started this cruel war against Kuwait; tonight, the battle has been joined.

This military action, taken in accord with United Nations resolutions and with the consent of the United States Congress, follows months of constant and virtually endless diplomatic activity on the part of the United Nations, the United States and many, many other countries.

Arab leaders sought what became known as an Arab solution, only to conclude that Saddam Hussein was unwilling to leave Kuwait. Others traveled to Baghdad in a variety of efforts to restore peace and justice. Our Secretary of State, James Baker, held an historic meeting in Geneva, only to be totally rebuffed.

This past weekend, in a last-ditch effort, the Secretary General of the United Nations went to the Middle East with peace in his heart—his second such mission. And he came back from Baghdad with no progress at all in getting Saddam Hussein to withdraw from Kuwait.

Now, the twenty-eight countries with forces in the gulf area have exhausted all reasonable efforts to reach a peaceful resolution, and have no choice but to drive Saddam from Kuwait by force. We will not fail.

As I report to you, air attacks are under way against military targets in Iraq. We are determined to knock out Saddam Hussein's nuclear bomb potential. We will also destroy his chemical weapons facilities. Much of Saddam's artillery and tanks will be destroyed. Our operations are designed to best protect the lives of all the coalition forces by targeting Saddam's vast military arsenal.

Initial reports from General [Norman] Schwartzkopf are that our operations are proceeding according to plan. Our objectives are clear: Saddam Hussein's forces will leave Kuwait. The legitimate government of Kuwait will be restored to its rightful place, and Kuwait will once again be free.

The New York Times, Jan. 17, 1991.

The War in the Middle East. A U.S. soldier walks past the bodies of slain Iraqis in the aftermath of the thunderous Allied military successes in the Persian Gulf conflict of early 1991. Hundreds of damaged oil wells burn in the background. (© 1991 Andy Clark, Reuters/Bettmann Newsphotos)

Iraq will eventually comply with all relevant United Nations resolutions, and then, when peace is restored, it is our hope that Iraq will live as a peaceful and cooperative member of the family of nations, thus enhancing the security and stability of the Gulf.

Some may ask, why act now? Why not wait? The answer is clear. The world could wait no longer. Sanctions, though having some effect, showed no signs of accomplishing their objective. Sanctions were tried for well over five months, and we and our allies concluded that sanctions alone would not force Saddam from Kuwait.

While the world waited, Saddam Hussein systematically raped, pillaged and plundered a tiny nation no threat to his own. He subjected the people of Kuwait to unspeakable atrocities, and among those maimed and murdered, innocent children.

While the world waited, Saddam sought to add to the chemical weapons arsenal he now possesses, an infinitely more dangerous weapon of mass destruction—a nuclear weapon. And while the world waited, while the world talked peace and withdrawal, Saddam Hussein dug in and moved massive forces into Kuwait.

While the world waited, while Saddam stalled, more damage was being done to the fragile economies of the Third World, emerging democracies of Eastern Europe, to the entire world, including to our own economy.

The United States, together with the United Nations, exhausted every means at our disposal to bring this crisis to a peaceful end. However, Saddam clearly felt that by stalling and threatening and defying the United Nations, he could weaken the forces arrayed against him.

While the world waited, Saddam Hussein met every overture of peace with open contempt. While the world prayed for peace, Saddam prepared for war.

I had hoped that when the United States Congress, in historic debate, took its resolute action, Saddam would realize he could not prevail, and would move out of Kuwait in accord with the United Nations resolutions. He did not do that. Instead, he remained intransigent, certain that time was on his side.

Saddam was warned over and over again to comply with the will of the United Nations, leave Kuwait or be driven out. Saddam has arrogantly rejected all warnings. Instead he tried to make this a dispute between Iraq and the United States of America.

Well he failed. Tonight twenty-eight nations—countries from five continents, Europe and Asia, Africa and the Arab League—have forces in the Gulf area standing shoulder to shoulder against Saddam Hussein. These countries had hoped the use of force could be avoided. Regrettably, we now believe that only force will make him leave.

Prior to ordering our forces into battle, I instructed our military commanders to take every necessary step to prevail as quickly as possible, and with the greatest degree of protection possible for American and Allied service men and women. I've told the American people before that this will not be another Vietnam, and I repeat this here tonight. Our troops will have the best possible support in the entire world, and they will not be asked to fight with one hand tied behind their back. I'm hopeful that this fighting will not go on for long and that casualties will be held to an absolute minimum.

This is an historic moment. We have in this past year made great progress in ending the long era of conflict and cold war. We have before us the opportunity to forge for ourselves and for future generations a new world order, a world where the rule of law, not the law of the jungle, governs the conduct of nations.

When we are successful, and we will be, we have a real chance at this new world order, an order in which a credible United Nations can use its peacekeeping role to fulfill the promise and vision of the U.N.'s founders.

We have no argument with the people of Iraq. Indeed, for the innocents caught in this conflict, I pray for their safety.

Our goal is not the conquest of Iraq. It is the liberation of Kuwait. It is my hope that somehow the Iraqi people can, even now, convince their dictator that he must lay down his arms, leave Kuwait and let Iraq itself rejoin the family of peace-loving nations.

Thomas Paine wrote many years ago: "These are the times that try men's souls." Those well-known words are so very true today. But even as planes of the multinational forces attack Iraq, I prefer to think of peace, not war. I am convinced not only that we will prevail, but that out of the horror of combat will come the recognition that no nation can stand against a world united. No nation will be permitted to brutally assault its neighbor. . . .

And let me say to everyone listening or watching tonight: When the troops we've sent in finish their work, I'm determined to bring them home as soon as possible. Tonight, as our forces fight, they and their families are in our prayers.

May God bless each and every one of them, and the coalition forces at our side in the Gulf, and may He continue to bless our nation, the United States of America.